P9-ECO-129

ECONOMICS IN ONE VIRUS

*The generous support of the Lazy L Foundation
helped make this book possible.*

ECONOMICS IN ONE VIRUS

AN INTRODUCTION TO ECONOMIC
REASONING THROUGH COVID-19

RYAN A. BOURNE

Copyright © 2021 by the Cato Institute.
All rights reserved.

Print ISBN: 978-1-952223-06-8
eBook ISBN: 978-1-952223-07-5

Cover design: Faceout Studios, Molly von Borstel.

Library of Congress Cataloging-in-Publication Data

Bourne, Ryan, author.
  Economics in one virus : an introduction to economic reasoning
  through COVID-19 / Ryan A. Bourne.
    pages   cm
  Washington, D.C. : Cato Institute, 2021.
  Includes bibliographical references and index
  ISBN 9781952223068 (paperback) | ISBN 9781952223075 (ebook)
  1. LCSH: COVID-19 (Disease)—Economic aspects—United States.
  2. COVID-19 (Disease)—Government policy—United States.
  3. Economic policy—Case studies. 4. United States—Economic
  conditions—2009– 5. United States—Economic policy—2009–
  LCC RA644.C67 B68   2021
  DDC 362.1962/41400973—dc23   2020054419

Printed in the United States of America.

1000 Massachusetts Avenue NW
Washington, DC 20001

www.cato.org

CONTENTS

INTRODUCTION

Nothing brought home the fear associated with COVID-19 more than my baby niece exhibiting symptoms of the disease.

Just a year old, one evening in late March 2020 she developed a 104°F fever. She was restless and uncomfortable for much of the night, before the hacking, dry cough associated with the disease started. Later came vomiting and shivering. Doctors by telephone urged her parents to keep her home and comfortable and only call for help if her symptoms worsened.

They did worsen. The next day, she struggled to breathe. This time she was rushed by ambulance to the nearest hospital, an experience she'd repeat two nights later. Observed in outdoor COVID-19 tents to avoid risking infecting others, she was admitted and stabilized on both occasions but wasn't tested for COVID-19 because of limited testing capacity in the UK at that time.

Slowly she recovered. Yet three weeks later, a body rash developed and a fever came again, requiring a third admittance to the hospital. Doctors said her symptoms matched those of other children who had recovered from COVID-19 and then suffered from a secondary condition known as pediatric multisystem inflammatory syndrome.

Those were scary times for my family. We often overlook the anxiety people have had to deal with owing to this disease or its threat, even beyond the losses of life Americans have had to endure. But, with my niece now recovered and happy, I recognize that although we were unlucky that she experienced such severe symptoms at her age, we were more fortunate than many families. Hundreds of thousands of others whose loved ones contracted this virus in the United States, particularly those with elderly relatives, have suffered dreadful losses.

But it hasn't just been the health impacts or fear of the disease that have shaken the country. My guess is that the virus called SARS-CoV-2, which causes the disease COVID-19, coupled with our social and political reaction to it, has profoundly disrupted your everyday life, too, even if you haven't had a family member contract it.

Maybe you lost your job. Maybe you had to work from home and juggle what you do for a living with playing teacher to your kids. Maybe your business failed or barely survived with the help of a government loan or grant. Maybe some dream vacation or wedding, or opportunity to perform in a concert or take part in a sporting event eluded you. Almost everyone's finances, freedoms, and future have been altered by this pandemic.

In fact, soon after the first confirmed U.S. infection in January 2020, ordinary households were forced to reassess the sort of daily choices they usually make on autopilot. Questions arose: How often should I go to the grocery store? How much food should I store at home in case a family member becomes sick? Which means of transportation is safest for me to use to get to and from work? When should I see my grandparents again?

True, we implicitly face those same questions every day, even in "normal" times. We just don't usually have to think about them much, at least not all at once. We answer through our instinctive decisions and habits—rules of thumb that we develop for how to behave as we weigh the costs and benefits of changing our routines. Yet this virus and its fallout have been pervasively disruptive. By fundamentally changing the calculations about what we wanted and were able to do, it exposed the sheer scale of choices we usually make unthinkingly.

Politicians have been forced to confront unusual choices as well. Almost all decided to answer the question "Does this virus necessitate a public policy response?" with a resounding "yes."

But that answer itself raised questions: What are we actually trying to achieve when enforcing policies that aim to reduce the spread of the virus? Should activity be explicitly locked down or is guidance sufficient to achieve that? What businesses and activities can and should safely operate while the virus threatens people's health? What costs should various members of society be forced to bear to reduce the spread of this disease, and for how long? How much money should be invested in medical innovations, such as treatments, vaccines, or COVID-19 tests? To whom should economic relief be delivered, and how much?

They may not seem so, but all of these questions, just as with all of the other individual choices that this pandemic has posed, are, at heart, economic. For at its most basic, economics is about choices. It is about weighing different options or alternatives in the face of constraints.

Yes, the stories we see if we click on the economics section of a newspaper's website may be about the headline unemployment figures, the latest gyrations in the stock market, or another GDP forecast. But economics as a subject is much broader—it provides frameworks for assessing the decisions we make and the incentives that drive them, as well as tools and methodologies for considering the impacts of those choices.

Ordinarily, those of you outside of Washington, DC, may not care much about the underlying economics of most choices politicians or bureaucrats make. Most probably won't affect you directly, while those that do may have a modest impact on your life. It may be rational to ignore how and why they were made.

SARS-CoV-2, however, has probably caused you to sit up and pay more attention. This time, the range and consequences of decisions policymakers are making has been profound. And, one way or another, we have all been affected by them. It therefore helps to have some mental tools to understand what is driving the choices being made, what assumptions or uncertainties underlay them, and how to consider the costs and benefits of different options.

Economics can provide that toolkit, and this book seeks to introduce you to it. It is written for people whose attention has been captured by this pandemic and the extraordinary choices confronting it has necessitated. It aims to provide those of you with little to modest familiarity with economics the opportunity to view our predicament through an economist's lens. Using the case study of COVID-19, I hope to introduce essential economic insights and ideas by highlighting how they have been or could be applied in considering the challenges associated with this pandemic. Even experienced policymakers have been forced into thinking afresh, given the extraordinary events we have seen. Think of this book, then, as a guide to economic first principles, explained through the example of the pandemic.

As such, this book does not intend to provide comprehensive answers to what the policy response to the pandemic should have been. For a start, coming to firm conclusions would often require knowledge about the disease that falls far outside an economist's wheelhouse. Our understanding of this virus and its impact from a medical and epidemiological perspective is still rapidly evolving. Much of this book was written during the early months of the pandemic; the first draft was a product of lockdown. I have tried to continually update it to reflect our best knowledge. But by the time this book is published, some of the scientific evidence I must take for granted here will be outdated, altering some of the assumptions laying behind the examples. I urge readers to remember, then, that this is an economics book and not an epidemiological one.

In any case, no one person would have the expertise to answer all the questions posed. Nor is there necessarily always a correct answer. The pandemic introduced a whole range of competing tensions and uncertainties, with moral concerns that go far beyond economic reasoning. Some tradeoffs are difficult to measure, at least at this stage. I can offer tentative conclusions and insights given what we know now, but when I do so, I aim to show my work or at least highlight the key drivers of my reasoning.

What I can do with more confidence, however, is offer readers an insight into the economic way of thinking. Soon after this pandemic unfolded, I realized that so many aspects of this experience were providing almost textbook examples of basic economic insights. This book is my nonexhaustive attempt to compile them as an introductory text to economics, through the prism of this ongoing crisis.

The title of this book, *Economics in One Virus*, is a play on one of my favorite books, *Economics in One Lesson,* by the late economist and journalist Henry Hazlitt. Hazlitt's work took a profound insight from French economist Frédéric Bastiat and illuminated it by showing how one central mistake led to a host of other economic fallacies.

That central mistake was about how bad economics considers only the seen and not the unseen effects of any given action or policy. On issue after issue, Hazlitt highlighted how commentators—and even economists, too—often ignore the broader or secondary effects of actions or decisions, leading to all sorts of faulty conclusions about their desirability. "The bad economist," he concluded, "sees only the direct consequences of a proposed course; the good economist looks at the longer and indirect consequence." I hope, in invoking a similar title, that I have not fallen foul of his insight myself.

Like Hazlitt, I don't pretend that most insights here are novel. I am very much a second-hand dealer in economic ideas. This book differs from Hazlitt's in two important ways, however. First, Hazlitt's text was light on data. These days, the empirical revolution in economics means that it would be remiss of me not to back the key economic insights I present with evidence and statistics where necessary. Second, where Hazlitt used multiple case studies to illustrate one lesson, my task here is more daunting: to use one case study—our dealing with this virus—to exemplify 16 crucial economic concepts.

Those looking for a comprehensive roadmap for what should be done to alleviate the pain and suffering from this disease and its economic fallout may well leave this text disappointed. My more modest hope is that by the end of this book, even those readers who were previously uninitiated in economics will at least appreciate some of its central insights, how they apply to this pandemic, and how they may be used to confront future economic and social challenges facing the United States.

1

WHAT DOES IT MEAN TO BE ECONOMICALLY "WORSE OFF" DURING A PANDEMIC?

An introduction to economic welfare

To say COVID-19 has had differential impacts on families' economic situations would be a gross understatement.

For some families whose members' jobs were unaffected, work continued even during the most restrictive periods of lockdown. The only difference was less eating out and travel and more sourdough baking and Zoom happy hours.

Wages actually rose initially for workers in high-demand grocery retail and delivery companies, for example, with certain companies offering compensation—or *hazard pay*—for employees willing to bear the risk of contracting the virus at work.[1]

Households with workers in leisure and hospitality were at the other end of the spectrum. The number of positions in that broad industry fell 47 percent across the United States in April 2020 alone—a decline of a massive 7.7 million jobs.[2]

Heartrending stories about family businesses struggling could be heard everywhere. One owner of a rafting company told me they had had 97 percent of their capacity booked for summer when they were shut down by the National Park Service because of SARS-CoV-2 just before their season started. Unlike some inner-city restaurants that can pivot to take-out services, there is little company owners like this could do except refund customers, hope they rebook in the future, and struggle to survive in the interim.

Unsurprisingly, given the initial hunkering down at home and forced closure of businesses across the country, most indicators used for families' economic well-being turned sharply negative after the pandemic hit.

More representative data for the whole population show this clearly. Work by the Pew Research Center from April 2020 suggested that 43 percent of American adults saw someone in their household lose a job or take a pay cut due to the outbreak.[3] Some could weather that storm more easily than others. Just 23 percent of low-income households sailed into the crisis with rainy-day funds that could help cover their expenses for three months, for example, compared with 75 percent of upper-income Americans.

There was a major policy response to all this devastation, too, however: Congress plowed $2.2 trillion into a relief bill that massively expanded unemployment insurance, sent out $1,200 checks to more than 80 percent of tax filers, and provided hundreds of billions of dollars in support to businesses to maintain payroll.[4] Large numbers of households gained a lot from these programs, others gained little, and future taxpayers were made worse off. The net effect on families' finances from all these impacts is heavily dependent on their personal circumstances.

The economic impacts of the pandemic are complex and multifaceted. Yet what is clear is that, whether we are discussing financial well-being or job security, plenty of people have struggled during this crisis on what we'd consider conventional economic indicators. That is what made one phone conversation I had back in April 2020 all the more surprising.

Your Bank Balance and Economic Welfare

It was late in the evening and I was on a call to a UK friend, whom I'll call "Dave" to protect his identity. Now Dave is a big consumer of news. He was well aware of the headlines about the sorts of broad economic impacts we've discussed, which were also afflicting Britain. Back then, the UK was in a government-mandated lockdown similar to much of the United States.

Yet as we discussed the economic fallout from the crisis, he made quite a remarkable claim. When I asked him how he, personally, was coping, Dave confidently and unambiguously claimed that he was actually "economically better off" as a result of this pandemic.

Dave isn't a hand-sanitizer manufacturer or an epidemiologist who's being hired by a top consultancy to model the path of the virus. He's neither a friend of Joe Exotic from the popular documentary *Tiger King*, able to profit from lucrative TV gigs, nor is he an Amazon worker who gained from the company's temporary hazard pay policy. In short, there was little reason to assume the pandemic would be economically good for him.

So I was somewhat taken aback by his remark. He was the first person I heard who claimed to be better off as a result of a global pandemic that had put people around the world under effective house arrest and generated huge job losses. So I pressed him to explain exactly what he meant.

"Well," he replied, "my spending—on restaurants, going to the cinema, buying tickets to football [soccer] matches—has fallen dramatically. Outside of basic bills, my outgoings, I reckon, have fallen by 70 percent or more. Yet I'm getting the same wages, as I can work from home. So I'm actually saving far more money than I was before the lockdown. I looked at my bank balance the other day and I was shocked by how much was in there. I'm much, much better off than I would have been."

I had no reason to doubt Dave when he claimed he had more *wealth* than before this crisis. That is, because he was lucky enough to have enjoyed steady wages from employment, his spending decline and lack of need to borrow meant that his extra savings grew; as a result, the total value of all his assets had grown while his debts remained steady. On paper, then, he was indeed a financially wealthier man than if this crash hadn't occurred. In that sense, he was, by one definition, financially better off.

But did he feel better off? "Absolutely not," he replied. Dave is a social guy. He usually plays on a rugby team and goes to the gym, bars, restaurants, and the movie theater regularly. I could tell from his social media presence that he was bored stiff during the full lockdown period. He was pining for the pandemic to be over. So how would an economist reconcile his feelings with the claim he was "economically better off"? Isn't this a case of there being a clear disconnect between economics and reality?

Well, no. For despite people constantly conflating economics with money, economics does not, in fact, start and end with our bank balance, or even our wages. Remember what I said in the introduction? Economics is really about choices. One pretty obvious consequence of both the virus itself and the drastic policies used to contain it is that we have faced a much more limited range of choices about how to live our lives during this pandemic. These constraints undoubtedly made Dave worse off.

It Matters Who Decides

Economists' starting point is usually that individuals are the best judges of what is good for them. Our actions tend to represent what we prefer to do, given the circumstances, financial constraints, and time constraints we face (economists call these actions our *revealed preferences*). In economic jargon, we assume that people seek to maximize their *utility*—that is, they try to get the highest possible value from their actions—including in their day-to-day decisions.

Think about going to an ice cream parlor. If I were asked to pick two scoops of ice cream and our seller had all the flavors in the world available, I might choose to have one pistachio and one hazelnut—my favorite combination. It would be pretty reasonable to assume then, that this combination, under these circumstances, showed the choice that maximized my well-being from eating ice cream on that particular day.

But suppose instead that I'd walked into the shop and the seller told me he only had peanut butter, a flavor that I detested, but that it was government orders that I instead buy three scoops, even though, faced with the unpleasant option available, I'd prefer to not spend the money at all.

It should be obvious that in some "real" sense, I'd be worse off in this situation than before: I am being forced to consume a flavor I dislike, even though that's not how I'd best like to use my money. That I end up with more ice cream doesn't compensate for that in terms of my overall well-being.

A similar phenomenon explains what went on with Dave and this pandemic. At least in part, he was being forced by circumstance into behaviors he'd usually reject. Just as my buying more ice cream when made to doesn't make me better off, the fact that Dave saved more and became financially wealthier when circumstances and policy forced him to didn't make him better off either.

Dave was in an unusual position. He had always had the option to live the lockdown lifestyle, if he had wanted to. His job allowed him to have worked from anywhere, including home. Nothing stopped him from staying in except to visit the grocery store once per week and to exercise once per day before the pandemic hit. There was no law that said he couldn't have lived this way and saved the extra money, thus becoming better off in the financial sense.

But despite having that option, he rejected it. He actively chose to spend that money on going to restaurants, to the movies, or on vacations, rather than save it. He wanted to hang out with family members and friends and to play rugby on the weekends. Faced with the choice of watching savings accumulate in his bank balance, or living more for today, he chose the latter.

In economic terms then, the pandemic overall has clearly made Dave *worse off* than before because he has been forced into a lifestyle and wealth combination that he would ideally prefer to reject. His personal *economic welfare* (a term economists use to mean how well someone is doing) fell, even though his bank balance was healthier. He was economically poorer than he was pre-virus, despite the status of his finances.

Our Ideal Choices Are Context-Dependent

Now, of course, Dave's choices were personal to him. Economists recognize that *value is subjective*—that the value of any good, service, or time to us is determined by our individual judgment of how far the product or action goes toward meeting our own needs.

In simple terms, although Dave was worse off with this new combination of lifestyle and wealth than before the pandemic, that doesn't mean that everyone who might have been financially healthier would have preferred their old lives back. Others might not have previously had the option of living the way they did under lockdowns and found they actually preferred that lifestyle. Perhaps, for example, the lockdown enabled them to spend more time with their children in the mornings, which they valued highly and which they couldn't conceivably have enjoyed before.

But there is another piece to this jigsaw puzzle in thinking about what enhances Dave's well-being. Dave's preferences were also context-dependent. Although he might have preferred to live his old lifestyle rather than his pandemic one with the virus absent, that need not mean he'd have preferred to live his old lifestyle in the presence of the virus, which imposes new risks.

Just as I might decide it is best for me to eat peanut butter ice cream if I were starving and there is no other food store open, Dave may have made very different decisions to maximize his well-being when a potentially deadly virus was on the loose than he would have made in the pre-pandemic world.

With the virus around, it may well have improved his economic welfare somewhat (relative to the even bigger fall in welfare he'd face from not changing his behavior at all) to sacrifice rugby and avoid seeing his grandparents for a while, because he valued both his health and the lives of his loved ones highly. Our preferred choices, in other words, are contingent on circumstances and the constraints these circumstances bring.

Dave may well have preferred to live the hermit lifestyle of lockdown given the existence of the virus even if governments hadn't mandated it, and even if this was a lifestyle he had rejected beforehand. When the world around us changes, the rational choices we may make about how to behave change too.

The really important point here, though, is that economic welfare is clearly not the same as financial well-being, even though the two are often used synonymously in public debate. "The economy" is, in fact, "us" and the choices we make. It is not just about our incomes or even formal activity that occurs in markets with prices.

Aggregating to the level of the whole economy, a country's economic welfare is therefore a much broader conception than just dollars and cents, or *gross domestic product (GDP)*—a measure of the value of all final goods and services produced domestically. Although GDP may be a reasonable enough guide to the path of a country's economic welfare over long periods of time, it can prove inadequate and misleading in circumstances like this when the constraints on our decisions have fundamentally changed.

Nationally, for example, when talking about how much worse off we are as a result of the pandemic writ large, commentators often use GDP as a proxy—a close-enough measurement—for our decline in well-being. But as we've highlighted, households became much worse off for reasons other than the fall in market production, because of the health impacts on those affected, the liberties they lost, and the non-market activities they no longer felt safe engaging in due to the virus.

Think about how much worse off you felt by not seeing family, not being able to help out with a charity, losing time as a single person to find a partner, or the missed chances to develop your sports skills during those early phases in the pandemic.

None of these things appear in measured GDP—economists consider most of them "nonmarket leisure"—but not being able to do them clearly has a large cost to your economic welfare. You'd have paid money to maintain these freedoms if you could have done so safely. The decline in GDP during the crisis compared with before the crisis is therefore just a subset of the bigger loss of social economic welfare—the economic welfare of the whole community—that we have endured as a result of this pandemic.[5]

Yet just as GDP ignores the value of the broader losses to economic welfare arising from living with the virus, its fall also partly reflects new choices we choose to make to avoid a yet greater fall in economic welfare coming from lost lives and heartache. Just as I may gorge on peanut butter ice cream when I am famished, the public may well really want to swallow at least some of the medicine of social distancing to avoid the possible death or ill health of themselves and their family and friends.

As economist Justin Wolfers wrote for the *New York Times*, social distancing lowers GDP by reducing the degree of formal activity that can feasibly occur.[6] But if it works, and we collectively value the beneficial impacts more than the additional GDP lost as a result, then our economic welfare will actually be higher than it would have been if behavior had remained unchanged, *given the circumstances we face.* We have to therefore be very careful in how we think about economic welfare and how it interacts with conventional measures of economic activity such as GDP, especially when comparing across very different states of the world.

Wolfers puts it this way: let's suppose that social distancing overall works to save hundreds of thousands of lives. If the pharmaceutical sector had developed a pill that had the same impact as social distancing in terms of saving lives, people would have probably been willing to pay a lot for it. This would show up as a big gain in GDP. But social distancing, as a nonmarket activity, does not show up in GDP, despite similar benefits. Even if not everyone were willing to pay for it, the GDP gains of the social distancing pill would at least somewhat have offset GDP losses elsewhere.

Using GDP as a metric for our well-being during the pandemic may therefore have both understated the economic welfare losses to society compared with the pre-pandemic world, and also failed to capture how social distancing improves welfare relative to bigger losses we might have endured if our behavior had remained unchanged in the presence of the virus.

Think about it this way: suppose a country was attacked by a hostile foreign power and, to defend its territory, its citizens went to work in munitions, as watchmen, and enlisted in the army as part of a broader war effort. The economic welfare losses resulting from the constraints of the war would vastly exceed any GDP loss that might occur (in fact, GDP might remain high because of all the measured activity). But economic welfare might be lower still if peoples' behavior had not changed in response to the attack. In the same way, people staying at home to avoid spreading a disease during a pandemic may lead to economic welfare losses that exceed the large GDP losses *relative to the pre-pandemic period.* This action might be preferable in welfare terms compared to having people continue as normal, however, given the reality of the virus, which could result in large numbers of additional people dying. During a pandemic then, there's good reason to think GDP is a very bad metric for assessing economic welfare.

So far we've talked about individual and societal choices in much the same way, as if the whole country making choices is just the sum of all individual action. But governments have also taken steps to constrain our behavior and choices beyond our voluntary action, ostensibly because they didn't trust us to do what was best for societal welfare.

What justifies such constraints on our behavior? One rationale is that, if free to do as we please, certain activities that have negative impacts on other people will be engaged in too much. Failure to account for these impacts—to "price them in" when we make decisions as individuals—is said to reduce overall *social welfare* (the welfare for the whole of society) relative to what we can ideally achieve. As we shall see, this has been the primary justification for restricting our liberties during this pandemic.

ECONOMIC LESSON

Economic welfare is a catch-all term for how well people are doing and is a broader conception of well-being than just financial well-being at the household level or GDP at the national level. In regards to the impact of SARS-CoV-2, people's finances or national GDP can give a misleading impression about what is happening to economic welfare. The pandemic, by constraining people's choice set, is likely to have made many households and the country much worse off than their finances or GDP alone would suggest, relative to a pre-pandemic world. However, given the reality of the presence of the virus, we might actively prefer to adopt behaviors we'd usually shun that lower our financial well-being or GDP, which suggests these new behaviors serve to enhance our economic welfare in these peculiar circumstances.

ECONOMIC TERMS INTRODUCED

- **hazard pay:** additional pay for the undertaking or performance of work duties that are dangerous or risky
- **wealth:** the market value of all the assets someone owes less their debts
- **revealed preferences:** the idea that people's behaviors and purchasing habits allow us to infer their true preferences
- **utility:** the satisfaction we get from consuming certain goods or services, or their usefulness to us
- **economic welfare:** a synonym for well-being, which includes financial well-being but is a broader term for how we are doing in other ways too
- **value is subjective:** the idea that value derives not from any intrinsic properties of a good or activity, or the labor that has gone into it, but from individual preferences
- **GDP:** the annual market value of all final goods and services produced domestically
- **social welfare:** the economic welfare of the whole community

2

SHOULD I BE FREE TO RISK INFECTING
YOUR GRANDMA WITH A DEADLY VIRUS?

An introduction to externalities

The fact that Dave feels so much worse off as a result of this pandemic shows how ordinarily people's freedom to pursue their own desires and dreams helps enhance their economic welfare. But not all decisions we might make freely are good for society as a whole. That's particularly true when it comes to a potentially deadly virus.

There's still huge uncertainty about how this coronavirus originated. Much informed opinion originally traced it to Wuhan's wet markets, which contain a plethora of animal species in close proximity, thus making it a potential breeding ground for the transmission of diseases across species. Experts think that this particular virus originated in a bat but might have evolved to latch onto human cells via a pangolin, cat, sheep, or even a pigeon.

More recent evidence has cast doubt on the theory of the Wuhan market as the actual source of the pandemic. Researchers Shing Hei Zhan, Benjamin E. Deverman, and Yujia Alina Chan have suggested that the SARS-CoV-2 genome is evolving too slowly compared with previous viruses to imply that it is still new to human transmission.[12] This, coupled with a lack of evidence of infected animal samples in the market, suggests the virus's jump into human hosts might have occurred before the Wuhan market outbreak, in a rural area, or (more speculatively) via a research lab working with collected samples. In any case, it remains true that events in the Wuhan market amplified the spread of the virus.

It doesn't matter for purposes of exposition here whether the virus jumped into our network of human beings via some undercooked bat soup, the handling of an illegal sale of pangolin, traces on a surface in an unhygienic environment, an interaction between someone else and an animal, or even a mistake from a lab. The important point is that somebody's activity in that market, seemingly rational to them, had catastrophic and global social consequences.

When deciding to attend that market on the particular day transmission occurred, the individuals in question undoubtedly underestimated how their choices would affect others. They weighed in their minds the private costs to themselves of traveling in or selling their products (the monetary costs, lost opportunities of using their time for other purposes, etc.), perhaps even being aware of some of the health risks to themselves in that environment. But they clearly did not give much consideration to how their actions might infringe on others' well-being or to the catastrophic economic and social consequences of their actions.

Going Viral: An Externality Problem

This is perhaps the most extreme example imaginable of what an economist would call an *externality*. The basic concept is that some purchases we make or some activities we engage in impose costs or provide benefits to other people outside of that transaction for which no appropriate compensation can be paid. For a *negative externality*, like the activity that propelled the virus into the community in Wuhan, the individuals involved did not face anywhere near the full social costs of their decisions. Clearly their market activity that day was not optimal for society. Yet there is no obvious or conceivable way those individuals could be made to compensate us for the consequences of their actions. The implication of a genuine negative externality is that market activity, left alone, may generate too much of the consumption or interaction than is ideal for society overall.

Unfortunately, the risk of zoonotic viruses (those that jump from animals to humans) developing is ever present. Barring obvious actions, such as closing high-risk wet markets or eliminating risky lab experiments, it's unclear how policies by governments might seek to protect against them. Many activities involve human interaction with other species, and we have no way of knowing, until there's a mass outbreak, where the risk of externalities lay. Some externalities are, therefore, sadly inevitable. But once SARS-CoV-2 was spreading, it seemed obvious that we faced a much broader externality problem, one where some changes to our behaviors and policies might help.

COVID-19's first reported case in the United States came on January 19, 2020, when a 35-year-old man turned up at an urgent care clinic in Snohomish County, Washington State.[3] The man had a cough and felt feverish and had recently returned from Wuhan. Just two months later, by March 19, 2020, there were more than 13,000 confirmed cases within the United States—and undoubted legions more people actually infected, given the lack of early testing and those infected who did not display symptoms.

The rapid escalation of confirmed cases in just two months highlights something that is trivially obvious: viruses spread. But in the case of COVID-19, features of the disease meant that it spread much more easily and rapidly than some other viruses. Not only was it fairly contagious (it was estimated that each infected person, on average, passed it to between 2 and 3 additional people prior to social distancing), but those infected could transmit the disease before they displayed obvious symptoms or despite not displaying symptoms at all.[4]

The implication here is that people going about their ordinary day-to-day activities could lead to a rapid growth in infections, and ultimately deaths, at least until enough people had recovered and gained immunity (if, indeed, immunity is permanent or at least long-lasting—something now evidenced yet uncertain, given admittedly rare reports of individuals suffering repeat infections). Given that people tend to value their lives and health very highly (see chapter 4), the potential social costs of normal behavior in the presence of the virus would therefore vastly exceed the private costs to individuals of deciding on their behavior.

Without accurate testing every day or so to check whether we are all carrying the virus, that means that my decision to go out and socialize risks my spreading the virus to others, or others spreading it to me, without even knowing it. We thus have no way of knowing in advance who should pay whom for the risks they are imposing on others. While ordinarily we might presume the case for freedom, economists, such as the University of Michigan's Justin Wolfers, have therefore described SARS-CoV-2 as one giant negative externality problem.[5]

Just like with pollution, the idea here is that when choosing the extent of our social activity, private individuals acting alone will consider their own risks and benefits but take insufficient consideration of the risks of infecting others, not least because they will not know whether they themselves are infected. They will consider the private costs of their actions but take insufficient account of the external costs of their behavior. As a result, too much human interaction will occur relative to what is best for society. The outcome, in economic terms, will be inefficient.

In this case, we will get more infections and deaths than is optimal (the concept of an "optimal" number of deaths might seem controversial—let's park that thought for now). Private action that does not sufficiently consider these costs will ultimately manifest itself in more mild illnesses for many; quite horrible short-term health experiences for others; hospitalizations; potential long-term neurological, heart, or lung damage; extended periods of symptoms for a few; and elevated mortality, especially for the elderly or those with linked comorbidities. In other cases, the externality might not be realized until the virus has been transmitted through a network of people through asymptomatic or mildly symptomatic spreaders.

In fact, the negative externalities of ordinary social behavior during this pandemic were broader than just these direct health impacts. Modeling by economists Martin Bodenstein, Giancarlo Corsetti, and Luca Guerrieri suggested that, absent meaningful social distancing, a higher rate of COVID-19 infections could affect core sectors' ability to function.[6] If important industries such as transportation, energy, or health care faced the prospect of sudden high levels of sick workers from a large infection peak that was caused by unchanged behavior, then the economic welfare damage beyond the harm to the individuals affected could be huge.

So, as well as risking infecting other people directly, social activity in a pandemic risks infecting workers who are essential to a functioning economy, bringing broader external costs that we might not consider when we are deciding our own plans.

In fact, one externality has especially worried policymakers throughout this pandemic. It was believed that leaving things to voluntary behavior might lead to infections and hospitalizations so numerous that severe COVID-19 caseloads would exceed the intensive care capacity of hospitals. Hence it was thought that more people would die unnecessarily through a *congestion externality*—that is, infection numbers being so high that people might not be able to get hospital beds or intubation equipment even if necessary, or else people with other health conditions might not be able to access care as resources were diverted to dealing with COVID-19.

Avoiding this scenario, which happened in Italy, was the stated motivation behind "flattening the curve" as a policy objective of lockdowns in the early days of the pandemic, which was intended to spread cases out to avoid hospital systems being overwhelmed.

Adding them all up, it is thought that there are potentially large negative externalities associated with human social interactions during this pandemic.

How My Behavior Threatens Your Grandma

Suppose it was a nice hot sunny day here in Washington, DC. The virus was still circling and there were absolutely no government restrictions on activity. When deciding whether to head for a walk on the National Mall, visiting a few retail stores or a bar en route, I might implicitly think about the costs and benefits to me of my social activity.

Yes, there is a risk I could get infected with the virus by being around and interacting with other people. But compared to other demographic and health groups, my risk of dreadful outcomes from this disease, given that I have no known preexisting conditions, is very low. On the other hand, I would really enjoy getting out for some sunshine, buying some new clothes in a store, and seeing some friends for a drink. I value the benefits of going out highly.

I will try to be respectful of the risks I pose to others, obviously. Yet I don't have any major symptoms, except a slightly sore throat that I put down to last night's whiskey. So I might feel confident I am not carrying the virus. But the truth is that I do not know whether I'm a carrier, absent an instant test. Perhaps I already picked up the virus from a container from the takeout food I ordered midweek. Or maybe the lady who served me at the grocery store three days ago, or a recent taxi driver, transmitted the virus to me, and I'm in the presymptomatic stage. I cannot know for sure whether I might sneeze or cough or breathe and unwittingly spread the virus while I am in a store or bar.

If I overwhelmingly worry about the costs and risks to me, perhaps I take insufficient account of the risks of my behavior to others. Again, if I get too close to your grandma in a store while I am not wearing a mask, or else get too close to someone else who might work in her care home or live with her, that means I risk potentially infecting her indirectly without even realizing it. Yet I would not feel the cost of that eventuality, nor is there any feasible way for me to compensate her for my behavior. It probably wouldn't even cross my mind to consider how I might contribute to hospital congestion or increase risks for workers in crucial industries.

This isn't a false concern, either. Lots of people with mild infections might, absent government intervention or at least guidance, decide to go about their lives paying insufficient attention to the welfare of others. We certainly saw some such behavior from younger people in Florida bars during the early stages of the pandemic. There have been some well-documented examples of others deliberately seeking infection because they thought the virus was a hoax or that getting infection early was best for them personally too.[7]

Although academic studies have suggested that Black Lives Matter protests and a Trump campaign rally in Tulsa might not have led to an initial spike in infections on net, this has been put down to offsetting behavior elsewhere—others staying home more or closing their businesses to avoid protestors and rally attendees.[8] In interviews, many protestors and Trump supporters made clear they thought it was worth taking the risk with their health to protest injustice or to attend a rally. The fact so many still thought, months into a pandemic, that they were only risking their own health, and not that of their families who often chose not to attend, is perhaps the clearest evidence we'll get that the externality problem is real: people often don't sufficiently consider the costs or risks they impose on others, especially given some of the indirect externalities we've outlined.[9]

Now, it's worth being crystal clear here about what the externality is and isn't. An externality, to reiterate, is a cost or benefit imposed on others for which it is impossible to charge compensation. It is nothing to do with the risk judgments of individuals. Two households might have decided to bear the risks of COVID-19 infections by getting together to share Thanksgiving. If a member of one household then infected a member of the other household, this wouldn't be an externality—it was a risk the individuals bore willingly and knowingly. The externality is the risk to other people outside of these households resulting from the meet-up: their colleagues at work, the staff who served them in hotels en route home, or the congestion at hospitals if any of those household members subsequently required medical treatment.

So, the primary externalities with this virus are the passing on of the disease to third parties, the potential congestion of large numbers of cases in hospitals, or the knocking out of essential industries through a major spike in infections. There is no way to charge people who put others' health at risk in these ways. The externality then is the external costs of the spread of illness, the longer-term damage to health of contracting the disease, the deaths, the risks of infecting people further along a social network, or the more indirect costs associated with contributing to key workers being sick or hospitals running over capacity.

The externality is not, as commentators claim, the cost to taxpayers associated with providing any health care to deal with the disease. People often claim these types of costs are externalities of smoking and drinking, too—that is, that someone getting lung cancer from smoking and requiring Medicare treatment is costing others, thus justifying government intervention. But these fiscal externalities are just a reflection of how we pay for health care, which can be changed at any time.[10]

It's also worth being clear on the implication of the externality framework. That we identify an externality problem should not mean that governments ban the activities generating the externality entirely. That would almost certainly be worse for societal well-being, because almost all activities have benefits as well as costs. Just as it would be disproportionate to ban driving because it causes pollution, so it would be disproportionate (and highly damaging) to put everyone in isolation pods for months to stop the spread of SARS-CoV-2 entirely. Society would collapse.

No, what the externality framework implies is that economically free choices might lead to too much disease spreading relative to what is best for society—*although the optimum quantity is not zero.* The policy conclusion from that should be to find the least disruptive way to ensure we get to a level of activity that balances the social benefits from additional activities with the social costs they impose.

Policies to Get the Right Level of Social Activity

Economists have a long history of experience advising governments on this, as approaches to alcohol, tobacco, pollution, or dealing with common resource problems show.

Despite a tendency for economists to reach for government interventions to deal with externality problems, it's worth noting that often markets do find ways to deliver compensation to others for the external effects of people's actions. There was a famous instance in Manhattan, for example, where a new building threatened to destroy a view of the Empire State Building for owners of a loft apartment block.[11] The loft owners banded together to raise $11 million to pay the developer not to build. When property rights are clear and the costs of transacting relatively low, externalities cease to be a problem because people bargain or trade. Government policy can sometimes help by reducing the cost of transacting or by assigning property rights.

Sadly, externalities often get misused to justify government interventions when markets already deal with the problem too. For example, governments around the world have banned smoking in bars, citing the dangers of secondhand smoke for customers and bar staff as a negative externality. But provided staff and customers have good information on the risks, their freedom to choose where to drink or work should mean establishments have to offer higher wages to workers or lower prices to drinkers to compensate each for the dangers they are putting themselves in by going to the bar. In other words, in a world of good information and property rights for the establishments, the externality is already accounted for and compensated for within markets.

But these examples also serve to show when the case for government action is stronger: when coordination for bargaining is difficult or property rights are unclear. In these instances, economists tend to advocate taxes and regulations.

The first line of thinking is often to try to devise corrective taxes on the offending activity, set at just the right level to ensure private individuals consider the costs they impose on others when undertaking those actions. Take, as examples, the popularity of "sin taxes" on tobacco for secondhand smoke, or carbon taxes to deal with the externality problem of carbon emissions. The aim, again, is not to ban smoking or carbon emissions entirely but to price in the external costs of the activity to try to ensure the level of activity that does occur is *socially optimal*.

Other times still it might be less costly to impose regulations on those who are worst affected by the activity. A new airport might produce noise pollution that imposes costs on the households below the flight path. But nobody forces those victims to live there indefinitely. It might be more efficient, in other words, to mandate that the houses be fitted with better noise-proof windows or to pay the affected residents to move rather than impose regulations requiring costly innovation for quieter airplanes or the banning of flights at night. We generally want the least-cost avoider to bear the cost—that is, the party that can achieve a given reduction in damage or risk at the lowest cost possible.

A key insight from economist Ronald Coase is that all externalities are two-sided like this. Because there are costs of transacting between parties to bargain and compensate, having the government impose the full liability on one party as the polluter or externality spreader can often be worse than doing nothing.[12] His famous theorem's main conclusion is that determining the best approach to dealing with an externality problem is always an empirical question specific to the circumstances. That is, theory alone doesn't get us very far.

Now, in reality, designing policies to correct for externalities is a lot thornier than textbooks suggest. Externalities are difficult to calculate and might not occur for all levels of an activity (if I smoke one cigarette in your presence, I probably do little damage to your health; if I smoke 100 a day on the other hand . . .). Other times they are trivial. Sometimes an activity might produce multiple externalities in different directions, such that the best course of action is still doing nothing. Often, governments themselves cause externalities, or at least politics does: think about how people might vote for a candidate who implements destructive, wealth-destroying trade policies that make you worse off without ever compensating you.

Finally, sometimes externalities are much more difficult to deal with because they are also what economists describe as *collective action problems.* These are instances where there are community-wide impacts of particular actions, meaning everyone would be better off if certain behaviors were adhered to, but at an individual level, there are incentives for individuals to deviate or "cheat."

One example given by the economist Sam Bowman is of sea fisheries, where all fishermen would be better off in the long term if each individual fisherman limited their catch to keep fish numbers plentiful. But if others are limiting their catch, there are incentives for each individual fisherman to overfish and the best outcome can therefore break down if enough people act according to their own interests. In these instances, many economists argue that the case for government action is much stronger, such as by setting legally enforceable and tradable fishing quotas.

The work of Nobel prize–winning economist Elinor Ostrom showed that private communities can, in fact, come to agreements on these types of problems, negating the need for government intervention in many cases. But as Bowman has explained, the types of arrangements Ostrom describes are more likely to emerge slowly within small communities, so they might be less feasible for acute problems, such as infectious disease control.[13]

Dealing with Externalities from SARS-CoV-2

If you grasp all these potential problems with the externality framework then you are ahead of a large proportion of professional economists. For many, it seems to suffice to point out an externality exists and then demand government action to correct it, without thinking through whether this action actually improves outcomes or what the cost might be. And although, clearly, SARS-CoV-2 is an example of an externality challenge, there are still two specific and obvious problems with this simplistic externality framing of the virus for the purposes of public policy.

The first is that it is incredibly hard to think of solutions that correct for the externality that would work efficiently in theory and would be easy to implement. With significant early uncertainty about how the virus was spread, which activities were high-risk, and when and what health costs were imposed on others, pricing in the externality, for example, would be extraordinarily difficult across different activities.

Imposing a tax on all social activities to deter the risk of spreading the virus is nearly impossible, although some targeted taxes could help reduce seemingly high-risk practices.[14] Raising the price of using public transportation, for example, through lowering government subsidies or taxing ticket prices, may deter the use of mass transit, particularly if operators adopted surge pricing to prevent packed trains.

One early study suggested the subway might have been a key vector for the virus in the initial spread of SARS-CoV-2 in New York City.[15] Other studies have found strong evidence that the early higher prevalence of COVID-19 in black populations can be accounted for, in part, by their higher use of public transit than the general population, while U.S. counties with greater use of public transport relative to telecommuting saw higher death rates early on.[16] So, for a high-risk activity like this—being in close proximity to others in congested buses or railroad cars for extended periods—a tax or charge could help reduce people's willingness to take public transit.

Introducing fines or taxes for not wearing facemasks in indoor public places, failing to separate tables in restaurants, and for traveling to areas of high rates of infection or failing to quarantine upon return could all likewise help proxy for dealing with the externalities of socializing or travel. One could imagine, too, that new technologies might be used to facilitate congestion-based pricing on other public transport or in large public spaces.

On the flip side, governments could offer tax breaks to companies that encourage remote work or temporarily subsidize sick pay so that fewer infected people would intermingle with others at work. Some governments in East Asia encourage quarantine for those who have come into contact with infected people by paying them to isolate or by imposing large penalties on them for breaching the rules.

Some of these policies would be simpler to administer than others, although all face difficulties. There is also a high degree of uncertainty about what the level of the charges or subsidies should actually be—if we were trying to get to the socially efficient level of activity, these charges should reflect highly localized risks, vary at different stages of the pandemic, and change when behavior evolves or the virus mutates.

What about setting frameworks for property rights? Some have suggested making businesses financially liable for infections on business premises through the courts. This, supposedly, would encourage them to invest in providing safe environments with good social distancing practices. But this too clearly has a range of problems. How can one really assess whether someone contracted the disease at work or in a store? And should businesses be really on the hook for potentially ruinous compensation claims if an employee or customer turns up and infects lots of other people? It seems unlikely that small restaurants would always represent the least-cost avoider.

In fact, given the higher risk they face, the least-cost avoiders, to avoid most of the highest costs associated with the externality here, might be those particularly vulnerable to the worst health care impacts or hospital congestion, such as the elderly, or large-venue activities such as concerts or sports events where many social interactions occur.

It may be, then, that differential levels of regulation by demographic or industry are better than blanket rules. But this raises all sorts of problems regarding equity and the fact that individual risks within demographic groups may vary a lot.

In fact, it is really difficult to target the genuine externality problem in the absence of widespread testing. That's in part because there is a collective action problem here. Everyone might be better off if there was widespread mask wearing or modest social distancing that helped get the virus to a level where clusters of cases could be easily identified. But coming to an agreement between the whole population is logistically impossible and some individuals have strong incentives to deviate from the behavior that might be best for society as a whole, perhaps because they themselves are at low risk from the disease or because their livelihood depends on more social interaction.

While it might be rational for people to voluntarily curb their interactions when the disease has widespread prevalence (and so they or their families face high risks), the incentive to ignore social distancing or mask wearing conventions is high when the disease prevalence is low. But, due to the way the virus spreads, too many people might therefore "cheat," leading to the bad social outcome of widespread disease prevalence. Everyone would be better off if we could all stick to the conventions or rules, but the incentives to deviate from them are strong for a lot of people. That's why many economists supported the state for imposing laws that punished those whose behavior deviated from the rules.

Of course, even if the government has the power to police mandates on social distancing, being able to do so in the absence of an intolerable surveillance state is impossible. So instead, governments imposed quite stringent initial lockdowns to try to eliminate as much person-to-person contact as was feasible, alongside more-targeted regulatory measures on certain activities.

These entailed closures of public schools; the shuttering of nonessential businesses; and stay-at-home or shelter-in-place orders, which asked people to stay home unless it was necessary to go out—such as to buy food, gas, or medical supplies, to receive medical attention, or to get to work. Some governors imposed further, more-specific restrictions, even on outdoor exercise activities and on what could be bought in stores that were allowed to be open. Governors were worried about a spiraling immediate crisis threatening the viability of health care capacity, and they emphasized how these extraordinary policies were necessary for confronting the congestion externality.

But just as with other bans and crude restrictions, these measures are very costly. Their broad scope—eliminating lots of nonrisky activity too—almost certainly banned activities that didn't pose any externality risk. In the presence of meaningful negative externalities from the virus overall, lockdowns might indeed have been better than doing nothing in terms of their impact on social economic welfare, but that's a low bar for public policy.

After reopening, and with more suggestive evidence of their effectiveness, guidance and mandates for mask wearing became a key policy tool to try to deal with the externality; the evolution of this policy is discussed at length in chapter 7. If the efficacy of the mask is high, this can help solve or mitigate the externality problem in a relatively low-cost way. That's because the main benefit of a mask—if it works—is to stop an infected person who is asymptomatic from easily spreading the disease—in other words, it targets the externality directly.

Given the uncertainty about who is infected, however, mask wearing again requires a very high degree of compliance to be fully effective. Guidance alone then might not be enough if there is reason to think a sizable chunk of people won't comply with the advice to wear masks. But, again, policing mask wearing is costly and intrusive, too, even for the government. There are no easy answers.

The Positive Externalities of Immunity

The second problem with looking at SARS-CoV-2 as a simple negative externality problem associated with human interaction, however, is that it ignores the potential *benefits* associated with someone contracting the virus.

That sounds crazy. How can it be beneficial to have someone contract the virus? Well, just as negative externalities exist, so do *positive externalities*. Someone who wipes down a crosswalk call button with a sanitizer wipe might be doing so in order to protect themselves from getting infected. But they might also be preventing others from becoming infected. Hence there are broader benefits to society from their actions, for which there is no obvious means of offering, in a credible way, a reward to them.

There is also a *positive externality* that arises from someone having contracted and recovered from the disease. That's because, once someone has recovered, they have immunity to being reinfected (at least for a time) and so are unable to spread the disease to those who are susceptible to infection. This, of course, reduces risks to others, as well as providing a source of labor and support to those yet to be infected.

That might sound counterintuitive. But it is, of course, the thinking behind why governments mandate or subsidize vaccinations for diseases. Once someone has been vaccinated, they have a very high chance of being immune to a virus, or are at least less likely to get bad symptoms and so be highly infectious, meaning there are fewer people in the population who can spread the disease to unvaccinated people or to those for whom the vaccines were ineffective. A vaccine, in other words, has a positive externality, bringing external benefits beyond those enjoyed by the individual obtaining the injection. That's why many governments subsidize them.

In the same way, someone who has recovered from COVID-19 benefits other people who are yet to be infected because others can effectively free ride off interacting with them. It is why one potential endgame of this pandemic is so-called *herd immunity*, a situation where enough people have immunity (having recovered from infection or having been vaccinated) that any further outbreak of the virus fails to accelerate because there are too few individuals susceptible to infection.

Might there be a way of trying to deal with the highest-cost negative externalities while society benefits from these positive externalities?

Obviously, a vaccine offers one route. But before that was available, some economists suggested that because the health risks to younger and less-vulnerable people were lower compared with older people and those with comorbidities, we should have isolated high-risk individuals for longer and imposed less-stringent restrictions on the activities of low-risk individuals. That way the net effects on society might have been preferable to a crude lockdown—benefits would have been achieved at much lower cost. Indeed, economic modeling from economists such as Daron Acemoglu suggested a more-targeted approach could have improved economic welfare.[17] Some economists have even advocated subsidizing the social activities of low-risk groups.[18]

But society in practice operates very differently from models, where people can be easily contained. Our interactions in reality are a messy mix of interlocking networks. High-risk groups often live in multigenerational housing with low-risk people. Low-risk workers serve high-risk groups in care homes and hospitals. One economic study of nursing homes found that despite visitor restrictions from mid-March 2020, staff operating across different care homes created links among those homes that help explain the spread of COVID-19 cases.[19] Areas of high community transmission of the virus eventually appear to seed the virus to those working or living with more vulnerable groups, too, with predictable consequences.[20]

And, of course, there was and is huge uncertainty about who was high-risk and low-risk, given health conditions we might not even have been aware of, uncertainty about which preexisting conditions made the disease worse, and a lack of clarity yet as to the longer-term health consequences of the disease itself.

To complicate matters further, the optimal policy balance between dealing with the negative externalities and realizing the positive externalities depends on medical innovation and capacity, too, which is highly uncertain.

If we knew there would be an effective vaccine or increasingly effective treatments, then the ideal restrictions early on would be much tougher, because any lives saved today will be more likely to be lives that are saved permanently. If, on the other hand, there was never to be a medical solution, insulating the most vulnerable groups and preventing health care capacity being exceeded at any given time from a major spike by moving caseloads and deaths around might have been the best we could do. We might actually have desired, in that case, much looser restrictions than we saw initially, even acknowledging the negative externalities outlined here, because these ill effects would eventually be realized anyway.

Policymakers were more optimistic about medical innovation than that. In developed countries, most initially tried to suppress the virus, rather than mitigate its worst effects. They were hopeful that the lockdown would buy time for a vaccine or medical innovation, or else improved treatments, meaning that averting deaths then meant lower total deaths from the pandemic. At the time of writing in late December 2020, the rollout of vaccines with high apparent efficacies has begun, although how smooth that will be, how many people will be willingly vaccinated, and how robust those vaccines will be to mutations in the virus remains to be seen.

Framing the virus issue as if it were a simple negative externality economic problem in need of correction then doesn't get us very far in thinking about the best policies to deal with the virus. To really get a grip on how to approach it, we need to think about the risks and benefits of certain activities, rather than thinking about interactions per se. We have to consider the policy and behavioral approach that would minimize the overall economic welfare costs of the pandemic (which incorporates the impacts on health, economic activity, and our liberties).

Approaching the issue in this broader way, it will almost certainly have been the case that the ideal precautions that needed to be taken or imposed must have entailed at least some restrictions or deterrence on high-risk and low-risk groups alike. In different situations, such that we mitigated against the largest negative externalities in the early stages of the virus, we will realize the positive externalities as immunity develops naturally or through medical innovation.

It is right, in other words, that we as a society take steps to reduce the risk of me infecting your grandma. The social costs of normal behavior in the presence of a deadly virus are very large indeed. But it is highly likely that policies that minimize the overall costs to society (health and economic) from this virus would have always entailed tighter constraints on certain activities than others, including (as best evidence now suggests) access to nursing homes and very tight restrictions on large public gatherings, especially those held in buildings where people project their voices (churches, concert halls, etc.).

At the start of the pandemic, though, we had far less information about which activities were risky. In the face of uncertainty, policymakers decided to press an emergency precaution button that not only mandated closures for obviously high-risk activities (indoor bars, clubs, restaurants, concerts, and sporting events, for example) but also closed businesses deemed nonessential. They often also ordered people to stay home unless it was necessary to go out.

Or did they? Of course, in a legal sense it was most definitely governors across the country that shuttered much of the economy, eliminating businesses' freedom to choose how to operate and individuals' scope to engage in personal leisure, travel, and entertainment activity. But the analysis of externalities so far implicitly assumes that individuals would accurately judge the risks to themselves, while not sufficiently considering the broader social consequences of their actions.

But what if, at that early stage at least, the public's perceptions of the risks were such that they changed their behavior much more drastically than we might have expected? What if the perceived private costs of normal behavior were so high for a critical mass of people that voluntary behavior created an effective shutdown of much of the economy anyway?

ECONOMIC LESSON

Externalities exist, and sometimes government policies can be used to improve societal outcomes in light of them. However, they are often difficult to correct through policy. In the case of SARS-CoV-2, there are clearly negative externalities associated with activities that spread the virus, but there are also positive externalities from someone recovering and becoming immune to it. This messy reality means that the best approach is likely to depend on the risks of activities and the availability of technologies, such as the timing of vaccines—factors that were inherently uncertain in the early stages of the pandemic. A better framework now is to think in terms of risks and the overall costs and benefits of more marginal approaches to reducing the total economic welfare costs of the virus.

ECONOMIC TERMS INTRODUCED

- **externalities:** instances where the overall social costs or social benefits of the activity exceed the private costs and benefits but where it is infeasible to set compensation within markets to account for this
- **negative externality:** costs on third parties that cannot be compensated for within markets
- **positive externality:** benefits to third parties that cannot be compensated for within markets
- **collective action problem:** situations where economic actors would be better off cooperating but fail to do so because of individual incentives

3

DID WE CLOSE DOWN THE ECONOMY?
An introduction to public and private action

On the evening of March 15, 2020, an unofficial fan account of Walt Disney World, Florida, on Twitter shared a picture of large crowds huddled together to watch the "Happily Ever After" nighttime show at the company's Magic Kingdom theme park.[1]

That evening's display took place two weeks after Florida Governor Ron DeSantis had declared a state of emergency due to the spread of SARS-CoV-2. Yet here were hundreds of Americans and other tourists packed tightly together for 30 minutes or more on a balmy Florida night to see some fireworks.[2]

The picture became a major news story and the day's Twitter storm, drawing the righteous ire of, among others, Walt Disney's own great-niece, Abigail Disney. Her tweet—simply saying "Are you f***ing kidding me?"—expressed the exasperation many felt that Disney-goers were ignoring social distancing recommendations despite warnings about the risk of spreading a highly transmissible virus. As with spring break parties at Florida's beaches a few days later, the picture was taken as clear evidence of Americans' lack of concern for the health of others. This was perceived as an obvious example of the externality problem.

The lesson taken, repeated over and over online, was that Americans were selfishly unwilling to voluntarily socially distance to anywhere near the extent necessary to reduce the transmission of the virus. Government shutdowns, the likes of which had been implemented in Europe, would be needed, given the negative externalities of the virus spreading. Paternalistic government and unprecedented government orders, it was thought, were needed to save us from ourselves.

A small fact, however, was omitted in all this coverage. Walt Disney World had, in fact, announced two days earlier on March 13 that it would close its Florida theme parks after the evening the photo was taken. Far from Disney itself requiring the government to guide it toward responsible public health decisions, the company was ahead of the governor's curve. The Florida stay-at-home order and mandate for closure of nonessential businesses were not announced until April 1 and only became active on April 3. Disney had closed its theme parks voluntarily a full 18 days beforehand.

Private Action Led Public

This points to an important truth. Although externalities from this virus are a real problem, when the perceived private costs of continuing as normal are high enough, a lot of people and businesses will change their behavior dramatically without government intervention.

Disney, in this case, was perhaps worried about the huge reputational damage of being the site of a future superspreader event. Or perhaps the decision was more purely consumer led: Disney expected park attendance to plummet so much that it would be financially disadvantageous to open.

Whatever the explanation, they were not the only business shutting down activity voluntarily. Household names were already canceling events, scaling back their operations, or adjusting how they provided their services to protect customers and workers.

Cato Institute executive vice president David Boaz has pointed out how events such as South by Southwest, March Madness, the Masters Tournament, and the Boston Marathon were all canceled before the Centers for Disease Control and Prevention's (CDC) March 15 recommendation that gatherings of more than 50 people be prohibited.[3] Temporary closures of nationwide chains, such as Nike, Urban Outfitters, Lululemon, and Abercrombie & Fitch preceded state orders to close businesses too.[4]

Other businesses adjusted *how* they operated in the face of the public health threat. McDonald's announced that franchisees should close dining rooms and offer take-out services only. Starbucks closed some stores and only offered to-go services at those remaining open.[5] Major tech firms had told employees to work from home from the very first days of March. My employer, the Cato Institute, instituted mandatory teleworking 12 days before DC Mayor Muriel Bowser's nonessential business closure went into effect on March 24. As of writing this (December 2020), there are no plans to reconsider a return to regular office work until spring 2021 at the earliest.

In short, overwhelming numbers of businesses and nonprofits embraced radical social distancing in the form of business premises closures and working-from-home arrangements before government mandates compelled them to close. Yes, we can find businesses and activities that did not voluntarily close and that would have remained open were it not for government lockdowns. But to a large extent, lockdown regulations in the form of stay-at-home orders and nonessential business closures codified changes that had already begun in much of the market sector across the country.

That raises an obvious question: Why were businesses and nonprofits closing before governments compelled them to do so? In some cases it was undoubtedly due to the *expectation* of government orders to follow, or observation about what had happened in China and then Italy. But there's another, simpler explanation: in the face of the public health threat, enough consumers and workers were hesitant about stepping foot in buildings or commuting into cities where they risked infection. Those businesses affected, faced with collapsing demand and nervous workforces, saw it was no longer profitable or good for staff morale to keep their premises open.

If you want evidence that some business closures were consumer-driven rather than driven by government orders, think about airlines. Due to complex logistical requirements and then mandates by Congress to fly existing routes as a condition for their bailout, airlines didn't cancel all their domestic internal flights.[6] Yet still the flights that did run were often largely empty in May and June 2020. People quite simply did not want to fly between American cities, even when they had the chance. If airlines could have cut services further, they would have.

This might sound counterintuitive given the last chapter about externalities. But when the private risk of an activity is perceived as high enough (such as the risk of dying from an infectious disease, or risking your elderly family member's health, or being liable for a customer's death), workers, customers, and businesspeople will likely decide to curb activity drastically anyway. In other words, if the perceived private costs of activities are large enough, then people might make decisions closer to what is socially optimal, or even curb activity far beyond the ideal level. Without making a judgment on whether the social reaction to COVID-19 in those early stages went too far, it's certainly the case that "we" appeared to close much of the economy, even before government orders.

Americans' Behavior Changed Dramatically

The evidence for this is overwhelming. Data from OpenTable shows that seated diner numbers from restaurant reservations had already fallen a full 73 percent in the median state (compared with last year) by the time state governments mandated that restaurants close.[7] Georgia saw an incredible 93 percent decline by March 18, the day before Atlanta's mayor first restricted restaurants to providing take-out only, which was the precursor to a statewide regulation (see Figure 3.1).[8]

Smartphone data analysis from economists at Indiana University shows that Americans' travel outside their state, county, and even their homes had fallen dramatically too.[9] In fact, time spent at home grew more strongly in U.S. counties that were recreation and tourist destinations, highlighting how collapsing demand was pushing people onto the sofa. Major declines in out-of-state travel and social mixing occurred even in five states that had not introduced lockdowns by early April—Arkansas, Iowa, Nebraska, North Dakota, and South Dakota—showing clearly that this impact was not about formal regulations.

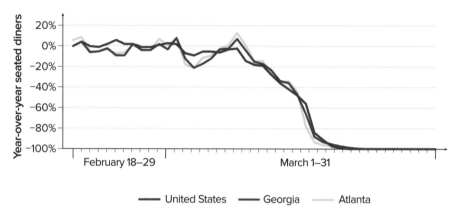

FIGURE 3.1

Seated diners from online, phone, and walk-in reservations on OpenTable, as a percentage change from the equivalent day last year

Source: OpenTable, "The State of the Restaurant Industry," https://www.opentable.com/state-of -industry.

To see just how dramatic the nationwide change of behavior pre-lockdowns was, consider the state of Missouri. By April 6, the day its governor's stay-at-home order became effective, the time that Missourians spent outside the home had already fallen by 21 percent compared with January (Figure 3.2).[10] Time spent on transit and at work similarly had fallen dramatically well before the governor's order too. Across other states, a big decline in time outside of the home preceded even closures of public schools, although these no doubt compounded both time spent at home and business closures.

In terms of consumer spending, the cliff-edge for Missouri had long passed before people were told to stay home. Spending on restaurants and hotels, transport, and entertainment all saw dramatic declines prior to April 6, with spending reaching its lowest level on March 30. True, St. Louis County had instituted a stay-at-home order on March 23, but as Figure 3.3 shows, the overwhelming majority of the decline in spending in the state occurred even before that order.[11] If anyone *closed* the economy, it was the population of Missouri.

This story generalizes to other parts of the country. As Harvard University economist Raj Chetty's team's work has concluded, "high-income

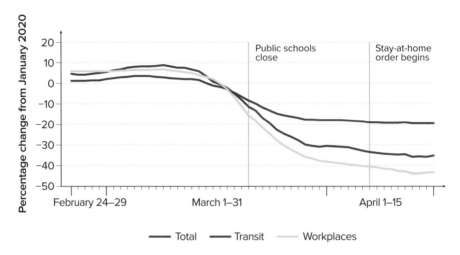

FIGURE 3.2

Time spent outside the home in Missouri, percentage change from January 2020

Source: Opportunity Insights Tracker, "Time Spent Outside the Home," www.tracktherecovery.org.

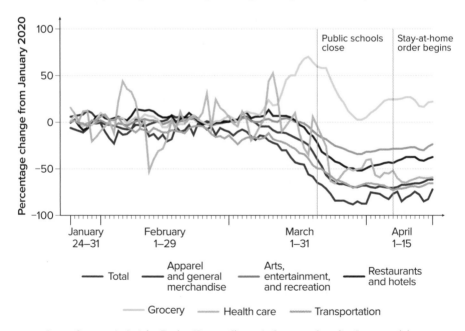

FIGURE 3.3

Consumer spending in Missouri, percentage change from January 2020

Source: Opportunity Insights Tracker, "Percent Change in Consumer Spending," www.trackthere covery.org.

individuals reduced spending sharply in mid-March 2020, particularly in areas with high rates of COVID-19 infection and in sectors that require in-person interaction."[12]

Now, this is not to say that federal and state governments didn't play an important role in these shutdowns. Large falls in mobility and consumer spending occurred around the time that a national state of emergency was declared by the federal government on March 13. While not compelling behavior, this provided a signal as to the seriousness of the public health threat and was accompanied by widespread media coverage of the virus. Those same Indiana University economists find state emergency declarations were important too—they attribute 55 percent of the uplift in time spent at home between early March and mid-April to state declarations, with the other 45 percent coming from voluntary changes in behavior.

The key point is that there's little evidence that specific government lockdown regulations (stay-at-home and nonessential business closure orders) were the *primary* driver of that initial dislocation—at least in those early days of the pandemic. Economists William Evans and Christopher Cronin, for example, examining footfall across industries from cell phone data, conclude that "between 74 and 83 percent" of the decline in attendance at retail outlets, entertainment venues, hotels, restaurants, and service businesses was due to "non-regulatory responses by individuals and businesses."[13]

Yes, subsequent government orders to close dine-in premises, entertainment industries, and other establishments compounded industry-specific downturns. Stay-at-home orders and public school closures led to more behavior on the extremes, too—such as people avoiding care for genuine medical problems, or avoiding even retail deemed as selling "essential" goods. But these impacts are dwarfed by the behavioral change preceding government action. A paper from the Department of Agriculture and Resource Economics at Berkeley, for example, estimates (again using cell phone data) that average travel distances had already fallen by 16 percentage points, human encounter rates by 63 percentage points, and nonessential business visits by 39 percentage points before the first statewide mandate came into effect.[14]

It's not just in the United States, either. Sweden did not impose business closures or stay-at-home orders but saw similarly sharp travel declines. Data from Citymapper shows mobility in the Swedish capital of Stockholm had fallen by 70 percent by the start of May compared to normal.[15] Travel to the vacation island of Gotland had fallen 96 percent between April 8–10 compared with the same period in 2019, despite there being no government travel restrictions.[16]

Comparing Sweden with Denmark, a country that did an extensive lockdown, shows the primacy of voluntary action. Cornell University economists, using transaction data from a large Scandinavian bank, found that overall spending fell 25 percent in Sweden and by a slightly higher 29 percent in Denmark in the early period of the pandemic.[17] Lockdowns, in other words, probably restricted economic activity relative to what would have otherwise occurred. But these impacts appeared to be marginal compared with how people willingly responded to information about the virus in those early months.

The rationale for stay-at-home or nonessential business closure orders was to reduce the transmission of the virus and so its reproduction rate—that is, the average number of people who will contract the contagious disease from one infected person. But if the mobility and economic data are evidence that people were interacting less anyway, then we would expect this reproduction rate to have been falling prior to these government regulations.[18]

The reproduction rate in a locality is incredibly difficult to measure. But there is at least some indicative evidence that, yes, it was falling quickly even prior to lockdowns:

- Data from U.S. states showed big falls in the rate prior to stay-at-home orders and nonessential business closures.[19]
- An official government report in Switzerland estimated that the rate had fallen from 1.8 to 1.1 between March 7 and 17, prior to government-mandated business closures.[20]
- Some analysis that worked back from deaths and hospitalizations in the UK implied that infection rates there may even have peaked prior to lockdowns, suggesting the impact of

voluntary social distancing behavior was greater there even than in Switzerland in reducing the transmission of the virus.[21]

We must treat such data cautiously and remember that government actions may still have been needed to get the reproduction rate of the virus below one—a necessary condition for falling infections. But, clearly, the impact of voluntary social distancing was dominant.

The Badger State Experiment

Wisconsin provided a good test of what was really driving behavior—people or government—when, on May 13, 2020, its supreme court overturned the state's "Safer at Home" order. Overnight, the Badger State became the only state without major SARS-CoV-2 public health interventions in place. Everything could open, even restaurants and bars. In fact, this was an unusually good *natural experiment* of the impact of government restrictions. Usually, lockdowns get lifted precisely because public health is improving, making assessment of the causal impact of removing them difficult to ascertain.

But research comparing Wisconsin in the 11 days after the ruling with a weighted average of states it had tracked closely beforehand found remarkably little economic impact of the court lifting the lockdown.[22] Except for a temporary, modest decline in time spent at home in the immediate 4 days after the decision, phone data from Wisconsinites revealed no real evidence of less time spent at home full-time, hours spent at home, or even changes to part- or full-time work behavior compared with similar states.

There was no good evidence that Wisconsinites suffered worse health outcomes due to the ruling, either—little surprise given that the restrictions didn't much change behavior. Again, this suggests voluntary social distancing trumped government policies in affecting health outcomes, at least in the early phases of the pandemic.

Now, none of this evidence of the primacy of voluntary behavior means, of course, that simply not having any public health interventions would have been optimal policy. It still might be the case that in the presence of such a big externality problem, coercive action through facemask mandates, stay-at-home regulations, or closures of certain businesses to deal with real collective action problems related to the highest-risk activity might improve on voluntary actions for public health outcomes and raise economic welfare overall.

Certainly, it does not mean that stay-at-home orders and business closures did not further reduce transmission of the virus. The Berkeley study, for example, suggested that lockdown mandates caused average distances traveled to fall by an additional 7 percentage points, nonessential visits by around 2 percentage points, and human encounters by around 3.5 percentage points. This, they estimate, saved 23,000 to 30,000 additional lives across the United States in March and April, of the total 48,000 to 71,000 they believe were spared as a result of both voluntary social distancing and government action.

Research shows that the propensity to engage in social distancing behaviors is lower in low-income communities, when individuals are less able to work from home, or when individuals have reduced access to outside space.[23] Formal government regulations and relief packages might therefore have larger effects in changing behaviors for some people in these groups, such as by deterring use of more-risky transit in poorer urban areas.

The flip side to this is that lockdowns further constrained market economic activity. In fact, by banning or restricting high-risk and low-risk business activity alike, mandating business closures or ordering people to stay home prevented activity that would otherwise be undertaken at low risk. Even for businesses that would have initially closed anyway because of collapsing consumer demand, formal lockdowns prevented those business owners from innovating and experimenting to find new ways to operate their premises in light of customers' increased preferences for safety.

Some evidence supports this: surveys of small businesses showed most companies shuttered during lockdowns expected to be open within a few days of mandates being lifted.[24] While this may in part have reflected an updating of the assessment of risks from business owners and customers and some pent-up demand for services, it does suggest lockdowns snuffed out additional activity from that which was voluntarily shuttered.

Evans's and Cronin's research, for example, unsurprisingly finds that state restrictions on eat-in dining did reduce traffic to restaurants, hotels, and other retail beyond that from voluntary declines in consumer and business behavior. In Florida, Texas, and California, the proportion of small businesses open rose when reopening occurred and then fell again when certain activities were ordered to reclose following spikes in COVID-19 cases in early July. So business-closure mandates are likely to have worsened job prospects too, although there's academic disagreement on the scale of the impact, particularly if you control for other factors—such as the size of the tourism industry in a state.[25]

What we can conclude by synthesizing these disparate findings is this: behavioral change stemming from knowledge and fear of the virus drove a large and effective shutdown of much economic activity even before politicians across the country mandated one in those early stages of the pandemic.[26] Yes, formal state-level lockdowns then compounded these impacts. But the initial driver of the shutdown was voluntary behavior.

In fact, some scholars in other countries speculate that their governments faced pressure to mandate formal shutdowns from businesses themselves. As consumers and workers stopped traveling and went out less frequently, companies faced financial ruin. An official mandate to close enabled some of them to access business interruption insurance or at least benefit from SARS-CoV-2 related support policies, which would not have been delivered without the government being seen to be responsible for closure. In some cases then, far from being imposed on most businesses, formal lockdowns may have been desirable to them, at least in the short term.

What this evidence highlights is a perfect example of one of the challenges economists face when assessing the impact of public policies. It is not always simple to ascertain how far laws or regulations affect particular outcomes because laws themselves can sometimes end up being a codification of voluntary behaviors and customs, at least to start with.

We therefore require more-sophisticated statistical methods to assess the true impact of a policy rather than simply looking at the timeline or correlation between two variables. Hence, this is why economists often use *difference in differences* research methodologies to seek to answer these questions. This is an approach that tries to assess the impact of a policy over time by taking the average change in outcomes after the policy is implemented in one state, and taking away from this the average change in outcomes over the same period for a similar state that did not implement the policy.

When it comes to assessing what caused that initial economic downturn, we also have to be careful not to overinterpret what has gone before as a guide for predictions of what will happen in the future. It would have been very tempting to take the evidence above as a slam-dunk indication that almost all of the economic downturn was caused by the virus itself and conclude that reopening would have had little to no GDP benefit because of entrenched changes to voluntary behavior.

Certainly, as we shall see in chapter 16, since individuals were willing to "pay" to avoid the virus by not engaging in market activity, we would not expect—and did not see—a full and complete recovery after policymakers reversed business closures and stay-at-home orders. Even when movie theaters and restaurants reopened, customer numbers remained far below normal. While the virus still percolates, that will continue to be the case. But that does not mean the impacts of removing lockdowns were symmetric with implementing them. We know that consumers' and businesses' behaviors are shaped by ever-changing perceptions of the risks they face. Clearly, many consumers and business owners revised their perceptions of risks during lockdowns or took active steps to reduce the risk of their actions, and so engaged in more activity after lockdowns were lifted than immediately before. These reassessments change people's tolerance for curbs on their liberties, making it politically more difficult to reintroduce tough lockdown controls over time.[27]

This was particularly true of younger people, for whom the costs of lockdown were arguably largest and who (it soon became clear) faced the lowest relative personal risks from the disease. Data on the demographic distribution of infections certainly suggests that many young people were more willing to quickly renormalize life after the initial lockdowns were lifted. In states such as Florida, California, and Texas, the demographic profile of new positive cases of the virus after that initial reopening was much younger.

External factors might also have changed perceptions. We saw a willingness to abandon social distancing during the protests of George Floyd's death, even in cities that still had extensive lockdown laws in place. The lack of any clear apparent spikes in the number of infections following this, or even the mere example of mass gatherings, probably emboldened others to engage in more social activity. Trump's quick apparent recovery from COVID-19 in October 2020 no doubt changed some people's attitudes about to how to live during this pandemic, particularly given that Trump used his pulpit to tell people not to be afraid of the virus. So we cannot assume people's behaviors in trying to avoid the virus will remain unchanged over time, even if it is clear that the initial shutdown of the economy was largely voluntary.

In fact, the economist Ed Glaeser and his colleagues believe the public might have updated their views on the risk of the virus precisely because of those initial government restrictions being relaxed.[28] His work on restaurant openings echoes the findings presented here that voluntary behavioral change explains almost all the initial downturn in activity. This implies lockdowns had little impact early on in containing the virus. However, he concludes that the lifting of lockdowns *did* matter, appearing to signal to people that it was safe to socialize again, particularly in places with lower cumulative cases of the virus up until that point. By the end of those initial lockdowns, then, the government restrictions did have a meaningful impact on behavior and market activity. Although for most states it is difficult to discern a massive jump in activity on the day that reopenings occurred, the gradual change in policies did appear to support changing sentiment toward the virus, thus leading to a greater normalization of activity.

Of course, as the pandemic continued, the public, armed with better information, experience with the virus in their region, and more scientific knowledge, continually updated their prior beliefs about the risks they faced. It is clear that many individuals became fatigued by the self-imposed and government constraints on their lives, deciding to recalibrate their risk tolerance. If it is confirmed that the virus is highly seasonal and case numbers keep rocketing in winter and decrease again in spring, behavior might change dramatically again as one season rolls into another. Many states saw more business closures as news of case spiking in the South hit the news through July 2020—even in places where local transmission was not spiking, such as Maine and New Hampshire.[29] People's behavior, in other words, adapts to their fears and perceptions of risks.

The crucial point in thinking like an economist here, however, is the need to carefully distinguish between the impacts of public and private action. Commentators have a tendency in public policy debates to just assume that changes to laws are the dominant driver of economic outcomes and, in this case, the path of the disease. People looked at the anecdotes of the Walt Disney World crowds and the Florida spring break beaches early in this pandemic and concluded that mandated closures of businesses and stay-at-home orders were the most important tools for curbing the transmission of the virus.

But consumers and businesses were, in fact, responsible for much of the initial economic shutdown, changing their behavior dramatically as knowledge of the virus spread and emergencies were declared. We, with governments following shortly behind, chose to take drastic action to potentially save lives or avoid infection. Still, today, we change how we act depending on our perception of risks of the virus, irrespective of the state of government policy. Exactly the same phenomenon—of significant voluntary behavioral change, particularly in areas with high levels of infection—has played out in Japan, a country that did not impose any lockdown.[30]

But deciding whether that societal response was truly worth it, given the risks we actually faced, will hinge to a large degree on the controversial topic of how much we value averting the loss of human lives.

ECONOMIC LESSON

Public policies can sometimes cut against the grain of behavior, curbing activities in pursuit of goals that consumers, businesses, and households wouldn't otherwise seek to pursue. Other times they can be a codification of what we are doing anyway. In the case of shutdowns and SARS-CoV-2, it is clear that businesses and much economic activity were shuttering or constrained through changed private behaviors, even prior to state-government-mandated business closures and stay-at-home orders. Disentangling the impact of the virus on behavior from the impact of government policies on behavior is a key task of economic analysis trying to assess the wisdom of public health interventions.

ECONOMIC TERMS INTRODUCED

- **natural experiment:** a study in which the treatments imposed on the subjects of the experiment are not decided by policymakers or researchers but rather unexpected or random events. In the case of this chapter, Wisconsinites were subject to both lockdowns and then no lockdowns in quick succession, due to an unexpected state court decision.
- **difference in differences estimation:** a statistical technique that seeks to estimate the effect of a policy on an outcome by comparing the average change over time in the outcome variable for an area experiencing the policy, compared to the average change over time in a control area that did not implement the policy

4

HOW MUCH WOULD YOU SPEND TO SAVE MY LIFE?

An introduction to the value of a statistical life

C an you put a price on a human life? New York Governor Andrew Cuomo did not think so, at least when faced with the escalating difficulties of the pandemic in New York.[1]

"I want to be able to say to the people of New York," he said on March 20, 2020, "'I did everything we could do.' And if everything we do just saves one life, I'll be happy." Such logic would dictate that there should be no limit on how much New Yorkers should collectively sacrifice through lost economic welfare to prevent an individual New Yorker from dying. In fact, at one stage Cuomo explicitly claimed, "a human life is priceless, period."

As a professional politician, Cuomo was empathizing with those who were worried for their vulnerable loved ones. The New York state death toll from COVID-19 was accelerating. Hundreds of lives in the state were about to be lost daily. Debate was bubbling about whether preventing this loss of life was worth the societal costs of voluntary social distancing and lockdowns.

Cuomo was appealing to our moral sensibilities, then, to push his preferred policy of suppressing the virus through stringent lockdowns.

He was not the first politician to appeal to our hearts, nor will he be the last.

In one sense too, his instincts were right. The holes in families' lives from lost loved ones suggest individual lives are *immeasurable* in terms of their value, if not priceless. It is uncomfortable to even consider, as a mental exercise, the limit on how much others in society should be asked to pay to try to save your parent.

Yet in the cold light of day Cuomo would surely recognize that it's silly to pretend that public policy can place an implicit infinite value on every life. Despite people often expressing disgust at economists for pointing out this hard truth, none of us live our lives in ways suggesting that we consider their continuation infinitely valuable.

When you drive on the highway, you implicitly calculate that the risk of dying in a car accident was worth bearing for the journey's benefits. Individuals around the world become seafarers, construction workers, engineers, or dispose of hazardous materials while receiving wages, which shows that eliminating the elevated risks of death these activities bring is not infinitely valuable to them.

Public policy is the same. Governments develop safety regulations, inoculation programs, and fire protection services to lessen death risks. But we neither spend unlimited amounts on them nor mandate that businesses commit unlimited resources to safety.

Take speed limits as the classic example. We could nearly eliminate road deaths by capping motor vehicle speeds at five miles per hour. But the lost time and business activity resulting from that regulation would be tremendous, making people poorer and leading to hardship and worse health outcomes. Therefore, for any given regulation, we accept that there is some boundary between an acceptable and unacceptable cost to save lives.

That's because spending money comes with a big *opportunity cost* to society—a term that economists use for the highest-value alternative use of a resource or funds. If governments dedicate more resources to preventing accidental deaths, that means fewer resources are available for other projects or less money is left in the private sector, where it could potentially do more to raise economic welfare.

It's understandable why it may rankle with our moral instincts to think about placing a limit on the resources used to save someone. For the noneconomist, that upper limit on how much we'd be willing to spend can sound an awful lot like putting a value on a human being—of judging a person's intrinsic worth.[2]

Less than two centuries ago, a price was being explicitly put on the heads of the ancestors of many of today's African Americans. The moral distinction between trading lives and tradeoffs in regard to saving them can sometimes seem blurred, particularly for families facing the consequences.

Public policy choices, however, are not about putting a dollar value on people but are about claims on others' resources. Once you acknowledge that we, as a society, are unwilling to collectively spend unlimited sums to save the life of just one person, what we are really haggling over is the limit of what we are willing to pay, rather than the principle.

So how do we decide what is the right amount? That's a controversial topic. If you were a social planner who cared little about the individual, then you might say the correct price on a human life should be how much it would cost to replace a dying person with a new one, which would give a very low figure indeed.

Thankfully, economists have more respect for individual dignity than that. For years though, economists instead put an effective value on life that had similarly perverse moral implications. That approach—dubbed the "cost of dying"—calculated the value of a life by the value of lost lifetime earnings should the individual perish.

Given our lives are about more than work, this method grossly understated the value we would place on avoiding death. What's more, it leads to obvious moral travesties. Under that old methodology, retired or disabled people's lives would have near-zero value. More recent attempts to use a variant of this methodology look at a richer conception of lifetime production, including people's contributions to the household.[3] But they can still suffer the same types of absurdities when it comes to those who are disabled.

The Value of a Statistical Life

Economist Thomas Schelling turned the thinking about this idea on its head.[4] Rather than calculate the cost of dying, he thought, why not observe how much people are willing to pay to avoid an elevated chance of death?

Such an approach clearly gives a more holistic assessment of the value of preserving life. Not only does it recognize that the value of avoiding death is subjective to each individual and circumstance, but it grants insight into the value placed on the continuation of all aspects of one's existence, not just work. When we make decisions about actual death risks confronting us, we aren't merely considering the risk of our forgone earnings but also the friendships, familial relationships, and experiences we'd stand to lose. As we saw in chapter 1, these have important value too.

Examining how much individuals would be willing to pay to avoid death risks, or how much they would need to be compensated for bearing an elevated risk of death, can then be aggregated and averaged across a population. This allows us to calculate the implicit value placed by a population on avoiding the probability of any one death from a given risk. Although aggregating and averaging inevitably hides some individual-level differences in people's valuation of avoiding risks, these numbers provide a reasonable estimate for undertaking cost-benefit analyses of a project, allowing us to quantify the economic value of the benefit of deaths averted if we go forward with a particular policy that diminishes the risk.

In practical terms, economists estimate these values from studies of actual labor markets. A lot of people work in environments that come with elevated risks of dying, such as coal mining or construction. After controlling for other aspects of the jobs, these people tend to be better compensated than those working in other comparable occupations because of the dangers of their work. Those *compensating differentials* in pay can allow us to assess how much people have to be paid to endure a slightly higher risk of perishing.

Suppose that, by examining risks and pay levels, we surmised that the average American in a given manufacturing occupation would have to be paid $2,000 extra to be compensated for a specific additional 0.02 percent occupational risk of death. We can use that information to compute, for this particular risk and population, the *value of a statistical life* (VSL).

This is the ratio of the amount the average worker in the population would need to be paid to bear the risk (through higher wages) divided by the death risk faced. In this case, that is $2,000 divided by 0.02 percent = $10 million per statistical life. This can be interpreted as the collective amount these workers would have to be compensated per life expected to be lost due to the risk (or, indeed, how much they would collectively be willing to pay to prevent the statistical probability of one of their group dying).

As it happens, this is around the middle value that studies actually find for the VSL in labor markets for modest at-work risks in the United States.[5] It tends to be higher here than elsewhere because American wages are higher. The $10 million VSL, in other words, represents an estimate of the implicit value that American workers tend to place on avoiding one death, derived from real observations about how much they, as individuals, would be willing to pay to avoid small, elevated mortality risks at work.

It's important to be very clear here about what this VSL means. This $10 million "value of a statistical life" is explicitly *not* the value of a human life. That workers would have to be compensated by $10 million collectively in lieu of a risk that implies the statistical likelihood of one person dying clearly does not mean that any one individual would accept $10 million in return for certain death! In other words, this VSL is a reasonable approximation only for similarly small risks to those found in labor market studies. You cannot extrapolate from values derived across a population for one risk and apply it to individuals for a very different level of risk.

It is understandable there is confusion about this, not least because of the name of the term the "value of a statistical life." University of Oregon economist Trudy Ann Cameron thinks the branding and units used for the VSL unnecessarily lend themselves to misunderstanding and distaste for economists, given that the public inevitably interprets it as the value of a life.

When economists say "value" here, however, they do not mean intrinsic worth but how much a population would need to be paid to bear a small elevated risk of death. When economists say "statistical," they are referring to the probability of a death, not its certainty for one person. When they use the term "life," they are referring to tiny risk reductions across many different people, rather than the impact on one identifiable, individual life.

The Value of a Statistical Live and COVID-19

It is worth bearing in mind how the VSL is calculated and how we should interpret it, because economists have utilized it in calculating the benefits of government lockdowns during the COVID-19 pandemic. Nonessential business closures and stay-at-home orders can be thought of as akin to regulatory measures that reduce death risks from the virus. Assessing their monetary benefits therefore requires not just an accurate estimate of the number of lives saved by the policies but some way of valuing those deaths that have been avoided.

To work out the value of these purported benefits, economists have been prone to undertake a simple calculation. First, they took the VSL from existing American labor market-studies (around $10 million) as if it were some universal truth. They then multiplied it by estimates from epidemiological models of how many lives would be saved by lockdowns (which, at least initially, some studies claimed could be 1–2 million). Most therefore concluded that we should be willing to bear one-off economic welfare costs of up to $10–20 trillion (around 50 to 95 percent of 2019 GDP) in order to avoid those deaths.[6] In other words, if the broader economic costs of lockdown are less than these benefits, then lockdowns were said to have been cost-effective.

As we will see later, just because lockdowns might be better than governments doing nothing does not make them optimal policy or even the most cost-effective means of reducing death risks. And there are all sorts of problems with the claim that 1–2 million lives would be saved by those lockdowns, as we shall see in chapter 5. Using that $10 million figure for VSL is not without controversy, either. Some economists and statisticians have assessed these VSL studies and found evidence that studies with more statistical power often see values that are 70–80 percent lower (implying the real observed VSL might be around just $2 million per statistical life today).[7] They argue that there is a publication bias, with journals more likely to publish papers with value of statistical lives that are very high.

But let's just assume for exposition's sake that the $10 million figure commonly used is a reasonable reading of existing evidence and that those epidemiological death projections were correct. Applying the VSL to COVID-19 implied that we should have tolerated extremely high economic welfare costs through policies such as lockdowns to avoid the deaths this virus would otherwise cause. To put it into context, one estimate of total marketable wealth in the United States is around $100 trillion, or five times GDP.[8] So to save 1 million statistical lives would imply that we should be willing to effectively sacrifice up to 10 percent of all U.S. wealth to save the lives of just 0.33 percent of the population.

These figures are so large that some economists have questioned whether using these old VSL figures for COVID-19 is appropriate. It might suit economists to act as if there is one true VSL that can be used for very different regulatory assessments. But can we really take values calculated from some people's willingness to pay to avoid small common risks of death at work and apply the results across the whole U.S. population in a global pandemic?

It would be reasonable to do so if the death risks were of similar magnitude to those observed in the labor market studies. It would be appropriate, too, if other conditions held: if the fatality risks were the same across the whole population, if people's willingness to pay to avoid those risks was nearly identical across demographic groups, and if the regulatory response proposed itself did not impact other fatality risks. But while those assumptions might hold reasonably well for, say, valuing the reduction in deaths from making a highway safer, they clearly do not apply well to COVID-19 and the economy-wide lockdowns in response to it.

It's now clear that the burden of death risks is not, in fact, evenly shared but falls disproportionately on the elderly and those with comorbidities. The VSL of $10 million may be a reasonable approximation for the collective willingness of the young population to pay to avoid COVID-19 deaths, given that the relatively small risks of death they face might be similar to those faced by their contemporaries in certain jobs (the Centers for Disease Control and Prevention's [CDC] most recent estimate is that the infection fatality rate from COVID-19 for 20–49-year-olds is 0.02 percent). But there is no reason to presume that a $10 million VSL is reasonable, on average, for the very old, who face substantially higher fatality risks from COVID-19 and whose lives are those that are overwhelmingly being saved. The CDC estimates the infection fatality rate for those over 70 is as high as 5.4 percent, for example. As we saw earlier, we cannot just assume the appropriate VSL will be the same as in labor market studies for populations facing this much higher death risk.

The health research company hVIVO was reportedly offering a hundred 18–30-year-olds £3,500 each (roughly $4,400) to take part in a human challenge trial for a COVID-19 vaccine in the UK.[9] Given that there is some evidence that the infection fatality risk for these groups may be around 0.02 percent, this implies a VSL used by the researchers of £17.5 million ($22 million), which is higher than the $10 million VSL figure cited earlier.[10]

But we know, from extensive research, that a lower VSL may be appropriate for the elderly, who are often not included in the working population studies used to calculate the $10 million figure. It is common, for example, to make adjustments to VSLs by controlling for life expectancy (instead using a "value of a statistical life year") or the health status of the population (via an approach known as correcting values for "quality-adjusted life years"). One paper that incorporates the life expectancy effect alone took a weighted average of the COVID-19 impact across the population by age to conclude that the appropriate average VSL for this pandemic, given the number of deaths in its early stages, was more like $3.35 million.[11]

But numerous studies show that the elderly tend to pay less to avoid death from a given risk than the middle-aged, even after controlling for life expectancy.[12] The appropriate value of a statistical life as applied to COVID-19 then is still likely to be very high but much, much lower than $10 million.

This makes intuitive sense—an additional year of life for an 85-year-old is likely to be less valuable, on average at least, than for a working-age person. We also might think it likely that older populations have more diverse and unusual preferences for their willingness to pay to avoid a given risk of death.

Consider a population of 85- to 100-year-olds in a nursing home, all with significant comorbidities. Let's say they have a median wealth of around $250,000 and an average remaining life expectancy of two years. Suppose we could move them all to a completely foolproof unit that would protect them from a 20 percent risk of contracting the virus and a 10 percent risk of dying if they did contract it.

Using the traditional VSL of $10 million here implies that the average elderly person in this group would be privately willing to pay $200,000 to avoid this 2 percent fatality risk. Applying this in the pandemic implies that society more broadly should be willing to bear such costs to eliminate this elevated death risk too. But how many elderly folk would really be willing to pay 80 percent of their wealth for a relatively small extension of life?

Some would no doubt pay to see family again; others would likely want to leave their money to their children and grandchildren instead and not prolong their relatively short remaining life, often in ill health. Just assuming this VSL holds across the population seems a stretch, though. In reality, not only do groups such as the elderly face much higher fatality risks from COVID-19, but their behavior in terms of willingness to pay to avoid any given risk might be very different too.

Perhaps the biggest problem with this simple application of the VSL to COVID-19, however, is the sheer scale of the lockdown intervention proposed. Usually the programs or spending to which VSL is applied in cost-benefit analysis are small enough that we don't really have to consider the broader societal impacts of the regulation. In this case, however, lockdowns, especially if sustained, would have a dramatic impact on incomes and health, which is likely to make many people less willing to pay to avoid the COVID-19 risk.

Another way of thinking about this is opportunity cost again. Usually in regulatory judgments that use VSL, we don't have to worry about whether one regulation might inhibit our ability to do anything else. But the scale of this intervention means it's not clear that the costs of lockdown couldn't be incurred for a much more effective way to save or improve lives at a societal level.[13] To put it another way: if economists were given $10 to $20 trillion and told to devise policies with the best chance of improving overall economic welfare at the height of the pandemic, would they have really chosen lockdowns?

Rather than judging the benefits of lockdowns in terms of lives saved and multiplying that number by the $10 million value of a statistical life, we should instead be judging whether lockdowns are the most cost-effective way to save a given number of lives in practice. While lockdowns may well have saved lives relative to governments doing nothing, we should really compare their effectiveness against other interventions.

Could we have saved a similar number of lives with much more targeted policies, such as sending out medical-class masks to all elderly people, paying nursing home workers and cleaners vast amounts to live in for a number of weeks, having taxpayers finance contactless delivery services, or mandating mask wearing at all indoor gatherings, for example?[14] One study estimated that eliminating staffing links between nursing homes alone could have reduced cases within them by 44 percent.

Economists do tend to value reducing fatality risks very highly, and for good reason: the choices we make at work imply that we highly value continuing our existence. It is right that we should therefore, as a society, be willing to contemplate high economic and societal costs today to prevent hundreds of thousands of deaths from occurring from an externality problem.

But Andrew Cuomo was clearly wrong in implying that human lives were priceless. And the precise level of costs that we should tolerate for mitigating COVID-19 death risks is far less clear-cut than economists suggested in the early days of the pandemic. Applying, crudely, the VSL derived from labor-market studies may have inflated the benefits of lockdowns significantly because fatality risks from COVID-19 are much higher for the elderly, for whom there is good reason to expect a much lower VSL.

So, was the introduction of lockdowns wise policy? In tackling that question, economists would have to do a much fuller assessment of the costs and benefits of these unprecedented interventions rather than simply estimating the value of any death averted. They would also have to compare lockdowns with completely different policy regimes to determine whether they were the best approach. Those are the subjects of the next two chapters.

ECONOMIC LESSON

Although it might make us uncomfortable to admit it, public policy cannot eliminate death risks at infinite cost. Economists attempt to assess how much we should be societally willing to sacrifice to reduce the probability of each life lost to a death risk using the "value of a statistical life." This examines how much private individuals are willing to pay to avoid fatality risks, or how much they would need to be paid to accept those risks, as a basis for answering how we should value reducing fatality risks for public policy decisions. In the case of COVID-19, this allows economists to place a monetary value on the deaths avoided through public health interventions, such as lockdowns. But the very high VSL derived from existing studies of labor markets is unlikely to be appropriate for COVID-19, given how death risks and willingness to pay to avoid death are likely to differ substantially across demographic groups.

ECONOMIC TERMS INTRODUCED

- **opportunity cost:** the value of the best alternative forgone as a result of a purchase or a decision
- **compensating differential:** controlling for other pay determinants, the difference in pay necessary to compensate workers for unpleasant or dangerous working environments
- **value of a statistical life:** the monetary amount that a population would have to be compensated by to tolerate the probability of the loss of one life given an elevated fatality risk to that population

5

WHEN IS A LOCKDOWN CURE WORSE THAN THE DISEASE?
An introduction to cost-benefit analysis

W e cannot let the cure be worse than the problem itself," Trump tweeted late on March 22, 2020.[1]

With economic indicators tanking, the president wanted to make one thing clear: state governors should not allow the economic costs of stay-at-home orders and nonessential business closures to exceed the value of the health damage the virus would do without them.

Trump was pilloried in the media for that tweet, including by public health experts and economists. Some denounced him for supposedly raising the idea of sacrificing lives for the economy.

But, read generously, Trump's musing was merely a variant of economist Thomas Sowell's uncontroversial insight that in policy there are no solutions, only tradeoffs. Making decisions brings inevitable costs. Logically, there must be some negative consequences of government lockdowns, and some point at which they might become self-defeating.

What aroused public controversy was not so much the content of Trump's banal statement but the belief that his expressing it reflected a conclusion that the lockdowns that were already in place were a mistake. Interestingly, most economists at that time disagreed with Trump that locking down compromised much in permanent economic welfare losses, at least relative to the value of lives saved by public health interventions.

For example, an Initiative on Global Markets poll of 44 economists by the University of Chicago Booth School of Business five days after Trump's tweet found near unanimity for the view that "a comprehensive policy response to the coronavirus will involve tolerating a very large contraction in economic activity until the spread of infections has dropped significantly."[2]

More pertinently, 89 percent of those polled agreed or strongly agreed with the view that "abandoning severe lockdowns at a time when the likelihood of a resurgence in infections remains high will lead to greater total economic damage than sustaining the lockdowns to eliminate the resurgence risk."

Economists tended to agree with my chapter 3 conclusion that voluntary social distancing drove much of the initial economic downturn anyway. They cited sincere public concern and voluntary social distancing as evidence that much of what appeared to be the costs of lockdowns were actually costs of the virus. Removing lockdowns, they believed, wouldn't lead to a meaningful economic rebound at that time but would lead to additional lives lost from higher transmission rates of the virus due to more socializing with family and friends.

Eventually, they thought, a worsening public health situation would reignite a deeper downturn in market economic activity too. It was common to hear the phrase, at least at that time, that "there is no trade-off between the economy and public health." Only by suppressing the virus and instilling public confidence that it was under control, it was thought, could a sustainable degree of economic normality return.

Indeed, simple cross-country correlations over the whole pandemic through December 2020 suggest, perhaps unsurprisingly, that those countries that have avoided significant health impacts of the virus have seen a healthier (albeit still depressed) GDP performance. But a blanket statement that there are no tradeoffs between public health and economic activity clearly doesn't apply in a near-term situation when prevalence of the virus is widespread. At that point, to lower the prevalence of the disease requires painful restrictions on economic activity, whether voluntarily or through government interventions. We therefore appear to face a distinction between the short-run (where trade-offs are real) and the long-run (where those polities that control the pandemic best enjoy better economic health too.)

Were the economists right about those specific early state lockdowns in the United States having economic benefits that vastly exceeded their costs? My honest answer is "I don't know, yet." Months later, we are still learning much about this disease, how far it has spread, and the risk factors for its transmission. Doctoral theses and detailed academic studies will be written on the role of initial state lockdown policies, with speculative theories developed for what would have happened in their absence and their effects on behavior afterward. Even after nearly a century, economists disagree on the economics of the Great Depression and New Deal during the 1930s.[3]

What I can say with confidence, however, is that there has been a lot of very bad analysis, or partial analysis, or both, on this question so far. Yes, it's hard to give a definitive answer on lockdowns' benefits and costs, but most assessments have looked at only one side of the equation; have utilized huge, unjustified assumptions; or have failed to consider realistic alternative policy regimes to lockdowns. My aim in this chapter and the next is not to provide a complete analysis of my own but to provide the reader with an economist's guide for how to think about this topic—including by highlighting the difficulties and uncertainties inherent in thinking through this question.

Before starting, however, it's worth highlighting the biggest red flag to identifying a bad analysis of lockdowns. The worst type of research on this will tend to produce a monocausal explanation—it will assume that everything that happens in a given period is due to one factor.

Lockdown skeptics sometimes have the tendency to ascribe the whole economic downturn through this pandemic to government policies, for example, ignoring that the virus clearly disrupted much private economic activity anyway. Even at the time of writing in December 2020, those most critical of how state governments reacted to the pandemic continue to talk of "lockdown policies" as shorthand for any public health interventions introduced since February 2020, even though a lot of the initial restrictions I describe as lockdown in this chapter have since been lifted in most places, either partially or fully.[4]

So defining what lockdowns are and what they are not is critical. For the rest of this chapter, I take lockdown to mean the widespread closure of nonessential businesses and schools, alongside orders for people to stay home, as was seen in those first three months of the pandemic in the United States. True, many public schools remained closed around the country for long periods after these initial months. Government restrictions on certain businesses, including their capacity, endured, while elsewhere they were reintroduced as the virus became more prevalent. But I define "lockdown" narrowly here to refer to that combination of policies in that early period, both to distinguish it from lockdowns seen in other countries (in which stringent restrictions on travel and strictly enforced quarantine rules were in place), and to avoid it being used too broadly to describe any changes in public behavior that shuttered activity compared to normal levels. Unhelpfully, the term has been used to denote everything from welding people into their homes in China to enforced isolation of asymptomatic infected individuals.[5]

Defining it that broadly risks ascribing all the hardship we have seen to government policy, rather than the broader impact of the pandemic. But it's certainly true, too, that some economists and epidemiologists on the other side of the debate can be guilty of the opposite—of denying the existence of any tradeoffs between public health interventions and economic welfare, so giving policy a free ride.

The truth, clearly, is somewhere between these extreme positions: substantial economic pain would have been felt irrespective of whether those early lockdowns were introduced, but they still shuttered a lot of additional economic activity, as the pick up in business, employment, and social activity post-lockdowns implies. For the purpose of analyzing the cost and benefits of lockdowns, then, it is important that we distinguish carefully the specific effects of those early government mandates as distinct from changes to voluntary behavior or other public health measures or guidance.

What's a Cost-Benefit Analysis Good For?

In theory, economics is a discipline well placed to assess whether lockdowns were worth it. One tool we have in our toolkit is *cost-benefit analysis*. This is an applied economic technique used to judge whether a project or government policy increases societal welfare, on net.

The approach, in essence, is to calculate the benefits of a policy in the broadest sense relative to an alternative world without it. A comprehensive analysis will account for direct or indirect benefits of the proposal, including any externalities associated with the policy, and convert all these impacts into common dollar units of societal economic welfare over a specified time period. The costs of the project are then summed up in a similar way. The analysis concludes by examining the ratio of benefits to costs.

A comprehensive cost-benefit analysis like this can serve two very useful purposes in policy evaluation. First, and most obviously, it can help to assess whether a project is sound—that is, whether the benefits exceed the costs. If they do not, then we know the policy is a mistake from the get-go.

Second, cost-benefit analysis can be extended to compare across policies such that, when we have scarce resources or have to make a choice between various proposals, we can review which path gives the highest benefit-cost ratio for any given budget. In other words, we can decide which approach gives the biggest economic bang for the buck.

Most early analyses of lockdowns just sought to assess whether their benefits exceeded costs. Economists estimated the value of the benefits of saving lives using the value of a statistical life (VSL) and epidemiological model estimates of how many lives would be saved if lockdowns were adopted. They then asserted that, because permanent GDP damage resulting from lockdowns would likely be lower than this very high value, lockdowns passed the basic cost-benefit test.

All too often, however, this type of analysis was written up as if it proved that lockdowns, as implemented, were the best possible policy. Yet this was clearly inadequate. Few economists early on sought to tally the broader costs of lockdowns in any meaningful way or take account of the limits of using GDP alone to assess them. Most didn't indicate where there was substantial uncertainty (i.e., in the epidemiological models); where different assumptions would have changed the conclusions (i.e., the assumptions of whether vaccines or effective treatments would be available in the longer term); or where the efficacy of lockdowns depended on what they were used for (i.e., whether suppressing the virus through lockdowns would allow us to then roll out a test-trace-isolate regime that meant COVID-19 cases and deaths averted from lockdowns wouldn't merely be delayed when the prevalence of the virus picked up again afterward).

There was scant thought given in such superficial analyses to ensuring that we were comparing like-with-like, either. For example, several analyses used the VSL to calculate the benefits of lockdowns (a measure of economic welfare) and used GDP to examine the costs of lockdowns (which is much more limited than economic welfare).

Finally, few people who undertook such analysis acknowledged that the uncertainties meant a wide range of potential outcomes. Politicians might have wanted to institute lockdown policies to avoid the small but catastrophic risk of a worst-case scenario, such as a situation where hospital capacity was completely overwhelmed by COVID-19 admissions. Ordinary cost-benefit analyses, with their headline results that reflected the average expected results from models, may miss this extreme tail risk.

Undertaking a full rigorous cost-benefit analysis of the early lockdowns seen in the United States is beyond the scope of this book. But I will outline the thought process an economist might go through when considering a more comprehensive assessment of those extraordinary measures seen between March and June 2020.

The Benefits of Lockdowns

The main purported benefit of early lockdowns was to avoid deaths by reducing transmission of the virus and preventing overcrowding from COVID-19 cases in hospitals. Calculating the monetary value of the deaths that were avoided therefore requires two key pieces of information: the value society places on avoiding the deaths and a robust estimate of the number of lives saved by the policy.

As chapter 4 made clear, the VSL used by economists is typically $10 million per life saved for ordinary day-to-day risks. But data on COVID-19 indicate that the elderly are far more at risk than other members of the population. The median age of death from COVID-19 in the United States appears to be somewhere in the 75–84 year range so far.[6] So, we should rationally adjust the VSL downward to reflect this. University of Berkeley economists have suggested that an age-adjusted VSL of $3.35 million per life saved may be more appropriate.[7] That is the value assumed here.

The next question is: How many deaths from COVID-19 were avoided because of early lockdowns?

Here, defining the *counterfactual* accurately is crucial. That is, we need to compare what we expect to happen under lockdown with a realistic assessment of what would have happened without it, over the same relevant timeframe. We have to try to strip away, in other words, deaths that would have been averted because of voluntary changes to behavior in reaction to the virus, thus isolating the impacts of government lockdown policies (stay-at-home orders, nonessential business closure orders, and public school closures).

Early epidemiological models from Imperial College, London, suggested that between 2.1 and 2.5 million American lives could be spared under a policy of "suppressing" the virus through lockdowns over the duration of the pandemic, for example, compared with a world where we let the virus rip through the population unmitigated.[8] But this unmitigated scenario is not a credible counterfactual. Extensive social distancing was happening prior to government orders, and so it would be wrong to suggest all lives saved compared with "doing nothing" can be attributed to government policies.

Michael Greenstone and Vishan Nigam of the University of Chicago concluded early on that sensible, society-wide social distancing—"combining home isolation of suspect cases, home quarantine of those living in the same household as suspect cases, and social distancing of the elderly and others at most risk of severe disease"—would alone have saved 1.7 million lives through October.[9]

Comparing a scenario where policymakers engaged in suppression across the country—with school closures, stay-at-home orders, banning large gatherings, and closing businesses—with mitigation (the Greenstone and Nigam assumptions plus physical distancing within the workplace, isolation of the elderly and vulnerable, and quarantining infected people and their recent contacts), Imperial's modeling implied that around 620,000 to 1.3 million additional lives would be saved by lockdown-like policies throughout the pandemic, with the higher number achieved if lockdowns were implemented when the virus was less prevalent. Even in these scenarios, however, between 84,000 and 470,000 Americans were still expected to lose their lives.

In reality, of course, the United States has not had a national suppression, or even mitigation, strategy but a patchwork of different approaches by states, albeit widespread state lockdown-like policies were adopted in principle in most of the country between March and very early June. Despite this, as of December 27, 2020, the Centers for Disease Control and Prevention (CDC) had estimated there were between 309,000 to 420,000 "excess deaths" in the United States since early February 2020, which is for now within the Imperial modeling predictions for what would happen even if we instituted suppression policies.[10] True, this number will still rise substantially—Yale scientist and network expert Nicholas Christakis estimates we could see a total of 660,000 U.S. deaths by the end of the pandemic.[11] But that even these numbers are at the low end of what Imperial projected with an extensive mitigation strategy suggests that their models might have been too pessimistic about the deaths we'd have experienced absent early lockdowns.

To add to this suspicion, Imperial projected that Sweden, for example—with various levels of social distancing—would see between 16,000 to 40,000 deaths over the course of the pandemic if it failed to adopt lockdown policies. However, the country has only experienced 8,279 deaths as of December 27, 2020, despite spurning these tougher suppression measures until recently.

What might have caused the models to be wrong? Perhaps, in time, the death figures will be closer to what they predicted once we account for any virus seasonality or mutations. But economists and analysts who have closely examined the modeling have commented on just how reliant these modeled simulations of human interactions are on arbitrary assumptions about how we'd behave—including rates of compliance with various social distancing measures, hospital capacity, and the proportion of businesses or other institutions that remain open. The simulations also do not contain specific modeling of the transmission of the virus in densely populated settings, such as nursing homes, hospitals, or prisons, which we know have been crucial vectors of the virus during this pandemic.[12]

Perhaps most seriously, many economists believe these epidemiological models failed to account for how far people and businesses would adapt to reduce the incidence of superspreading activities and interactions that would expose vulnerable groups to the virus.[13] People's behavior has changed dramatically, from greater precaution (such as hand washing and mask wearing) to large, active changes in lifestyle. Economic modeling has suggested that people will voluntarily engage in less activity when the prevalence of the disease is high, when there are fewer restrictions on infected people, and when there are prospects for a vaccine. Behavior, in other words, is adaptive and appears to have changed more dramatically than the models expected.

Looking at trends across many countries, some economists have even concluded that, over time, behavioral change may even tend to reduce the virus's basic reproduction number to around one, where it will fluctuate—that is, that the average number of people who will contract COVID-19 from any infected person will tend toward one over time as people update their behaviors in response to the state of public health.[14] This might explain why cases and deaths across countries implementing very different public health interventions nevertheless followed fairly consistent patterns through much of the spring and summer of 2020.[15] But it is also possible that the transmission through that period was reduced due to a seasonality of the virus, or people finding it easier to engage in outdoor activities. Whether behavioral change proves as powerful during the winter, or robust to recent mutations, is another matter. What we do know is that models that account for variation in different people's network sizes have also suggested that the transmission and death numbers that were estimated by Imperial if we had failed to lock down may be significant overestimates.

If this failure to account for behavioral change and differences in networks really means that Imperial's results of deaths without lockdowns were biased upward for the United States, then the estimated 620,000 to 1.3 million additional lives that would have been supposedly saved by suppression policies throughout the pandemic would be a vast overestimate.

That's not to say that those lockdowns we saw did not reduce the transmission and spread of the virus. Some empirical studies find a significant impact of lockdowns in terms of reducing caseloads and deaths. One, which controlled for demographics, access to tests, and the capacity of local health care systems, estimated that stay-at-home orders across states were associated with an overall 60 percent (between 18 and 80 percent, depending on the state) reduction in weekly fatalities three weeks after the orders were introduced, ultimately avoiding 41,000 deaths in that short time nationwide, which, given the way the virus spreads, could have prevented vastly more deaths after that as well as some of the knock-on externality effects on crucial industries we discussed in chapter 2.[16]

Several other studies back this up. One exploited the variation in the timing of local shelter-in-place orders in Texas to show that those counties that adopted orders sooner saw slower case growth.[17] Another paper that modeled Sweden as if it had undertaken a lockdown similarly found that the number of deaths would have been a third lower during the lockdown period had Sweden adopted that approach.[18] Finally, a paper by Penn-Wharton economists presented at a Brookings Institution conference in September suggested that, although the private responses did most of the heavy lifting, the combined impact of state stay-at-home orders, school closings, and nonessential business closures across the United States reduced deaths by 48,000 in the first three months of the pandemic.[19] Again, given how quickly the virus spreads, this may have avoided hundreds of thousands of extra deaths over a longer period, with the caveat that an outbreak of that size would almost certainly have seen voluntary social distancing behavior tighten further.[20]

So, those first lockdowns likely brought near-term economic welfare benefits associated with saving significant numbers of lives, albeit at a lower number than Imperial's modeling implied. The next question is whether those lives are "permanently" saved from COVID-19.

Basic logic would suggest that until a vaccine or effective treatment is rolled out, at least some COVID-19 deaths that were averted might simply occur at a later date once restrictions are lifted.

Yet it seems likely that lockdowns actually bought time for adjustments to protect hospital capacity, enabled some contact tracing programs to be set up, and produced a window to develop more effective treatments or a vaccine as we learned more about the virus. Indeed, news of successful early trials for vaccines and a range of new treatments that reduce the odds of severe forms of the disease or help those most sick (many of which were administered on Donald Trump as a COVID-19 patient), suggests that many people whose lives were saved by lockdowns will now permanently avoid death from this particular virus.[21] For example, the pharmaceutical company Pfizer believes its vaccine has 95 percent efficacy and it will be widely available to Americans in 2021. Other vaccine trials suggest similarly high efficacies—implying that avoiding COVID-19 cases and deaths now could mean that we will avoid them forever.

To summarize: lockdowns reduced contact between people and so reduced transmission of the virus and the number deaths from COVID-19. However, the degree to which we can say this "saved lives" for our cost-benefit analysis depends on what would have happened to behavior in the absence of those lockdowns and whether lockdowns allowed medical innovations or public health efforts to develop to maintain those saved lives even after the early lockdowns ended.

Given these large uncertainties, we may for now have to make do with a range of estimates of lives saved from those early lockdowns. At the low end, we'll take figures from the recent empirical analyses; at the high end, we'll use the lower bound of the estimates of lives saved as implied from the Imperial modeling. The range thus runs from around 40,000 to 620,000 estimated U.S. lives saved from those initial lockdown policies. Using the $3.35 million VSL, the monetary benefits of those deaths averted because of early lockdowns therefore range from 40,000 lives multiplied by a value of $3.35 million per life ($134 billion) through to 620,000 lives multiplied by a value of $3.35 million per life ($2.1 trillion). This equates to between 0.6 and 10 percent of 2019 GDP (the wide range reflects the depth of uncertainty).

Lives saved are unlikely to have been the only benefits of those lockdowns, of course. We know, for example, that some survivors of COVID-19 suffer permanent lung scarring, as well as chronic fatigue syndrome or damaged hearts. There are well-documented cases of "long COVID" too—people enduring the effects of their infection for months. Just as people would have a willingness to pay to avoid fatality risks, similar logic dictates they would have a willingness to pay to avoid these nonfatality risks, including the unpleasantness of the symptoms of the disease.

It is not great to lose your sense of smell or taste, suffer cognitive impairment, diarrhea, muscle problems, strokes, kidney damage, disease transmission to your unborn child or even to your living child, who might suffer the pediatric multisystem inflammatory syndrome described in this book's introduction.

In fact, the mere fear of getting the disease, even asymptomatically, may mean there's a VSL-equivalent (say, the value of statistical infection avoidance) for avoiding the nonfatality risk of being infected. Some workers will no doubt have benefited from improved mental health, for example, knowing that the closure of the business they work in kept them or a vulnerable loved one safer from the virus in a region that was strongly affected.

If lockdowns reduced transmission of the virus, then, it stands to reason that we should add up any gains from having fewer nonfatal health consequences too. Some of these will be benefits to economic production. James Broughel and Michael Kotrous estimate one benefit of early lockdowns—reducing permanent lung damage—at anywhere between $19 and $123 billion in value, assuming between 80,000 and 530,000 more people would otherwise have been affected.[22]

Using willingness to pay values commensurate with reducing other nonfatal risks (the value of a statistical injury), some economists even estimate that the economic welfare benefits from lockdowns of reducing transmission of these nonfatal risks may be of a similar magnitude to that of reduced deaths, simply because the number of COVID-19 cases avoided vastly exceeds the number of deaths avoided.[23]

Then there are other unintended benefits of lockdowns. Think about the reduced pollution for the period of the lockdown, including the restoring of natural habitats and more. It is beyond this book to seek to put values on any of these effects that turn out to be permanent, but they are real and should be included in any comprehensive calculations economists undertake. In all then, we can see that the estimated economic welfare benefits of lockdowns run, at the very least, into hundred of billions of dollars, if not trillions. This is truly massive compared to the impact of most ordinary economic regulations.

The Costs of Lockdowns

Just as with the benefits of lockdowns, assessing their costs requires answering the "compared to what?" question. As we have already shown, voluntary social distancing led to many business closures and job losses well before state governors issued their mandates.

In fact, it is particularly difficult to use data to construct a counterfactual when it comes to lockdown costs because even states that didn't formally lock down are interconnected economically with states that did. Examining differences in GDP or business activity between lockdown and non-lockdown states may therefore be misleading about the true impacts of lockdown policies.

There are four other difficulties with working out the costs of lockdowns accurately in terms of lost economic welfare.

First, separating out the temporary effects from the permanent is hard. Saving lives has a longer-term benefit, obviously, so the correct comparison when it comes to any costs of lost economic activity is that which is permanently lost as a result of the lockdowns. We should be careful not to count lost activity that is merely delayed as if it were permanently lost. Someone putting off a TV purchase during lockdown but then making it soon after produces an economic welfare loss, but it is conceptually very different from, say, restaurant or bar activity that will never occur.

Second, given the key benefit of the lockdown is saving lives, a like-for-like comparison requires us not just to compute the costs of lost GDP from lockdowns but to account for a broader assessment of lost economic welfare. So, as outlined in chapter 1, we must include the welfare impact of suspended liberties, any *scarring effects* on mental health or economic opportunity owing to the lockdown, the losses to lifetime knowledge from shuttered schools, and more. This is difficult because the value of certain activities is inherently subjective. Indeed, as a libertarian economist, I'd usually reject attempts to aggregate people's welfare across society in this way. But given the magnitude of the restrictions on our lives, a comprehensive economic analysis should at least try to account for these economic welfare losses.

Third, the costs of lockdowns are potentially highly sensitive to their duration and timings. Some of the costs of lockdown, such as the educational and friendship losses to children from being out of school, or the effects of certain workers being out of the labor force, are likely to become more damaging with longer lockdowns. But it is also likely that an on-off suppression policy of short lockdowns is likely to create a lot more uncertainty and economic inefficiency than one initial longer lockdown that gets the virus down to very low levels, thus enabling the introduction of a robust test-and-trace system.

Given that states began and eased off lockdown at different times and very different levels of infection, we therefore have to be careful about making conclusions about lockdowns as if they were a designed national policy. We know, too, that people's perceptions of risks from COVID-19 began falling during the lockdowns, so while at first the lockdowns probably had little marginal impact in reducing activity given people's fear from engaging in economic life, over time their depressive effect on formal market activity likely grew.[24]

Finally, if we think behavior adapts to the spread of the disease, as discussed in the last section, and that absent lockdowns the caseloads and deaths would have been somewhat higher, we'd also expect greater voluntary social distancing to result from a rapidly spreading disease, reducing economic activity in reaction. So the additional impact of lockdown may be smaller compared with an accurate counterfactual world than we imagine.

With those difficulties in mind, let's first consider the formal market economy. Bureau of Economic Analysis data show that GDP shrank dramatically during the second quarter of 2020 when lockdowns were implemented and rose significantly (but did not fully recover) after partial reopening in the third quarter.[25] As of the third quarter of 2020, the net effect is that GDP was down 2.8 percent relative to that stage in 2019 and about 5 percent below where it would have been had the crisis not hit.

How much of this impact owes to initial lockdowns, as opposed to changed behavior, is difficult to calculate. Most economists believe that, at most, a third to a half of even the near-term decline in activity in the early phases of the pandemic was purely due to lockdowns, as opposed to panicked changes in behavior from risk-averse consumers and workers. By restricting at least some activity that otherwise would have occurred, however, it is inconceivable that lockdowns didn't make many businesses unviable, eliminate plenty of good jobs permanently, and suppress new economic activity.

The precise impact of lockdowns on U.S. GDP, of course, requires accounting for the different timings of introductions and removals of lockdown measures at the state level too, given the states' very different contributions to economic output. Mercatus Center economists James Broughel and Michael Kotrous are the only people to have attempted to assess this, and they conclude that the initial lockdown measures probably cost somewhere between $255 and $464 billion in lost output (1.2 to 2.2 percent of 2019 GDP.)

This no doubt understates some of the longer-term costs of lockdowns, however. One source of potential longer-term difficulties was school closures. Those contributed to downturns in short-term GDP by making it more difficult for parents to work. But they also might have had much longer-term effects, too, if the loss of that schooling led to a reduction in what economists call *human capital accumulation*, the stuff between our ears that makes us economically productive. The worry is that sustained absence from school might scar the economic potential of the children affected, particularly those from poor socio-economic backgrounds, who might have less access to parental or information technology resources for effective substitute schooling during lockdowns.[26]

Then there's the loss of entrepreneurial activity. Ideas are generated in clusters, from human interactions and testing the selling of new products to consumers. If these opportunities are curbed even on the margins by lockdowns, perhaps because business people and entrepreneurs who could otherwise interact safely in person are restricted from meeting, or because school closures mean they are spending time parenting, then the loss of innovations for economic well-being could be large.

We have evidence that socializing is good for innovation. Recent research from economist Michael Andrews shows that states that enacted alcohol bans during Prohibition saw a significant decline in patents in previously wet counties relative to consistently dry counties.[27] The effects were bigger for populations more likely to frequent saloons too. Bars, in other words, were a source of collaboration and a place for exposure to new ideas. Who knows what opportunities were missed as a result of stay-at-home orders and people not meeting face-to-face?

Data show, unsurprisingly, that small-business formation collapsed during the period of lockdown, albeit rebounding afterwards. It's also likely that by banning existing businesses from opening, crude lockdowns prevented companies from finding innovative means of opening safely, in ways their customers could trust, so that over time the economic costs of lockdown grew larger.

None of this yet mentions the potential longer-term impacts of lockdowns on the psychology of businessmen and entrepreneurs either. It is almost certainly the case that most would-be entrepreneurs and business owners did not even consider the risk of their business being shut down for extended periods by state governments. The sheer fact that lockdowns have happened at all is likely to deter people from going into certain industries in the future, even after this pandemic is over.[28] If this precaution is excessive relative to the real risks, it could lead to very large longer-term damage to societal welfare. Of course, there's a risk, too, that politicians will find the allure of using lockdown-type policies for other policy goals, meaning their mere precedent has damaging longer-term impacts. Already, for example, some commentators have suggested the idea of "climate lockdowns."

Banned activities that add to economic welfare but that don't appear in GDP are real costs of lockdowns too. We value our liberties to engage in productive leisure activities that bring us happiness, from playing sports to attending religious gatherings or meeting family.

Restrictions on these make us worse off—if we'd be willing to risk doing them—and that's precisely why a VSL is much higher than people's lifetime earning potential from market activity alone. We value life because of the things we can do while living. So it makes no sense to count saving lives as a benefit of lockdown but fail to account for the lost value of living as a cost of lockdown.

Not being able to see loved ones, having to push off important events such as weddings or christenings, being restricted from traveling, not being able to develop your music skills, or having your time to find a partner curtailed during the window of life when you are fertile—all these things are likely to be extremely costly for some people. One of my friends had to cancel his bachelor party and wedding as a result of the lockdown; another probably won't have her ill father around to see her married; many a grandparent, including my parents, lost a quarter of a year of personal interaction with their grandchildren. It should be obvious that these losses compound any hit to consumption or earning potential. Therefore our economic welfare is sharply reduced.

True, a lot of this can't simply be chalked up simply as a loss from lockdown. Social distancing puts paid to much activity anyway. Who wants a big wedding celebration when grandma's health would be put at risk? But it is likely that at least some activities that could have been undertaken with safety precautions were nevertheless banned, resulting in significant losses to welfare, sometimes if only due to a lost option. In economic terms, the former chief economist to Trump's Council of Economic Advisers, Casey Mulligan, writes about all this as a loss in the productivity of leisure time.[29]

Then, of course, we have to add the unintended health costs of lockdowns. We know that although historically deaths fall during recessions, mental health, disability, and suicide trends tend to worsen after downturns end.[30] Medics have worried about "substantial increases in anxiety and depression, substance use, loneliness, and domestic violence."[31] Stated levels of distress were up during the shelter-in-place order period in San Francisco, and the *Washington Post* has reported that drug overdoses have surged.[32]

Locking down is also likely to have deterred people from going to health care facilities for checkups for conditions that are likely to turn out to be serious, such as cancers. The CDC has presented evidence of a decline in the number of vaccines for other diseases administered for children. Hospitals canceled lots of elective surgeries that are likely to worsen the health prospects of those affected.[33] Newer evidence shows that one consequence of nursing homes locking down hard to avoid COVID-19 deaths was greater levels of non-COVID-19 deaths.[34] Given the high VSL that we've seen, the cost of effects such as these on future mortality and morbidity also adds up quickly, so we should keep an eye on longer-term effects in the coming years, although excess deaths so far appear to correlate extremely strongly with where there are big COVID-19 outbreaks. Again, we have to be careful to remember that a lot of these impacts would have occurred without lockdowns, given people would still be worried about catching the virus, if it were running rampant. But it is certainly likely lockdowns will have compounded some of the impacts.

Finally, while a more speculative cost, it is certainly possible that lockdowns may have been a contributing factor to the riots and looting that followed the killing of George Floyd. Certainly, some were predicting riots, given the impact of quarantine on the human brain, as far back as March, based on historical precedent.[35] I noticed a lot more petty crime being committed here in Washington, DC, a few weeks into the formal stay-at-home order. Since the pandemic began, violent crime has spiked in major cities.[36] With weeks of people being cooped up inside, we cannot discount that lockdowns may have provided an aggravating condition for civil unrest, albeit triggered in the Floyd case by a genuine injustice. Crime, though, is costly—bringing both economic destruction and reducing societal trust.

Weighing It Up

$16 trillion. That's how much former Treasury Secretary Larry Summers and economist David Cutler believe the pandemic will ultimately cost the United States in lost economic welfare, even if the virus is largely contained by the end of 2021.[37] The economists reach that figure by adding up the projected impact of the pandemic on GDP, mortality, morbidity, and mental health. Yes, they use a higher VSL than I have in this chapter, adjusting for which would reduce this number to just under $14 trillion. But even this looks to be an underestimate for the total impact of the pandemic, given the valuable nonmarket activities we've lost and the innovation and scarring impacts we cannot truly even envisage so far.

Yet, I hope the one thing I've driven into you through this chapter is that we cannot blame the initial lockdowns from March to June 2020 for anywhere near the scale of this economic welfare hit. Not just because they are likely to have reduced transmission and deaths of the virus but because vast amounts of formal market activity and socializing would have stopped even without state lockdowns. South Dakota, for example, had limited dine-in restrictions on restaurants and no mask mandate as of December 2020 but still faced a greater depression in restaurant activity relative to January 2020 than the country as a whole.[38] The state did not adopt a lockdown in the early days of the pandemic but still saw a sharp GDP decline across the first half of 2020, not much different than many other states.

Outlining the sorts of considerations we must make for a comprehensive cost-benefit analysis of lockdowns has hopefully highlighted how difficult they are do well and how inadequate many existing efforts have been.

Given the assumptions in place when governors were making their initial decisions, it was perfectly reasonable for a rough-and-ready take to conclude that lockdowns would pass a basic cost-benefit test, especially given the uncertainties at the time. A respectable analysis could then have concluded that the societal economic welfare benefits of lockdowns would potentially run into trillions of dollars. Their costs were high, too, running into hundreds of billions of dollars, if not trillions. Yet given the predicted death tolls, driven by flawed epidemiological models, we can understand why politicians thought lockdowns were appropriate and why some economists reacted angrily to Trump's tweet suggesting otherwise.

But academic economists failed to indicate the huge uncertainty around these results. Not only would the costs of lockdowns have multiplied significantly if they lasted longer than necessary, but the economic case for them was partially dependent on assumptions of how much worse the death toll would have been with voluntary mitigation and whether the pause gained by lockdowns would be used to improve the testing regime, develop better treatments, or produce a vaccine to reduce the negative effects of the pandemic in the future.

Increasing evidence at this stage of the pandemic suggests that epidemiological models may have underestimated how behavioral change would mitigate the spread of the virus and so reduce the transmission of the disease. Lockdowns did reduce the transmission of the virus somewhat, especially through restrictions on places such as bars and gyms. Certainly, they imposed additional restrictions on economic activity too. But both their still-large benefits and costs were likely exaggerated in public debate because behavioral change did, and would have continued to, effectively mimic lockdowns in many respects, at least in those early months of the pandemic.

At the very least, economists must admit that those lockdowns were a crude way to protect lives. That's why it's necessary to remember the second important role cost-benefit analyses can play—to judge alternative policy frameworks against each other. For saying "the benefits of initial lockdowns are likely to have exceeded their large costs" should not be the end of the matter.

If two paths are extremely costly, the fact that one path is costlier doesn't make the less-costly path the optimal approach. Banning all cars might be costlier than having no rules of the road, but it doesn't mean that we cannot find a better intermediate solution, such as introducing laws that reduce the likelihood of accidents while retaining the benefits of allowing road travel.

Lockdowns were extreme emergency measures. They banned much high-risk and low-risk activity alike. Our aim should always have been to find ways of retaining the health benefits of social distancing while reducing the costs of restricting liberties and economic activity. This might have been easier if we could have identified clusters of cases because of widespread testing and introduced a robust isolation regime early. But even without this, it should have become easier to find a better balance between economic activity and public health as we acquired more information about the virus. In that sense, the recent re-adoption of lockdown-like policies in some parts of the country are a sign of failure.

Of course, that's not to say there is one conclusion resulting from analyses of every lockdown proposal in very different situations and other time periods. In fact, it could be argued that the case for lockdown-like policies is much stronger as of the end of 2020 than in spring 2020. With vaccines already being rolled out and the prospect of more highly transmissible strains of the virus spreading in the United States, anything that reduces transmission of the virus now has larger, more certain, public health benefits in terms of lives saved than policies adopted when COVID-19 first hit. In the UK and Ireland, one new mutation of the virus appears to be better adapted to circumvent existing mitigation efforts, too, spreading more quickly for any given restrictions on activity. So it might be the case that even tighter controls than were used in the spring are appropriate to avoid a catastrophic, rapid spread of the virus and the worst congestion externalities associated with overwhelmed hospitals.

At a societal level, however, we should have always wanted to minimize the overall economic welfare costs of this pandemic, rather than talking as if our aim was simply minimizing deaths or minimizing near-term economic damage, as if it must be a direct tradeoff between the two. World Health Organization officials now say that lockdowns should only be seen as emergency measures that buy time. For most of the pandemic, there have been better "middle paths."[39] But realizing them would have required politicians to do something they are not prone to do: to think on the margin.

ECONOMIC LESSON

Cost-benefit analysis is a useful economic technique for considering whether a project improves societal welfare and to compare the societal net benefits of different projects. To do cost-benefit analysis well, we must account for all the direct and indirect impacts of the proposed policy on societal welfare, account for externalities, and ensure that we compare like-with-like in both timeframe and measurement. When it comes to COVID-19, cost-benefit analysis can, in theory, be used to examine the efficacy of lockdowns. However, there are huge uncertainties that make it hard to weigh up the precise costs and benefits of those policies. Even if the societal benefits do appear to exceed the costs on reasonable assumptions, that doesn't mean the exact contours of the lockdown are "optimal policy." In an ideal world, we'd find the policy mix that minimizes the overall societal costs of the pandemic.

ECONOMIC TERMS INTRODUCED

- **counterfactual:** what would have happened in the absence of the policy, which provides a baseline for assessing the policy's true impact
- **cost-benefit analysis:** an economic policy evaluation technique that assesses the strengths and weaknesses of a project or policy, seeking to convert (as far as possible) its impacts into monetary values representing the costs and benefits to societal economic welfare
- **economic scarring:** longer-term damage caused to an individual or an economy's prospects by a shock or recession
- **human capital accumulation:** the buildup of a stock of skills, education, work habits, and experience that increases a person's productive capacity

6

WHY WAS I BANNED FROM GOING FISHING?

An introduction to thinking on the margin

've never really cared for fishing, despite my dad's best attempts to convince me otherwise. The very first day he took me to the local river, I caught a fair-sized sea bass—a piece of beginner's luck that would have had others hooked for life. But, in truth, I never really enjoyed having to hook into worms for bait or untangle fishing line. After that early foray, it seemed as if the thing I was most likely to catch on each excursion was a cold.

Nevertheless, preferences are subjective. My own experience is very different from others. Millions of people enjoy angling and it self-evidently brings them immense joy, just as others are obsessed with playing golf, or dancing, or posting Instagram stories.

Yet in many states, stay-at-home or shelter-in-place orders explicitly or implicitly banned going fishing. Despite the activity being extremely low-risk in terms of spreading the virus (given you can safely socially distance and undertake it on your own or just with fellow household members), politicians often made no such exemptions from the broader orders to stay home.

Fishing is not the only activity it made little sense to ban. In California, a man paddleboarding alone in the Pacific Ocean was tracked down by lifeguards and subsequently arrested for breaching the state's stay-at-home orders, even though he clearly posed an infinitesimally small risk to others while in the sea.[1] In fact, his arrest itself was infinitely more risky than the activity he was arrested for in terms of transmitting the disease.

It seems obvious that the benefits to public health of banning fishing or paddleboarding are tiny. The costs to those individuals for whom the activities are important, however, may be large. For a family that has been cooped up inside for long periods of time with young children indoors, the opportunity to fish in solitude outside may have been extremely welcome. But politicians had outlawed the activity.

In their defense, politicians would argue that there is a behavioral reason why some seemingly safe activities can't be allowed. They would say that any exemptions from stay-at-home orders are likely to bring some additional interactions between people, not least in traveling to the beach or fishing site. But mostly they will be wary of *peer effects*— the idea that some people going out and engaging in activities will influence others' behavior. Perhaps I may not be willing to take the risk of socializing as I once did, but if everyone else is out fishing or being active, it may influence my own risk preferences.

Yet we can find other absurd examples of regulations related to COVID-19 that suggest politicians' propensity to ban things is not just driven by fear of people being more willing to travel or socialize. In Michigan, for example, the state governor's executive order effectively banned the sale of goods not thought to be essential within large grocery and department stores.[2] Famously, customers quickly posted pictures online of aisles containing seeds for gardening that had been roped off from purchase.

Once in stores, the additional risk from someone buying these other goods is low, especially given that the regulations already imposed restrictions on customer numbers by store size. In fact, given that additional regulation, the roping off of certain areas might actually have increased the risk of close contact among patrons.

But daft rules that didn't help the public health effort did not end with seeds. Lockdowns across the country, at least in principle, stopped people visiting their empty second homes, from using their boats or jet-skis in solitude, and from having people visit at a safe distance in their gardens or yards.

All these features of the edicts brought minimal public health benefits but did impose economic welfare costs. These regulations were the product of incredibly crude thinking, of aggregating whole groups of goods and activities together to decide what to ban without considering the benefits and costs of each activity alone. That crudeness was perhaps best exemplified by the categorization of industries into "essential" and "nonessential" groupings—a listing completely unmoored from considerations of the relative risks associated with the spread of the virus.

Now think about all those people who had actually recovered from the virus early and were then, at that stage, immune to it. Many could have undertaken a raft of banned economic activities, including home visits for beauty, personal care, or gardening services, without posing any major risk of spreading the disease.

Hairdressers who had recovered could have undertaken home appointments at a time of high demand at little additional risk of infecting anyone. Other stores could no doubt have innovated to find ways to open relatively safely using personal protective equipment or other precautions, such as outdoor sales only.

But most of those original lockdown orders precluded lots of this activity or innovation. Although some people probably breached the law when they realized their activity did not bring large health risks, the orders themselves would no doubt have deterred many people from undertaking activity that could bring clear net benefits to society.

As we concluded in the previous chapter, doing nothing in the face of the virus could have been incredibly costly to economic welfare. Yet crude lockdowns themselves were incredibly costly too. Economists should look at this as an opportunity for an intermediate solution—for trying to identify the policy interventions that maintain the largest public health benefits at the lowest possible cost, or more accurately, to identify ways to minimize the total combined economic welfare costs of the pandemic.

The last chapter examined lockdowns as a policy regime, assessing their costs and benefits relative to not doing lockdowns. But in truth, there are many possibilities between the hard lockdowns we saw and doing nothing. Rather than simply applying a crude ban on much activity, what we really needed was for policymakers to examine the impact of individual components of lockdowns—not compare the whole bundle of interventions against inaction. We needed politicians to do something they don't usually do—to start to *think on the margin*.

When Should We Build a Highway?

Thinking on the margin is perhaps the key way that economists think differently from noneconomists, including most politicians. In simple terms, a lot of the time political decisions and policies are made using binary thinking, such as to ban or not to ban, or to spend or not to spend. Yet most meaningful decisions in life are actually not binary but are about whether more or less of an activity is desirable.

Let's consider an example. Lots of politicians like infrastructure spending in general and highway spending in particular. They repeatedly say that it is good for the economy and demand dollars be put toward it. And one of the talking points used in support of this view is academic work that shows that the construction of the interstate highway system brought with it rising productivity and so rising GDP.[3]

Yet if they were thinking on the margin, politicians would realize that evidence from past road building tells us nearly nothing about the desirability of new highways. Just because the first interstate highway system had big benefits relative to the costs of building it does not mean a second interstate highway system would too. In fact, this is precisely what economists have shown. Recent studies find that too many new highways were built between 1983 and 2003 and that those extensions to the system did not increase economic welfare.[4] That's because the cost savings to businesses and individuals of newer, better connections were relatively lower.

Economists would therefore judge an additional road proposal on whether the marginal benefits of the project (i.e., the benefits from the additional road being discussed) exceeded the marginal costs of the project. And if there were a set budget for road building, they would want to finance the projects where the benefit-cost ratios were highest.

We all implicitly think on the margin as second nature in certain circumstances. Take drinking alcohol. That first drink at happy hour might taste great. The second might be almost as awesome. But at some point most of us judge that having an additional pint of beer will have higher marginal costs than marginal benefits to us—that the hangover the next morning, or the additional alcohol impairing our future decisionmaking, combined with the monetary price, exceeds the additional benefit we get from drinking it.

Thinking on the margin, then, is how consumers usually decide whether to buy an additional unit of a good or service. If the consumer's marginal benefit (the additional benefit that a customer gets from purchasing the next unit of the good) is greater than their marginal cost (the additional cost to them of purchasing the good), then they will tend to purchase the good. Therefore, the maximum amount a consumer is willing to pay equates to their marginal benefit. They should theoretically continue consuming up until the point where this marginal benefit of consumption is equal to the marginal cost.

Sometimes we don't think on the margin when we should. Consider assessing whether you want to take up your pharmacy's offer of buying a second tube of $2.50 toothpaste in a half-price deal. Yes, the marginal cost of this new tube of toothpaste is just $1.25, reducing the average cost of both the tubes you might buy to just below $1.90.

But in the moment, deciding to buy the second tube also means spending 50 percent more on toothpaste than you were expecting, with the consequence of having less money to spend on other goods. You have to weigh up whether the marginal benefit to you of another tube of toothpaste right now exceeds the marginal cost of purchasing it.

The problem with many government policies is that they preclude such marginal thinking. Whether because of the clarity of binary rules or because politicians simply don't understand the reasoning, they instead implement bans and restrictions on activity that make society worse off relative to a world where decisions are based on weighing the marginal social cost and marginal social benefit of an activity.

Indeed, a key insight of marginal thinking is that the ideal amount of any activity will rarely be zero. Yet politicians talk and act as if lessening the occurrence of "bads"—pollution, crime, or collusion between companies—is *always* good and the failure to spend more on "goods" is *always* bad.

My colleague Diego Zuluaga highlighted a fun example of this.[5] Famous anti-communist Sen. Joe McCarthy (R-WI) once suggested that having even one communist in the State Department was one communist too many. Yet this was an obvious failure to think on the margin. The marginal cost of rooting out every last communist would have been massive. It seems incredibly unlikely that just one communist among all State Department employees could have such a damaging influence to justify the vast cost in time, resources, false allegations, and employee morale.

We could likewise eliminate lots of pollution by banning all industrial activity, most travel, and the burning of various fuels. But the cost of doing so would be huge. On the margin, it would soon become clear that reintroducing some activity, such as a power system to prevent many people dying of hypothermia, would be very, very good, on net, for society. Or, as another example, we might believe that providing government support for education has some positive impacts on society. But mandating another additional two years of formal schooling on top of existing mandates might have vastly higher marginal costs than societal marginal benefits.

Marginal Thinking in a Pandemic

The lockdown itself is a great example of this failure to think on the margin. Banning low-risk activities as part of stay-at-home orders because they are not "essential" means banning lots of interactions where the marginal benefits exceed the marginal costs.

Fishing in most uncrowded locations or paddleboarding in the Pacific Ocean are zero cost, or at least as close to zero as one can imagine. There are clear marginal benefits, on the other hand, for those engaged in the activities, whether from the vitamin D and open air, the positive impact on their mental health, or the opportunity to take children out and away from the house they have been stuck inside for weeks.

Likewise, it seems very unlikely—again, on the margin—that someone already in a grocery store taking the extra time to buy packets of seeds will add much risk of COVID-19 infection to anyone. The marginal cost of allowing seed buying within stores is very low. Yet these restrictions do harm to those who otherwise would buy them.

We could think of similar arguments in regard to beaches or public parks. A handful of people roaming free on the sand or on lawns are likely to bring tiny upticks in the risks of spreading COVID-19. Thousands of people packing a beach, on the other hand, clearly would raise the risks. A marginal approach would seek to limit numbers of people at the beach or advise them to keep socially distanced, rather than banning use of public spaces entirely, as was seen in many states.

Whenever governments ban activities or preclude behaviors entirely, there are lost societal benefits such as this. Even beyond the trivial examples of activities where most agree the restrictions went too far, full lockdowns, incorporating the closure of a range of businesses deemed nonessential, meant inadvertently preventing much economic activity that could take place safely on the margin.

Not that all marginal thinking points in favor of looser public health guidance or mandates, however. For many weeks during the initial lockdown, the most risky activity most people undertook each week was a visit to the grocery store. But at that time here in Washington, DC, there were no initial requirements from government or the retailers to wear facemasks or coverings within stores, or indeed limits on how many people could enter. The requirements by stores that came later, however, almost certainly had marginal social benefits that exceeded the marginal social costs. Having to wait outside for a short time or cover your face while inside would usually be a relatively small cost imposition on each individual relative to the potential benefits of stopping the spread of the disease.

Economists tried to alert policymakers to thinking on the margin in regard to lockdowns, often using sophisticated economic and epidemiological modeling. A few studies broke down the impacts of lockdowns onto different demographic groups, for example, examining the marginal impacts by age. In theory, stricter and longer lockdowns on older populations and shorter, weaker lockdowns on everyone else would have generated higher public health benefits at lower economic costs than a uniform lockdown.[6] However, as noted earlier, it is easier to isolate populations in theory than practice, and such an approach might have violated people's ideas of fairness.

Similar conclusions, however, were reached in studies that looked at alternative policy regimes. One found that economic welfare would have been much enhanced by a targeted testing and isolation regime, rather than indiscriminate lockdowns.[7] It should go without saying that ordering each uninfected person to stay home has a high marginal social cost relative to marginal social benefits, if we could otherwise use rigorous and regular testing to identify the infected and simply isolate them from others. This, of course, is theoretical—it merely assumes we could have instituted that alternative policy regime. As we will see in chapter 9, government failures meant that insufficient testing was done early on, meaning that the virus quickly spread through the population.

But that idea—of trying to isolate infectious people and reduce or eliminate activities likely to facilitate the spread of the virus for low economic benefit—is how an economist would approach this. One study, for example, broke down the implicit components of a lockdown and examined individual sectors to develop a GDP-to-risk index of industries. This helps to identify where closures had the biggest economic cost relative to public health benefit. That particular paper concluded that nonwork social activities were a big public health risk (bars, large gatherings, gyms, shopping without masks) and that keeping strict controls on these areas could allow relaxations with strong net economic welfare gains elsewhere.[8]

Since then, a study has used phone tracking mobility data for 98 million people in Atlanta, Chicago, Dallas, Houston, Los Angeles, Miami, New York, Philadelphia, San Francisco, and Washington, DC, in the early months of the pandemic to integrate the real social networks that were observed from peoples' movements into epidemiological models. It found that the outcomes of the model then reflected the trajectory of real cases reasonably well, suggesting that a small number of points of interest, such as restaurants, gyms, coffee shops, or religious gatherings may have been associated with seeding an overwhelming majority of infections. The study also found that grocery stores in lower-income areas appeared to see higher virus transmission than grocery stores in high-income areas in 8 of 10 cities, which may be explained by stores in the poorer areas being more crowded. The implication is that restricting maximum occupancy at these points of interest, or encouraging better ventilation or moving activities out-side, is likely to have been a much more effective policy for both containing the virus and protecting economic welfare than constraining people's mobility uniformly, such as through stay-at-home orders. Many activities that were implicitly banned from these blanket measures are low risk and so have low marginal social costs that are exceeded by their marginal social benefits.[9]

What happened after the initial, crude lockdowns was an implicit admission that the developers of these lockdowns did not think enough on the margin. Most reopenings occurred in stages. Lower-risk activities were allowed first, such as eating in outdoor restaurants with strict social distancing protocols. Mass gatherings, including concerts and sports events, were banned for much longer—these are, it is now believed, highly likely to have been the sources of superspreader events that possibly propelled infection rates. The marginal social costs of such gatherings are therefore highly likely to exceed the benefits.

But this type of thinking on the margin might have vastly more implications in the pandemic than just on when to relax lockdowns. It should also impact the timing and type of restrictions on activity through different stages of the pandemic. Banning a lot of activity in a particular state when there are no people infected or exhibiting symptoms would be hugely destructive from a societal perspective, for example, for a very small marginal social benefit. It would be much more cost-effective to adopt other policies, such as trying to stamp out the virus spreading from new arrivals.

In fact, quarantining new arrivals is another example of an area where thinking on the margin could be useful. A lot of states and countries, including my native UK, and indeed Florida and Washington, DC, during the early stages of the pandemic, made all new arrivals from certain places self-quarantine for a 14-day period. This type of measure, however, actively deterred people from visiting by restricting them from engaging in activity outside of where they were staying.

Was this too cautious? It's important to think on the margin here. Each extra day in self-quarantine (after the likely incubation period for the virus) brings a diminishing marginal social benefit in terms of reducing the public health risk but a rising marginal social cost in terms of the activities forgone by keeping that person stuck indoors. At some point, these values intersect—that should be the optimal average length of quarantine. This optimal length of time would no doubt vary depending on where the traveler was coming from, because this would impact the marginal social benefit that comes from mitigating the very different risks faced.

Did the choice of 14 days make economic sense? Several studies identified a median incubation period for the virus of just over 5 days and showed that virtually all individuals with symptoms developed them within 12.[10] Once symptoms begin, of course, you are advised to self-isolate for 10 days from that point. But not everyone who was infected develops symptoms. The 14-day quarantine therefore not only risked some infected people unknowingly going out into the community while still infectious after the enforced quarantine but kept lots of other people who were never infected locked up—at large cost, for no benefit.

A better system could be devised when rapid results from testing were more widely available. We knew that there was a very high possibility that those exposed and infected by the virus would not test positive for it straight away. Harvard experts thought there was a 100 percent possibility that you would falsely test negative for COVID-19 if you were tested on the day of your infection. You would still face as high as a 40 percent chance of a false negative four days after exposure to the virus.[11] This then declines to a trough of around 20 percent on days eight and nine.[12]

To reduce the costs of this type of quarantine policy relative to the benefits, then, why not have a shorter compelled quarantine—say of eight to nine days but with a COVID-19 test on that date? If someone tests positive, they would have to go into self-isolation for a longer period, whether they were displaying symptoms or not.[13] But for those without symptoms, the probability that they have the virus, after that long a period of self-quarantine and with a negative test result, would be extremely low. The marginal social benefit of keeping all those who would have tested negative in quarantine for another six days would be very small indeed, relative to the larger social costs.

Remember, one of the important takeaways of marginal analysis is that bans or efforts to quash "bads" entirely tend to be suboptimal.

The aim should not be to eliminate *any* risk of the virus being transmitted but to set policy such that, even in the face of this externality, we account for the costs that it imposes on others. Along those lines, it is possible to think of further improvements to COVID-19 mitigation measures, such as home isolation quarantines, that could raise economic welfare for minor uplifts in risks. For example, contact tracers might inform a cluster of people that they have been in close contact with someone who is infected and order those people to stay home. But if after, say, five days, none of a large group has exhibited symptoms or tested positive, then a risk-based home quarantine policy could conclude that it is highly unlikely anyone is infected, and so end the quarantine to eliminate the marginal social costs of people being told to stay at home unnecessarily.

By December 2020, the Centers for Disease Control and Prevention had acknowledged that a two-week travel quarantine damaged economic welfare, admitting that enforced quarantine after a week or so imposed significant marginal costs on peoples' lives without much marginal benefit to improving public health. It revised its guidance to suggest allowing people to leave quarantine after 7 days if they obtained a negative COVID-19 test result, or 10 days if they had no COVID-19 symptoms.[14]

Once we start thinking on the margin in regard to this pandemic, it is difficult to stop. We start to realize that politicians often talk about the impact of a regulation, such as a mask mandate, as if the alternative is that nobody is wearing masks, when the real *marginal* impacts of a mandate are the benefits to public health above and beyond the voluntary mask wearing we would see anyway, which we must then compare with the marginal costs of enforcing and policing the law. It took far too long to pivot to thinking about win-win measures that could have increased the ratio of economic welfare to economic risk for any given set of activities, such as mask wearing, better testing regimes, or other low-cost safety measures that helped screen for infectiousness, thus allowing people to undertake economic activities with more confidence. Thinking on the margins gets one infuriated that governors made those early blanket calls to shut down so-called nonessential businesses, rather than thinking about additional risks.

Yes, there were good public health reasons to mandate closures for mass entertainment activities, such as sports events, restaurants, bars, nightclubs, and movie theaters. There might also have been justification for temporary emergency limits on the numbers of people allowed in social gatherings or stores, or indeed for facemask mandates. A government message encouraging people to work from home may have been reasonable guidance too. Such principles drove many private companies' responses to this crisis, even prior to government action.

But orders to close all non essential businesses risked needlessly cutting off activity that might otherwise have occurred safely. That's not to mention the risks of inadvertently disrupting industries that, contrary to bureaucratic knowledge, were in fact important suppliers to other companies doing essential work.

Then there were the huge congressional spending packages. Lots of funding and relief spending was thrown around left, right, and center. But clearly some uses could have a much bigger payoff than others. Although there was great uncertainty over whether we could fund a robust test-trace-isolate regime, or a successful vaccine or treatment for COVID-19, the reduction in economic pain that any of these ideas could have delivered was always huge. We knew, too, that vaccines in particular usually take years to roll out, in part because they entail incredibly risky investments in manufacturing capacity specific to the particular vaccine.

Given the potential social benefits of any of these public health innovations compared to the upfront costs, the case for a huge investment in testing, treatment research, and advanced orders for vaccines was extremely strong. Recent research by Tim Johnson, a business professor at the University of Illinois Urbana–Champaign, and others, has used stock market reactions to vaccine progress to estimate that a vaccine cure that ended this pandemic and its uncertainty would be worth around 5–15 percent of global wealth.[15] The marginal benefits of any measures that encourage economic normalization by speeding up the end of this pandemic by just a few months then would be absolutely enormous, especially relative to the marginal costs of the investment, which were tiny in the grand scheme of things. And yet, as Nobel prize–winning economist Paul Romer has observed, governments around the world, including in the United States, spent tiny, tiny fractions on medical innovation and testing through this pandemic relative to more direct relief to households and businesses.[16]

And this was despite the fact that all the while the prevalence of the virus was high, the marginal benefit of additional "stimulus" was low in terms of its impact in reviving activity, especially relative to steps that got the virus under control.

Of course, we cannot blame politicians for all these mistakes and their failures to think on the right margins. We are blessed now with a degree of hindsight. SARS-CoV-2 was a new pathogen and there was massive uncertainty about how it spread, how lethal the disease was, who was affected, and which activities therefore put people at risk. Lockdowns, in part at least, reflected an emergency decision to shut as much down as possible until we knew more. But thinking on the margin can help guide us toward recognizing that, while pain is inevitable in dealing with COVID-19, it is only desirable to engage in actions up to the point that their marginal social benefit equates to their marginal social cost—that is, the point at which the additional pain of that measure is equal to the preservation of the value of life and health it delivers.

As knowledge about the disease has expanded, there have been changes to policies and regulations that reflect our growing understanding of the risks. But unlike most private business activity in a market economy, political decisions do not come with automatic feedback mechanisms that help policymakers adapt quickly in light of new knowledge or realities. When this virus hit, our political leaders were both dealing with radical uncertainty and trying to wrest control of the transmission of a virus across a complex system of human relationships.

ECONOMIC LESSON

Policymakers often fail to think on the margin—delivering crude bans on activities regarded as "bad," or endorsing ever-growing subsidies for programs regarded as "good." Economists, on the other hand, assume the optimal amount of any activity occurs when the marginal benefit is equal to the marginal cost. During this pandemic, many public health interventions showed a failure to think on the margin. Lockdowns banned much activity that barely affected public health but did reduce people's well-being. Quarantine policies often seemed designed to eliminate the risks of importing the disease entirely, although this is almost certainly economically inefficient. And spending on testing and medical innovations was arguably too low relative to the amount of the relief packages, given the huge marginal social benefits of ending this pandemic sooner.

ECONOMIC TERMS INTRODUCED

- **peer effects:** an externality effect whereby the actions or characteristics of a surrounding group affect the actions or characteristics of an individual
- **thinking on the margin:** weighing the costs and benefits of each additional change or action rather than basing decisions on past events or broad rules of behavior
- **marginal benefit:** the additional benefit from a unit change in an activity
- **marginal cost:** the additional cost from a unit change in activity

7

WHAT GOOD IS A PANDEMIC PLAN WITH
SO MANY UNKNOWNS?

An introduction to uncertainty and the
knowledge problem

t became the catchphrase for a failed presidential campaign. Sen.
Elizabeth Warren (D-MA) would regularly declare "I have a plan for
that" on the Democratic debate stage, irrespective of the economic
or social issue being discussed.

The Massachusetts senator wore her reputation for detailed policy
schemes as a badge of honor. "Child care unaffordable? Big corporations and billionaires not paying their fair share? Want more economic
and political power in the hands of the people?" her website said, "Don't
worry, Warren has a plan for that." You can still buy T-shirts embla-
zoned with that slogan.[1]

Warren's ambition did not end with plans to overhaul the economy, however. Even the seemingly intractable COVID-19 pandemic
was something she quickly developed a "plan" for, as far back as January 2020.[2] At least, that was when her first plan was published. A second
was forthcoming in March.[3] But that had an even shorter shelf life,
with a third plan published just a few days later, when it became
clear that the damage associated with the virus would be much more
serious.[4]

It is widely believed that achieving better economic and social outcomes requires a detailed plan from governments. As human beings we like to feel in control of events, even in the grip of a viral pandemic, and so we are drawn to the idea of someone, somewhere, with a clear roadmap to alleviate our suffering.

Plans are something we are familiar with devising personally. Before we shop for groceries, we might plan what meals we want to eat during the week. We plan how much we need to save for a deposit for a house or to put our kids through college. Businesses plan their product range and investment ambitions. It seems logical, then, that we might seek to engage in planning at a societal level through the political process for what type of economy we want or for what we'd do to stop the spread of a virus.

Yet, as Warren's continual updates to her plans show, when we plan for ourselves, we have some big advantages over politicians or government officials who are trying to control actions across complex personal and economic relationships.

For starters, we have better access to the local knowledge of our circumstances. Governments might plan for, say, improving childcare quality through regulatory requirements on providers. But only we as individuals might know really specific emotional or physical needs that our children have that will be ill-catered for by such an approach. Likewise, only individual providers in different markets might understand the viability of operating under a specific pricing point. No official would be able to acquire and account for that very local information of each person or area's needs.

Most of the decisions we make as individuals have relatively clear consequences too. I know that if I decide to eat at McDonald's this evening that it will probably taste as I remember it, that it will be affordable, and that it is a relatively unhealthy meal that I shouldn't eat too often. I cannot be absolutely certain all these things are true, obviously. Perhaps it will be cold by the time the order arrives, or the restaurant won't have what I want. But, generally, I have a strong idea of the risks and benefits of my actions, not least because I acquire specific knowledge through my lived experience.

The Knowledge Problem

Things get much more complicated when considering society-wide economic, social, or even public health problems, however. Economic Nobel laureate F. A. Hayek famously wrote about what has since been dubbed the *knowledge problem* that would plague any attempt to plan economic or social affairs for everyone.[5] Yes, he said, if some individual had full information, a complete knowledge of people's tastes and preferences, and a full understanding of the availability of resources, then at a given point in time they might theoretically be able to compute the best way for society to use its resources.

But no government official or politician has such knowledge or will ever be able to obtain it. Our preferences are extremely personal and, as we saw earlier, context-dependent. Knowledge of things such as the availability of workers, the best way to manage individuals, the durability of a specific piece of machinery, or some custom or practice that helps in accomplishing a minor task are dispersed throughout society, with a lot of important information accumulating in our individual brains. Some knowledge is tacit—we learn how to do things but could not possibly articulate it (think about how to catch a ball). This makes the information inherently uncollectible for any planner.

In fact, even if that information could be extracted at one point in time, human behavior constantly adapts to changing circumstances, often in unpredictable ways. As UK political economist Mark Pennington has explained, we are not just like "human elements" that respond to external stimuli in the same way, whatever the time or circumstances. We are, in fact, "creative actors" who are continuously innovating, looking to eke out new opportunities in an ever-changing world—and changing our tastes and preferences in light of new information or experiences. This is shown not least by the way entrepreneurs develop new ideas for products that we never even knew we might want. That makes the challenge of planning the economy more difficult still.

When it comes to COVID-19, the problems of planning are particularly acute. For policymakers were confronted with a more challenging environment than even that which usually afflicts economic policymaking. Not only did they have all of the long-identified difficulties about dispersed knowledge to face up to, but on top of that they were also faced with the novelty of the virus and a lack of experience of how modern society would deal with such a society-wide shock.

Retrospectively we can identify clear institutional and policy failures. When the virus hit, however, policymakers faced what economists John Kay and Mervyn King have described as "radical uncertainty."[6] They were confronted with a huge range of variables in which they knew *something* about the virus or how people might react to it but (initially at least) had extremely limited information to confirm or refute their beliefs.

To understand what economists mean by uncertainty here, we need to go back to 1921, when economist Frank Knight clearly distinguished between ordinary risk and uncertainty.[7] Risk, Knight said, arises when we do not know the outcome of a situation, but we do have good information on the probability that various outcomes might occur. Think about rolling dice as an obvious example. We have no idea what number will land face-up when we roll a die, but we do know that a fair die has a one-in-six chance that any given number will land face-up.

Uncertainty is a quite different phenomenon. It describes situations where we just don't have very good information to calculate the odds of different outcomes occurring in the first place.

Now, some economists think you cannot make this distinction between risk and uncertainty so clear-cut. Lots of daily choices have a degree of genuine uncertainty, after all, but we still estimate reasonable calculations of risks. But the application here to COVID-19 should be clear: when the virus arrived, there was a substantial lack of knowledge about its features and the implications of policy responses to it. Scraps of information and hunches were being used to make massive, society-altering decisions based on patchy context-specific evidence that we had, first from China and then from Italy.

Radical Uncertainty in a Pandemic

Just think about how much we did not know at the time the virus first hit the United States.

First, there was uncertainty about the virus itself. It wasn't clear exactly what the full range of symptoms were; whether it was transmitted primarily by aerosol or droplets; which risk factors made people particularly susceptible to dying from it; how contagious it was; how far the virus had already spread into the community; how quickly or in what forms it would mutate; what proportion of people carried the virus asymptomatically; what the longer-term damage to survivors would be from contracting it; whether its spread was affected by weather or humidity; when individuals were infectious (as opposed to being infected); how long immunity lasted for those who had recovered; or indeed whether populations had any form of existing, partial protection against it because of their previous infections from coronaviruses.[8]

Then there were huge uncertainties about the behavior of the public in the face of the virus. How much would people abide by guidance on handwashing and physical distancing? How long would the public tolerate voluntary social distancing and how extensive would behavioral change be? Would businesses and transport services voluntarily adopt safety protocols that helped prevent transmission of the virus? How easy would it be to contain the virus from your family at home? What effect would information about the virus or news of potential vaccines have in changing behavior? To muddy the waters further, answers to all these questions would likely differ somewhat depending on broader cultural factors or demographics in a locality, and indeed they might vary over time with the changing prevalence of the disease. There remains a huge uncertainty about which types of business or home settings are the primary locations of disease transmission.[9]

The epidemiological modeling of COVID-19 that informed policy therefore involved plugging in guesses for some of these variables based on very limited information about the virus and assumptions about human behavior. There was substantial resultant uncertainty about extremely important variables, not least the transmissibility of the disease and how it would respond to various public health interventions. As we saw earlier, at least for the early stages of the pandemic, scenario modeling appears to have vastly underestimated how much people's behavior would change when information about the virus was released.[10]

So outputs from those models, whether it be estimates of deaths, when peaks would occur, whether hospital capacity would be exceeded and, indeed, whether there would be a second wave of the virus, were inevitably strongly determined by things we just could not know with any degree of certainty.

Yet the uncertainty didn't stop there. There were also huge unknowns in regards to indirect issues associated with the public policy response too. Lawmakers had to grapple with all of the difficulties that come with imposing major policy change on the incredibly complex range of relationships that constitute a modern economy. What impact would closing schools have on people's ability to work and earn income, and how might these affect other health outcomes? Would temporary lockdowns lead to business bankruptcies and permanent job losses? Would all this lead to an increase in shadow economy activity? Which businesses were "essential" to continue operating to ensure that society continued to function and which businesses might be mistakenly thought of as being "nonessential" when in fact they were essential suppliers for other businesses? What would be the knock-on consequences of stay-at-home orders and nonessential business closures on landlords, banks, and other financial institutions?

There were, of course, complex interactions between economic and health outcomes too. Unemployment insurance was made more generous so that laid-off workers wouldn't find themselves financially destitute and incentivized to work in the shadow economy. Loans were provided to small businesses through the Paycheck Protection Program that would turn to grants if companies rehired workers, too, to try to protect existing job relationships and give workers in shutdown industries more security.

But these sorts of programs brought their own uncertainties: would generous unemployment insurance deter people from taking jobs in growing essential industries important to supporting the public health effort, such as in delivery or as contact tracers? And what impact would the pandemic have on work practices and the types of services people demand? If they changed substantially—with ongoing elevated usage of delivery services, increased working from home, or less travel, for example—then attempting to pause the economy and protect the jobs that existed as of March 2020 would be economically harmful rather than supportive.

On top of all this was the potentially momentous, yet uncertain, impact of medical innovation. We always hoped for some breakthrough in terms of a working vaccine or effective treatment. More recently, it seems that we have gotten better at treating the disease and high-efficacy vaccines are now being distributed and used. It was long uncertain, however, when a working vaccine would be viable, what proportion of the population would be eligible to receive it, whether the vaccine would merely reduce symptoms of people infected or provide immunity to infection, the proportion of the public who would willingly get vaccinated, and how long any full or partial immunity that it provides would last, especially with likely virus mutations.

Yet the optimal policy would change dramatically if or when we knew this information. It may have been the case, for example, that the complete absence of an effective vaccine would have meant that suppressing the virus for long periods didn't save many lives in the long term beyond those protected via avoiding hospital overcapacity but that the ongoing suppression period would have brought huge, prolonged economic pain.

I've labored through all the uncertainties here because that is what a responsible economist should do. But as we have seen in the discussion of cost-benefit analysis, there is a huge range of concerns social planners would have to consider to comprehensively plan the best approach to the health and economic fallout from the pandemic. Almost all aspects of that plan come with unknowable or highly uncertain probabilities of effectiveness. It's of little surprise, then, that Elizabeth Warren had to issue revised plans so quickly.

Markets versus Planning

Now one could say that social and economic life always entails a complex, evolving ecosystem of uncertainties that no single planner could fully comprehend. Policymakers attempt to circumvent this by using evidence of past relationships to try to ascertain the likely effects of particular policies. But they cannot possibly gather all the necessary information to remove all these uncertainties.

This is one key reason why economists do not generally support the idea of substantial economic planning or interventionism—whether that be in the form of industrial planning or state socialism. For economists, in fact, the debate about whether a market economy or planned economy is a better system is over—or at least it should be. Countries with more economic freedom and market exchange—characterized by private property rights, freedom of contract, market prices, and systems of profit and loss—vastly outperformed planned economies through the 20th century. Upon reunification in 1990, for example, GDP per capita in East Germany was one-third of the West German level.[11]

So-called "unplanned" market economies allow near-constant experiments by individuals and organizations trying out new ways of doing things. Our preferences, the relative availability of resources, and other forms of economic information, meanwhile, are not the preserve of some central authority. They are embedded in the prices of goods, services, and resources that reflect supply-and-demand decisions. The social desirability of new activities is communicated in a market system by the signals of profit and loss, which other economic actors can observe and act on.

Importantly, a market economy brings two huge advantages in a world of uncertainty and change. For not only does the inherent decentralization of a market economy harness much of that very highly localized information discussed earlier—a necessary condition for better economic outcomes—but in the profit-and-loss system it has a way of weeding out bad ideas or concepts that not enough people value highly. These signals incentivize the allocation of resources toward productive ends. Not perfectly or instantaneously, of course—an economy is a dynamic, adaptive system that has many imperfections. But, overall, this discovery process encourages the enrichment of society as a whole over time.

To repeat: the crucial ingredients for why a market economy tends to work successfully is the harnessing of decentralized knowledge and the built-in feedback mechanisms that encourage effective uses of resources and discourage ineffective or undesired uses. The economy therefore doesn't require central planning: a free market enables many hyper-localized plans to be tested, some of which succeed and some of which fail.

The ordinary superiority of the market highlights just why the pandemic is such a thorny problem, however. For as we saw in the discussion of externalities, this is a rare instance where private-market solutions alone might not produce the best possible results. When diseases are highly infectious, with costs borne by others from your behavior, containing the rapid spread of the illness requires very high levels of compliance at a societal level. So there is a much stronger case for behavioral nudges and the use of coercion than would be regarded as ordinarily acceptable.

The problem in determining what those coercive measures should be, when they should be implemented, and how effective they will be in achieving their goals, was, in this case, very difficult to judge, especially early on in the pandemic. Not only were policymakers operating in a world of uncertainty, but there were very few obvious rapid-feedback mechanisms to help improve policy quickly.

In the absence of good information about who was infected by the virus early on, for example, because of a lack of testing, policy was instead enacted as if everyone was potentially infected. That meant intrusive policies such as lockdowns and quarantines, as well as guidance on social distancing and handwashing. These imposed much larger costs than if a more surgical approach had been available. The absence of widespread testing meant there was no way of harnessing the highly localized information of individual circumstances.

In terms of when and for how long to implement these costly measures, the lack of widespread testing again meant that policymakers were working from out-of-date, partial information on the number of people actually infected, on top of second-guessing how people's behavior would change as a reaction to news about the virus. There was no way, then, that policymakers could set policy with any degree of precision—lifting restrictions or implementing them just at the right time. In a world of adaptive behavior, politicians couldn't fine-tune our actions to control the path of the virus any better than they could fine-tune the economy to prevent recessions.

The novelty of the virus meant there was almost an absence of evidence for the effectiveness of medical treatments and public health interventions too. Scientists had not conducted their preferred *randomized controlled trial* studies of what might work—experiments which seek to eliminate results bias by assigning people randomly to either receive the treatment being assessed or assigning them to some control treatment. Although this quickly began happening for medicines and therapies, there were no obvious feedback mechanisms to indicate the effectiveness of other public health interventions, particularly given the lack of variation in the types of policies adopted around most of the country.

Test, Trace, and Isolate

In scenarios like this, good and accurate information that can be acted upon quickly becomes incredibly important. If states had been in a position where they already had a test-trace-isolate (TTI) infrastructure in the first few weeks of the pandemic, that could have alleviated some of the large uncertainties outlined above.

As we discussed in chapter 6, an effective TTI framework, in principle, enables you to maintain much more economic activity than under the alternative suppression policies that politicians first opted for. That's because TTI allows a more surgical approach—removing from everyday life only those who have been infected or in relatively close contact with the infected, rather than imposing costly regulations or lockdowns on swaths of economic activity that could otherwise be undertaken safely.

But there's another potentially huge advantage of a well-functioning TTI regime. Tracing provides extensive information that enables us to quickly learn what sort of activities bring higher risks of virus transmission or which types of people are likely to spread the disease, as well as better knowledge on variables such as the incubation period of the virus. Via backward tracing, we can identify the sources and timing of local flare-ups, such as certain bars, public spaces, activities, or indeed superspreaders and their characteristics.

If used to inform the population quickly, this information provides crucial, indirect ongoing feedback that enables the public, especially those who are vulnerable or elderly, to adjust their behavior or whereabouts. Importantly, it also provides an evolving evidence base for other, more targeted policies or guidance—a source of error correction by learning from failures and obvious successes.

South Korea is perhaps the best example of a country that went down this TTI route. The country quickly built a huge range of new testing centers, harnessing the private sector to ramp up capacity. Alongside readily available testing and the isolation of the infected and their contacts, Korean public health authorities traced COVID-19 patients with extreme thoroughness from very early on. It is widely considered a success. As of December 27, the country has had 808 COVID-19 deaths (which equates to 16 deaths per million people compared to the more than 1,025 per million in the United States) and the country's unemployment rate, although somewhat elevated compared with the situation pre-pandemic, is still only 3.4 percent—a thoroughly respectable figure even in ordinary times.[12]

A large workforce of epidemiological contact tracers were given extensive access to a range of data sources for the population, including closed-circuit television footage and credit card data. Detailed information about the movements of the infected prior to their positive test result was even publicly disclosed to enable the population to adjust their behavior quickly. The tracing system therefore provided a stronger nudge to the public to avoid certain places or areas where testing alone might have missed infected people.

Economists David Argente, Chang-Tai Hsieh, and Munseob Lee highlight the example of how, on March 30, Korean public authorities disclosed that a COVID-19 patient had visited a coffee shop in the Mapo district on March 28.[13] As a result, nobody visited the shop on the day of the disclosure. Similar effects were observed on general commuting patterns—travel into districts with higher numbers of COVID-19 patients fell more than travel into other areas. By highlighting the whereabouts of the infected, and so where they may have infected others, the public avoided these places, reducing the probability of the spread of the virus beyond that which would occur from merely identifying direct contacts for those with positive tests alone.

In the absence of a vaccine, those economists, using a fairly standard epidemiological model, estimated that public disclosure information like this not only significantly reduced death numbers in South Korea but could eliminate 73 percent of the economic costs of a full lockdown for a city like Seoul, South Korea's capital. By reducing uncertainty and adjusting commuting and behavioral patterns swiftly to reduce the virus's transmission, TTI can therefore obviate the need for lots of restrictions on the safe continuation of economic life.

This policy regime still comes at a cost, of course, most pertinently in terms of lost privacy for those tracked. The publicly disclosed information was incredibly detailed. It would probably be illegal under current U.S. health privacy laws. Culturally, Americans would likely be far more hesitant about such government surveillance, not least because it may set a dangerous precedent for less justifiable policy uses. Having such specific information may also lead to an unjustified behavioral overreaction in certain areas, bringing near-term economic pain or stigma to areas or particular ethnic populations with large outbreaks.

Yet with the virus as a reality, we have to weigh these types of trade-offs against other policy regimes. As Larry Summers' work referenced in chapter 5 showed, the combined economic and health cost of the U.S. policy mix so far has been huge and I suspect that most Americans would have preferred the overall policy mix seen in South Korea, particularly over the longer term, when the scale and uncertainty of the curbs of liberties that come with Whac-A-Mole approaches to dealing with the virus become clear. Unfortunately, the United States did not even have the option to consider this alternative TTI approach because it had no such testing or tracing infrastructure in those opening weeks of the pandemic.

Once case numbers are too high in the community, a TTI regime becomes prohibitively expensive and impossible to manage. The only way to make it viable again then is to get caseloads back to such low levels through crude measures such as lockdowns that it becomes feasible to introduce it later. But the costs of achieving this are extraordinarily large—the United States already saw a quarter of the year (Q2) where economic activity fell by a third. Even this wasn't enough to get caseloads down to manageable levels for a viable tracing system, and the political will to suppress the virus evaporated quickly. South Korea itself is currently struggling with a winter outbreak, testing the limits of its previous approach.

Implications in a Pandemic

True, regular repeat testing of certain populations can go a long way toward obtaining the benefits of a full TTI regime, with the advantage of giving us good knowledge of the average infection duration (more discussion of this in chapter 9). Economist Larry Kotlikoff and epidemiologist Michael Mina have highlighted in a *Wall Street Journal* op-ed how Cornell University's twice weekly COVID-19 testing of all students, quarantining all those who tested positive, cut new case numbers per week there from 60 to 3.[14] But if that sort of surveillance testing regime is unavailable or unfeasible across the whole country, the knowledge problem and the lack of feedback mechanism identified earlier make suppressing the virus without immense economic costs incredibly difficult.

So is there any way for us to learn quickly how to best deal with the virus if we don't have TTI or widely available rapid testing? As Pennington writes, the comparison with the case for the market economy might better inform us of what not to do rather than giving us a detailed guide of what good policy would look like. In effect, in the absence of these policy regimes, we want to try to increase our likelihood of correcting errors.

One implication here is that too much uniformity early on should be avoided. Experimentation and varied approaches to trying to contain the virus, whether between nation states or U.S. states, provides valuable information about best practices that can then be adopted elsewhere. Central plans that do not allow variation depending on local circumstances, in contrast, risk entrenching systemic mistakes. The United States' system of federalism allows plenty of local variation on public health and economic policy, for the needs of New York are very different from those of Alabama. But even here the lack of variation represented a problem—most states adopted very similar lockdown measures in the initial phase of the pandemic despite clearly different risks from the disease as determined by a range of structural factors.[15]

Back in April 2020, Las Vegas Mayor Carolyn Goodman got a lot of heat for suggesting that she advocated that her city be used as a "control group" for COVID-19 policy.[16] In other words, behind the scenes she was advocating a much more hands-off approach to dealing with the virus, probably because the Las Vegas economy is so dependent on in-person activity.

But underlying her clearly self-interested stance, and despite the clear practical difficulties of having a non-locked-down island of activity in an interconnected country, she was right to worry that one great information problem associated with COVID-19 early on was how governors and mayors adopting similar policies might prevent learning about what actually worked. It's one reason why we were all so much more interested in different approaches abroad, from Korea's test-and-contact tracing regime, to New Zealand's strict quarantine for new arrivals, to Sweden's more hands-off mitigation approach.

A second implication from these insights about the market economy's advantages is that COVID-19 safety policies should be based on principles, rather than overly prescriptive rules. Individual business owners and building managers are likely to know far better how to manage simple physical distancing guidelines on their premises, or which spaces need regular sanitizing, than bureaucrats trying to write up detailed rules for how tables should be spaced or how often rooms should be cleaned.

As my colleague Chris Edwards wrote back in April 2020,

Businesses are separating workspaces, taking temperatures and screening health at work entrances, testing employees before they get to work, closing lunch rooms, installing workspace partitions, adjusting shifts, modifying production lines, changing entrances and exits, closing facilities and tracing contacts if workers test positive, placing materials down rather than handing them to others, sanitizing workspaces, having safety experts instruct workers, spacing bathroom urinals, wearing electronic bands to alert workers if others are too close, and providing masks, gloves, and hand sanitizer.[17]

Any top-down national plan on how businesses should have re-opened could not possibly have incorporated this highly localized knowledge. Every workplace is unique. Not only do companies themselves have to engage in trial and error, but businesses often learn from each other. Edwards highlights, for instance, how Volkswagen, having been flooded with requests from other businesses about the safety procedures it had implemented, shared its ideas online. Governments can provide useful information on the ways the virus can spread and can articulate the broad risks, but they cannot plan every workplace.

A third implication is that public health officials and politicians should be honest about the state of knowledge on the virus and the effectiveness of policies to stop it. Although a lot of information in society is dispersed, often only public health officials have access to datasets that can provide live real-time information about what we know or don't know when a new public health challenge hits. This is information that cannot be easily transmitted or observed at the individual level. Huge mistakes in the use or interpretation of public data or misrepresentations of scientific evidence more broadly can be highly damaging for both public health and economic activity.

Although there was uncertainty about how effective they were, this is why it was so damaging that public health officials ultimately misled the public on the potential efficacy of masks. Anthony Fauci, a key member of the White House coronavirus taskforce, now admits that public officials told a "noble lie" in suggesting masks might not be effective, not just because they believed that people who were asymptomatic might not be able to spread the disease but in order to prevent a run on purchasing masks that could have jeopardized their availability for health care workers.[18] This kind of non-scientific reasoning not only undermines the credibility of public health officials in giving advice or guidance, but it actively deters the sort of consumer and worker trial-and-error approach to innovation in providing cheaper masks that would have helped in the public health crisis.

The government can play a crucial role in providing advice on important behaviors that can mitigate risks (such as on ventilation and mask-wearing, for example). But these should be guided by the underlying science, not second-guessing how people will respond. At times, public health officials nationwide have put their own credibility on the line through this pandemic by trying to play behavioral scientists. Some even endorsed protests or indicated that it was fine for infected people to go out and vote on presidential election day, thus undermining public health laws and existing guidance for people to refrain from engaging in other activities that may be subjectively much more important to them, such as attending funerals or participating in sports.

Finally, perhaps the most important lesson about pandemic-related uncertainty, as Pennington has brilliantly explained, is to be extremely wary about the inevitable post-pandemic push for new detailed plans to ensure something like this never happens again.

Yes, there are things we can do, in theory, to help ensure the country is resilient in the face of unexpected public health shocks, whether that means facilitating flexible, adaptive health care systems, having decent stockpiles of masks and personal protective equipment, making advanced commitments to order vaccines or treatments to encourage their production, or else changing regulations to allow a quick development of future testing capacity. We can also use knowledge from retrospective studies to inform our understanding about likely public behaviors in the future.

But the precise nature of a new virus, or any other extreme risk, will not be the same in a future pandemic or other crisis as it is today. As we will see later in chapter 15, political incentives push hard to reward "fighting the last war," but the key takeaway from a world of such uncertain events is the need for overall resilience as an economy and society, rather than a prescriptive plan based on our last experience.

One aspect of this is to protect a dynamic, entrepreneurial market economy. This is the best way of producing wealth that gives us more resources to deal with any uncertain shock. Yet we should judge other proposals beyond this not by how they would have helped during this pandemic but whether they would allow us to adapt quickly in the face of a new crisis, providing those feedback mechanisms that help us shift resources to face up to a future threat that could take a very different form.

A key part of this learning process, when the COVID-19 postmortems are written, will be assessments of which countries or regions seemingly got it right this time. It will be tempting to look at policies and compare them with death numbers or economic outcomes over a given period as a slam-dunk argument for what worked and what to do in the future. But the radical uncertainty here means that some apparent success may have arisen more out of luck than judgment and may tell us little about how to prepare for next time. While different approaches adopted by various states or countries might be a rare source of variation to examine carefully during this pandemic, those cross-country and cross-state comparisons themselves must be handled with care.

ECONOMIC LESSON

Policymakers do not have access to full and complete information to generate optimal policy at the best of times, particularly given that so much uncertainty exists when it comes to complex, dynamic relationships among human beings. Obtaining good outcomes requires the harnessing of local knowledge to productive ends and some sort of feedback mechanism to weed out bad ideas—reasons why economists overwhelmingly support a market economy over government planning. When it comes to COVID-19, U.S. policymakers were faced with substantial uncertainty, including about the virus itself, public behavior, economic resilience, and medical innovation. These problems were compounded by the lack of a testing infrastructure to generate useful information and feedback mechanisms to allow the fast adaptation of policy or behavior to new knowledge. In the face of radical uncertainty about future risks, we need broad resilience, not detailed prescriptive plans for what to do when crises hit.

ECONOMIC TERMS INTRODUCED

- **knowledge problem:** the idea that the information required to effectively plan an economy is dispersed among individual actors and could not possibly be collected by a central authority, not least because a lot of human knowledge is tacit and nearly impossible to articulate
- **risk:** a description of a situation where we do not know whether a bad outcome will occur but we have sufficient information to accurately assess its probability
- **uncertainty:** a description of a situation where we lack sufficient information or knowledge to accurately assess the probability of an outcome

8

WHY DID PROTESTS AND MARCHES NOT LEAD
TO OBVIOUS SPIKES IN COVID-19 CASES?

An introduction to endogeneity

Perhaps we have sports to blame. For one of the more depressing parts of this COVID-19 pandemic is the obsession with cross-country or cross-state standings. The internet is filled with rankings on everything from population-adjusted death rates through to testing capacity being used as slam-dunk evidence of the efficacy of a particular government's policies.

Never mind that countries or states have different characteristics, including demographics, population densities, rural-urban balances, initial seeding of the virus, and industrial compositions, all of which might affect the spread and health impact of the virus. No, there appears an insatiable demand for simple lists, as if the numbers or trends of cases or deaths tell us who has done well or done badly.

Now, in part, this longing for comparators arises due to the problem discussed in the last chapter—of insufficient variation in approaches within nations. It would be politically impossible within most non-federal countries, not to mention ethically questionable, to tell one area of the country it must adopt policies considered more risky from a health perspective merely to obtain better information on what works.

Las Vegas Mayor Carolyn Goodman was harshly criticized for a reason. Although, as individuals, we might be willing to countenance taking part in a medical experiment for an elevated possibility of recovering from a disease, we understandably do not like the idea of politicians risking our health without our consent when we are healthy by making us part of a control group for a more risky approach.

One of the United States' great strengths, in general, is its federal system. Power residing with individual states and localities ensures lots of localized policy experimentation, with the power of exit for those who do not agree with their state government's choices. This, in theory, means ideas get implemented that are better suited to local needs. But perhaps more importantly, the differences among states provide a laboratory-like source of information on the impacts of some policies compared to others.

Yet, in the case of COVID-19, most states in the early stages of the pandemic implemented such similar policies, at least for a time, that journalists and economists naturally began to look further afield for comparators. After Italy became the epicenter of the European outbreak back in March 2020, for example, its path of deaths became a barometer by which other countries' media judged their home nation.

Cross-country comparisons, even on something as seemingly uncontroversial as death rates from COVID-19, turn out to be fraught with danger, however. We not only have to control for the stage of the pandemic, but it turns out that different countries count deaths and their causes very differently. France and Germany's death figures originally incorporated deaths in nursing homes, for example, while the UK's, up until April 29 at least, only included deaths in hospitals. Some countries required a positive test for COVID-19 for a death to be counted as attributable to the virus, while others recorded it as a COVID-19 death merely if it was suspected to be one.

For long periods of time, different countries had very different policies on who could access tests too. Then, of course, different countries have very different demographics—and we know age is a particularly important driver of death from COVID-19. Is it really right to compare, unadjusted, the COVID-19 death rate of a country with an old population to one with a young population? What would that comparison usefully tell us?

For these reasons, researchers have turned to looking at excess death data across countries as the best guide to the full impact on mortality of this pandemic—the uplift in the number of deaths in particular countries this year compared to previous years. This eliminates some of the problems of comparison but is itself clearly not foolproof in allowing us to draw policy conclusions. Some major public health interventions, such as lockdowns, can affect mortality through a variety of mechanisms other than reduced human transmission of SARS-CoV-2 (e.g., fewer people going to hospitals for other conditions, fewer road journeys, more depressions and suicides, etc.), although so far it seems that high excess deaths appear strongly correlated with COVID-19 prevalence in a state.

Where we face even bigger statistical challenges is when we try to use cross-country comparisons on death outcomes to ascertain the success of particular policies, such as lockdowns.

Do Lockdowns Reduce Deaths, or Do Expectations of Deaths Induce Lockdowns?

Lockdowns aimed to reduce deaths from COVID-19 by breaking up networks of human interactions, in turn reducing the transmission of the virus. It was initially feared that without lockdowns, the spread of the virus would be so rapid that caseloads would overwhelm hospital capacity, too, leading to increased numbers of avoidable hospital deaths from congestion.

It would therefore be naturally tempting to try to assess the effectiveness of lockdowns by simply tracking some estimate of the stringency of the lockdown by country and then examining the evolution of deaths before and after lockdowns were implemented—the variable that lockdowns aimed to reduce.

Yet by doing this type of analysis, we would have to be careful about what economists describe as an *endogeneity problem*. In very simplified terms, an endogeneity problem refers to there being some reason why the model you have in your head (in this case that lockdowns affect death rates by reducing human interactions) gets the causation from one variable (lockdowns) to another (deaths) wrong. This might be because there is some third factor driving both deaths and lockdowns, or because the causality in fact works in the opposite direction.

In this case, that initial decision by countries such as Italy and Spain to implement the most stringent lockdowns among developed countries was in large part driven by the high and escalating death toll in each country, as well as knowledge that the virus was more widely dispersed in the community already.

So we run into an immediate problem: the expectation of further deaths in part induced the emergency lockdown. To then see those high deaths materializing as evidence of the weakness of lockdowns in achieving their objectives would be mistaken. It should not surprise us that Italy had adopted most of its lockdown measures by March 20 but that deaths continued increasing and remained near their peak up to two weeks afterward.

Another way of putting it is that the decision to impose stringent lockdowns was not made independently of the likely path of the pandemic. It was precisely the prevalence of the virus in these countries and the dreadful outlook for deaths that drove both the stringent lockdown policy and the deaths. It would be extremely misleading to compare the increased number of deaths in Italy or Spain in the weeks after lockdowns began as clear evidence that lockdowns were less effective compared with less-stringent policies adopted elsewhere (although they might well have been).

Economists describe the precise endogeneity problem outlined here as *simultaneity*. Lockdowns affect potential deaths, but potential deaths can also impact the adoption of lockdowns. There's a two-way causation. In this particular case, then, the endogeneity problem might be a source of bias that leads to an underestimation of the effectiveness of lockdowns in reducing deaths, at least in the near-term after lockdowns are implemented.

Using Death Rates as Evidence of Risks Is Risky

One of the reasons why a lot of the statistical claims about COVID-19 are controversial is that endogeneity problems abound. Early on in the pandemic, it was worryingly common, for example, to hear people take the numbers of deaths within some age brackets from COVID-19, divide that by the total population of the group, and then use the low number to conclude that people in that group are less likely to die from COVID-19 than from being struck by lightning, being a victim of a shark attack, or something else that seems a relatively tiny risk.

The implicit mental model here is that becoming infected with COVID-19 is a matter of random chance and therefore the death rates observed so far represent an accurate representation of the risk of getting and dying from the disease. But this is obviously not true. Your chance of getting infected and dying of COVID-19 is influenced by both your behavior and policy. That there have been relatively higher infections and deaths in prisons or meatpacking plants does not necessarily tell us that prisoners or meatpacking workers have personal characteristics that make them more susceptible to the worst outcomes from the disease. It might simply be that they spend much time in a place that puts them more at risk of infection.

Another example comes in regard to ethnic disparities. We know that up until June 13, 2020, for example, the rate of hospitalization for blacks and Hispanics was more than four times as high as for whites, and those groups had higher death rates too. Yet that didn't necessarily mean black or Hispanic people were simply more predisposed to more virulent cases of the disease. In fact, the economists Joseph Benitez, Aaron Yelowitz, and Charles Courtemanche have found that higher death rates for black and Hispanic people in Chicago and New York was explained mainly by higher caseloads, rather than individuals being more likely to die when they did contract the disease.[1]

One particular danger with COVID-19 is that we may mistake evidence gathered under one policy and behavioral regime as evidence of general risks from the virus under a completely different policy and behavioral regime. That my probability of dying of COVID-19 is very low when I only go out once per week to the grocery store with a mask on tells me little about how likely I am to die of the disease in a world where everyone behaves normally, including gathering in sports stadiums or speaking loudly face-to-face with strangers.

It was obviously mistaken, then, to look at low death rates in certain states where there was widespread social distancing and conclude that because excess mortality was similar to that of an ordinary bad flu season, the virus itself brought with it only risks akin to the flu. This is one example of another driver of the endogeneity problem—*omitted variables*. We might draw bad inferences on the impact of X on Y if we fail to account for another factor, Z, which influences both.

Suppose a small stand sold umbrellas near a subway station. Examining trends on prices and the quantity of umbrellas bought over time might seem, in principle, a good means of assessing the price sensitivity of demand for them—that is, how much the quantity demanded changes when the price goes up or down. But suppose the seller actively raised prices whenever it rained, precisely because demand was higher on these days. Failure to account for this when analyzing the relationship between price and sales might make it seem as if demand was far less sensitive to price than it is in reality—that is, after we've controlled for the state of the weather.

When it comes to COVID-19 we face the potential for large omitted variable problems. If we fail to account for changes in behavior in analysis, for example, the impact of public policies on cases and deaths might be hugely exaggerated. Likewise if we fail to take account of other factors that could have a big impact on the spread of the virus in a city or state, such as the degree of immunity in an area from the first wave of the virus, then we might reach similarly faulty conclusions about the effectiveness of policy later on.

We saw in chapters 3 and 5 that behavioral change in light of information about the virus was extremely important in driving changes in its transmission. Yet some people still talk as if government policy can explain everything. Looking at trends of what happened to the virus after lockdowns were introduced, a story commonly told is that European countries and New York were hit hard and then used stringent lockdowns to quash the caseload.

The flip side inference from this for a long time was that removing lockdowns would lead to huge outbreaks again. Yet for most of the late spring and summer, through to the end of September, those places that were initially hard-hit saw sustained low caseloads and deaths, perhaps because of entrenched changes to behavior facilitated by the summer weather and ongoing caution about the disease. It was seemingly only when the cooler weather arrived and more activities began to take place indoors again that cases and deaths started rising substantially to the extraordinary levels that were seen in November and December. Looking at trends in cases and deaths during lockdowns as a guide to what would initially happen after lockdowns were lifted would, therefore, by ignoring seasonality, have given us faulty information about the likely impact of reversing the policies.

Another good example here is the public debate over whether mass protests would ignite a spike of COVID-19 cases. Other things being equal, getting close to other people at marches or rallies would be expected to lead to higher transmission of the virus. There is suggestive evidence, for example, that geographic areas that hosted more National Hockey League games, more National Basketball Association games, and more National Collegiate Athletic Association basketball games during the early months of 2020 saw more cases and increased mortality.[2] Yes, any protest transmission would likely be mitigated by mask-wearing and being outside. But large groupings of people getting together would be expected to raise COVID-19 risks by creating a lot more networking for potential transmission of the virus.

Nevertheless, in the weeks after the initial Black Lives Matter protests, media outlets pointed out that caseloads and deaths did not appear to spike in cities with large protests. Was this a case of finding out that the virus was more difficult to transmit than we'd imagined? Perhaps. But economists identified what might have been an important omitted variable: the behaviour of nonprotestors. As urban protests continued, nonprotestors spent more time at home, both because of curfews imposed within their cities but also because they wanted to avoid any trouble or even risks associated with the virus. These effects were sharper when there were media reports of violence or the protests were more persistent. The protests then led to a reaction by nonprotestors that meant overall interactions did not spike significantly because stay-at-home behavior for the cities as a whole increased, explaining why cases and deaths appeared not to spike.[3]

It would be wrong then to conclude that protests themselves didn't increase the risks associated with the virus for participants. What mitigated this uplift in risk across the population was the behavior of other people.

In the introduction, we heard that Henry Hazlitt identified the mark of a good economist as someone who sees the unseen. Yet still, too many people close to public policy talk as if certain activities occur in a vacuum. Much of the discussion about children returning to schools, for example, was conducted as if their interactions in classrooms were purely an additional risk of spreading the disease. The implicit alternative that school returns were judged against seemed to be children being in perfect isolation at home, with any outbreaks at schools held up as evidence against their wisdom.

But children's lives don't occur in a vacuum outside of school. The alternative for many children may well have been having them be cared for in commercial settings, hanging out a neighbor's house, or being tended to by grandparents, some of which might entail more risky interactions in terms of the worst risks associated with the virus. Before assessing whether having children attend school increases or reduces transmission of the virus then, we have to accurately account for what would happen if schools remained closed and try to work out the net impact of school reopenings relative to the most likely alternative. It seems likely that, given how schools act as hubs in networks, their reopening could well significantly increase the transmission of the virus in a given area. Certainly, that appears to have been the recent experience in the UK. But simply pointing out instances of outbreaks in individual schools or summer camps is a necessary but not sufficient condition for showing that this would have been the case in the United States. We have to compare the overall transmission in a community to the relevant counterfactual of the likely transmission of the virus absent the school opening, not implicitly assume a nirvana where no children would spread the virus if schools remained closed.

Policy Can Shape Where Transmission Occurs

We have to be particularly careful about using simple data on cases to make firm conclusions about where people are at risk from the virus too. Some commentators, for example, used the fact that 42 percent of

COVID-19 deaths, as of May 26, 2020, had been in nursing homes or assisted living facilities as clear evidence in favor of loosening lockdown restrictions and placing more stringent protection measures on the nursing homes themselves.[4]

Again, the implicit belief here is that the virus is equally likely to be transmitted to all people within an area. So the 42 percent figure is taken as evidence that the relative risk of catching the virus and dying from it in nursing homes is much, much higher than elsewhere.

We know, of course, that COVID-19 is much more deadly for older people with comorbidities, so therefore it should not surprise us that a relatively high number of deaths appear in nursing homes. But what those people who used the 42 percent figure to advocate for policy change simply assumed was that the proportion of total deaths in nursing homes was unrelated to the public health policies in place elsewhere or unrelated to nursing home numbers within the state.

That may well have been the case, but we cannot tell from this simple statistic alone. It may instead be the case that lockdowns substantially reduce network links among a population outside of nursing homes much more so than it does among those within it, such that the policies inflate the relative probability that any death that does occur, even among the elderly, will be in a nursing home. And, of course, if a particular state has a much larger nursing home population than other states, we may expect the nursing home share of deaths in that state to be higher than average.

Think about it this way. Suppose there was a known group of roving outlaws and bandits moving across the country, committed to ransacking any properties they could and stealing people's personal items. As a consequence, vast swaths of the population decided to stay home to defend their properties and installed home protection equipment, such as cameras, barbed-wire fences, and alarm systems. But those whose jobs were deemed essential in keeping society functioning were still expected to go out to work when they could, including as communal carers in nursing homes.

As with the virus, those living in nursing homes in this situation might be more vulnerable to the bandits to begin with. The elderly in these homes tend to be frail and so less likely to be able to defend themselves from any thieves. But because nursing homes also have to be accessible to nursing home workers, who come and go frequently, the buildings might also be more vulnerable to attack from ambushes from the bandits.

In this scenario, we would not take a high proportion of nursing homes being ransacked relative to ordinary homes as obvious evidence that the security measures on other properties were unnecessary. But that is precisely the claim that people who used high nursing home deaths as evidence of the case for relaxation of lockdowns wanted to make. They may well have been correct, in other words, but the simple evidence of the share of total deaths that occurred in nursing homes does not prove it. In fact, following the relaxation of the first lockdowns, the proportion of overall COVID-19 deaths made up of nursing home residents fell somewhat.[5] This suggests that looking at numbers of deaths according to the setting in which they occurred as if it was unbiased evidence of the relative risks of that setting is dangerous. The distribution of deaths is also impacted by policy and changes to behavior, including the lockdowns and later actions taken to protect nursing homes.

Nevertheless, policymakers often seem to not even comprehend that their policies go a long way to explaining where transmission of the virus is likely to occur. Back in May 2020, New York Governor Andrew Cuomo said it was "shocking," for example, that most new COVID-19 patients were people who had been staying at home.

But why exactly was this a surprise? If much social activity is outlawed and other social interactions minimized for all except for "essential" workers, then of course it's far more likely a nonessential worker will catch the virus from someone in their home or apartment block— via that person's work, visits to the grocery store, or more. In other words, the lockdowns themselves made any given case more likely to be one contracted at home. It would obviously be extremely risky to conclude from this that lockdowns, by keeping people at home, caused more deaths than would have occurred without them. The virus is transmitted by people, not places (although it does, of course, appear to spread more easily in certain settings).

Correlation Is Not Causation

In economics, we therefore have to be extremely careful in thinking about causation and the underlying mechanisms that have driven a given outcome. Simple *correlation* analysis, where you compare two variables across states or time, can be instructive about some underlying causal trend at work. But correlation alone does not prove *causation*, and you must be aware of the possibility of omitted variables that make interpreting your results as causative misleading.

Economists Klaus Desmet and Romain Wacziarg examined a wide range of correlates between COVID-19 cases or deaths and structural and demographic factors early in the crisis, for example.[6] Particularly striking was that areas with high proportions of minorities and lower proportions of Trump voters appeared to be more heavily affected by COVID-19 cases and deaths in the opening months of the pandemic.

But did that really show that minorities or those who voted for Hillary Clinton in 2016 were just personally more susceptible to the disease? That seems unlikely, particularly because other work on behavior has suggested that "as Trump voter share rises, individuals search less for information on the virus, and engage in less social distancing behavior, as measured by smartphone location patterns."[7] It seems that there were other factors that were omitted here.

Desmet and Wacziarg's own work points toward some potential mechanisms that a simple correlation analysis would ignore. An area's population density had, at that time, a strong impact on COVID-19 cases and deaths, for example, as measured by how urban the area was, how heavily public transportation was used, and the types of housing arrangements. The disproportionate impacts on certain ethnic groups might therefore have had relatively little to do with race or political affiliation but may, in part, merely reflect where people live. Indeed, more recent evidence suggests the early geographic variation in the pandemic across the United States is much better explained by geographic conditions, such as population or density, than either behavioral responses or government policy.[8]

Where people worked was also crucial. One economic analysis of frontline workers (those in industries that remained open in March and

April who could not work from home) found the cohort to be, on average, less educated, with a "higher representation of disadvantaged minorities, especially Hispanics, and immigrants."[9] A more sophisticated statistical analysis that sought to ascertain how the virus impacted particular demographic groups would therefore need to control for this occupational exposure before you could conclude that there must be biological or lifestyle differences driving the variance.

Another potentially huge example of omitted-variables bias in pandemic data comes from reading too much into official case fatality rates of COVID-19 over time, a mistake that is made, mercifully, less and less these days. The case fatality rate measures the number of people dying from the virus as a proportion of the total number of people diagnosed to be infected with the disease, usually through a positive diagnostic test.

The economist Jeffrey Harris, for example, has pointed out that the Los Angeles County Department of Public Health at first discouraged testing, even on those presumed to have the virus, if they did not appear to have complications, to avoid running out of what was then a scarce resource.[10] A lot of cases therefore went unconfirmed. But when tests became more widely available, the department relaxed its position and began testing nearly anyone with or without symptoms who wanted to be tested.

The problem with using the path of the case fatality rate as a meaningful indicator of the effectiveness of policy over time should therefore be obvious. If a state or locality increases the number of people being tested, then it is likely to catch more asymptomatic cases or mild cases where the individual's life is not imperiled. Testing more people will put a downward drag on the case fatality rate, not because public health outcomes have improved but because more people are being confirmed to have the disease through testing, meaning that the number of positive cases rises relative to the number of people dying from the virus.

As Harris concludes: "Data from partial voluntary testing can give a misleading picture of the state of the epidemic if standards for testing have been recently changing. . . . Data on case fatality rates can serve as an indicator of the degree of penetration of voluntary testing. When case fatality rates are unusually high, testing penetration is likely to be low."[11]

This is yet another example of an endogeneity problem. If you were to look at the path of the case fatality rate and attribute all its movement to public health or medical interventions alone, as if it reflected us better treating the disease and saving more lives, you would have reached very faulty conclusions. The ramping up of testing, alongside medical interventions, created the statistical illusion that the true fatality rate of the virus was falling, even though nothing real may have changed. In this case, looking at just the case fatality rate in a timeline with other policies is likely to suggest that the policies have been far more successful than they have actually been.

In an ideal world, we would have had comprehensive, or at least relatively stable, high levels of testing throughout the duration of the pandemic, so that statistics such as case fatality rates and infection numbers were meaningfully comparative across time. Of course, even then official cases would have been unlikely to pick up all true infections, given the large number of asymptomatic cases and the fact that testing is voluntary. So we should not pretend that even if testing capacity had been ramped up nationwide the official case numbers would be an accurate reflection of the number of true infections (certainly, antibody test results in certain places imply that the true infection rate has been many times higher than the testing we have seen).[12] What sustained high levels of testing would have allowed, however, is more insight into the dynamics of the pandemic in terms of trends in infection rates over time. In fact, if tests had been widely available for the whole population, testing could have been used as a tool for reducing infections by identifying those who were infectious and thus allowing them to isolate sooner. As economist Alex Tabarrok has explained, there's good reason to think that there is an inverted-U shape of COVID-19 cases as testing numbers increase. At first, conducting more tests leads to finding additional cases, but when testing is widespread and regular enough, conducting more tests actually reduces COVID-19 cases because the testing regime itself helps reduce transmission of the virus by isolating more infectious individuals.

But federal and state governments were slow off the mark in developing widespread testing availability—a fact now seen as a key reason for failing to get to grips with the virus early, resulting in the devastating economic and social consequences we have experienced.

ECONOMIC LESSON

Ascertaining whether a policy is successful usually begins with comparing policies across countries or time with the outcome it aims to change. But assessing correlations between a policy and some outcome may lead to faulty policy conclusions if they are interpreted as a causal relationship without thinking hard about the mechanisms or other variables that might drive the results. In the case of COVID-19, assessing lockdowns' effectiveness by looking at crude death numbers might be misleading if lockdowns were introduced *because* death numbers were expected to rise, or if we ignore major changes in behavior. Public health interventions themselves might affect the relative risks of different groups becoming infected or dying, which might then get misinterpreted as certain groups being more susceptible to the disease or "at risk." Likewise, we might overinterpret a falling case fatality rate as evidence of the success of public policy if we ignore omitted variables, such as the ramping up of testing.

ECONOMIC TERMS INTRODUCED

- **endogeneity problem:** instances where the model in consideration has a faulty view of causation, perhaps because of the omission of some other variable or because the potential direction of causation runs both ways
- **simultaneity:** situations where the explanatory variable is jointly determined with the dependent variable. For instance, X causes Y, but Y also causes X, leading to a potential bias in estimating the effect of one on the other
- **omitted variable bias:** situations where failure to account for another variable leads to faulty conclusions about the impact of the variable being examined
- **correlation:** a statistical measure to describe the size and relationship between two or more variables
- **causation:** the relationship between cause and effect

9

WHY COULDN'T I GET A COVID-19 TEST BACK IN FEBRUARY AND MARCH 2020?

An introduction to regulatory tradeoffs

Need a Coronavirus Test? Being Rich and Famous Might Help" boomed the *New York Times* in mid-March 2020.[1]

Resentment among those who thought they had the virus but couldn't confirm it was bubbling nationwide. Celebrities, from Hollywood actors through to members of Congress and National Basketball Association stars, were somehow obtaining diagnostic tests for COVID-19 and publicly declaring their results.

But ordinary people in hard-hit areas such as New York, California, and Washington were being turned away. Unless they had met the initial Centers for Disease Control and Prevention (CDC) guidance of having been to a global COVID-19 hot spot or had been in direct contact with someone who was infected, most people with symptoms had been unable to access tests for the virus through February.

Unsurprisingly, those sick at home, not knowing whether the virus was the cause of their symptoms, were beginning to ask questions. The hashtag #CDCWontTestMe began to circulate on Twitter. It struck at the nerve of basic unfairness that basketball players and supermodels were able to get tests but that teachers, pregnant women, and even paramedics were not. Stories began to proliferate of infected people searching for tests for days and weeks, only to eventually end up in a hospital extremely sick. And all the while the wealthy and famous were able to successfully hunt down tests, both here and abroad.[2]

Populist politicians pounced on these apparent inequities. New York Mayor Bill de Blasio attacked the Brooklyn Nets for testing all players, despite four of their roster actually testing positive. Sen. Rand Paul (R-KY) ran into sharp criticism from his Democratic counterpart Sen. Kyrsten Sinema (D-AZ) for roaming the Senate following a pending COVID-19 test, which later proved positive, despite him not having symptoms.[3] Paul correctly pointed out that if he'd followed guidance to a tee, he would not have even been eligible for a test and so "would still be walking around the halls of the Capitol" spreading the virus even during the period he ultimately self-isolated.[4]

Media write-ups were keen to suggest this was all evidence of money buying access—of the rich seemingly jumping the line to get testing. But looking at these stories through the lens of health inequalities was to mistake the symptom for the cause. The well-heeled having better access to testing was not an indictment of income inequality or even the differential quality of one's health insurance; it was instead a manifestation of a bigger problem—a severe shortage of available, reliable tests. Shortages of products and their restrictive rationing almost always lead to secondary shadow markets where those with money and influence are better able to access goods.

The FDA's Regulatory Failure

In this case, the United States as a whole, and some states in particular, were dealing with a lack of reliable tests because of the regulations of the Food and Drug Administration (FDA).

This supposed consumer protection agency, which has sole discretion over which tests can be used and sold for the purposes of interstate commerce, actively made it harder for private and government laboratories to develop their own diagnostic tests in the very early stages of the pandemic. As a result, up until February 29, 2020, the FDA had only approved one COVID-19 test for use in the United States. That test proved to be both faulty and got distributed to the wrong places.

Earlier we discussed externalities, which are sometimes dubbed a *market failure*—the term being used to describe situations where free markets supposedly fail to achieve the most efficient possible allocation of resources. That depends on the feasibility of the benchmark, of course. Yet here was a clear example of a *government failure*—of policy reducing economic welfare relative to what market activity alone could have delivered, because numerous reliable diagnostic tests were already available elsewhere around the world.

What explains this catastrophic failure? As my colleague Michael Cannon has pointed out, the FDA discouraged private and government laboratories from developing tests; actively prohibited private and state labs that had created tests from using them; and prohibited any U.S. lab, health care provider, or consumer from purchasing diagnostic tests that were readily available in other countries.

Why would a regulator want to prevent widespread testing at the start of a pandemic? The answer is that the FDA was particularly risk averse and made a huge error in its cost-benefit analysis of testing regulations.

When Secretary of Health and Human Services Alex Azar declared a public health emergency on January 31, in theory he gave the FDA the flexibility to speed up diagnostic tests. But in practice the regulations they adopted for universities, hospitals, and research labs made it more difficult to deliver a viable test.

Following the emergency declaration, these labs had to go through a rigorous process of receiving Emergency Use Authorization for any tests they developed. These polymerase chain reaction (PCR) tests were well known, and labs would ordinarily have been able to use them without FDA approval, provided they were for noncommercial use. Yet the FDA explicitly introduced a higher hurdle than normal during the pandemic, because of the supposed higher risk associated with faulty testing.

Given the potential for inaccurate tests to give a misleading impression of developments of the pandemic across the country, the FDA prioritized efficacy over speed and quantity. The result of those early regulations was a huge, devastating delay in tests becoming widely available. The FDA was banning the use of lab-developed tests for clinical diagnoses without agency approval. At the same time, the one test it had approved—the CDC test that had been approved on February 4—had a huge problem of generating false or inconclusive results.[5] In fact, this CDC test ultimately had to be reformulated to become viable at all. That process was also held up by the FDA's emergency regulations, which said tests could only be used in the specific form approved.

These regulations meant labs ended up weighed down by the laborious and risk-averse Emergency Use Authorization process. Foreseeing the vast effort required, some decided against developing tests despite having the capability to do so. The *Washington Post* reports that one academic clinic—the Mayo Clinic—had to put a third of its 15 rapid-response team members to work solely on the FDA's data and paperwork demands.[6] A laboratory at the University of Washington ran into some absurd well-publicized regulatory difficulties because they had not burned copies of their application onto disks or mailed a hard copy to Washington, DC. While all these labs were going through that bureaucratic process, they were not able to put their tests to use, and the virus was spreading across the United States unchecked.

Clearly, this ramp-up of regulatory hurdles was a bad call. Retrospectively, it should be obvious that the regulatory costs and benefits in the early stages of the pandemic pointed strongly toward the case for more *permissionless innovation* with testing.

The United States had a relatively narrow window in which to try to get to grips with the spread of the virus to avoid devastating health and economic consequences. Every three days or so, caseloads were doubling. Given how quickly the virus's footprint was growing, every week that went by without widely available testing became more and more damaging. The cost of risking alternative faulty tests was therefore relatively low (the alternative was very limited numbers of tests rather than widespread availability of accurate tests), but the potential benefits to discovering tests that could identify cases earlier, in turn leading to the isolation of those infected, was huge.

Labs should have been able to experiment with their own tests by default. The CDC's own test was faulty, after all, so the counterfactual at the time, against which to weigh regulatory risk correctly, was barely any testing capacity. As economist Casey Mulligan has explained, the relatively short time period of a pandemic and the large costs of delay make reaching for perfect efficacy a fool's errand.[7]

This is especially true of diagnostic testing in the early stages of a pandemic. Science journalist Ed Yong has described the testing failure as "the original sin of America's pandemic failure."[8] He concludes that if "the country could have accurately tracked the spread of the virus, hospitals could have executed their pandemic plans, girding themselves by allocating treatment rooms, ordering extra supplies, tagging in personnel, or assigning specific facilities to deal with COVID-19 cases." Testing, in other words, would have gone a long way to solving the informational problems associated with COVID-19 outlined in chapter 7. Unbelievably, working diagnostic tests developed in the United States were being used in Sierra Leone before the FDA allowed them to be used here.[9]

We will never fully know what a counterfactual world without these regulations would have looked like, or how many American lives could have been saved. What we do know, when we compare outcomes here to other countries where testing and contact tracing were rolled out quickly, such as South Korea, is that the health and economic welfare costs of the policies used instead of testing and contact tracing were extremely large.

Mistakes Repeated Again

Did regulators learn their lesson from this episode? Sadly, a similar regulatory mistake was repeated not long afterward. Even in July 2020, with the potential gains from a regular testing regime well recognized, the FDA was delaying the newer "cheap, paper-strip tests for coronavirus that report results at-home in about 15 minutes" because of regulations that demanded similarly high accuracy for these tests to standard polymerase chain reaction tests.[10]

Again, because the agency thought of testing as a tool of medical diagnosis rather than for screening, it implicitly started from the assumption that more-accurate tests were always preferable (in this case, in terms of the sensitivity of the tests in picking up traces of the virus).

In turn, the agency was ignoring the advantages associated with having widespread availability of rapid, cheaper, less-sensitive tests sooner in isolating those most infectious in terms of the virus. The FDA, in other words, was once more prioritizing efficacy in detecting COVID-19 rather than thinking through the overall costs and benefits of delaying the authorization of this new type of test.

Yes, it's true that the rapid-strip tests at the time had a higher false negative rate for detecting COVID-19 than PCR tests, meaning more people would be wrongly told they weren't infected than if the same population undertook the PCR tests. If all else about the tests, such as their cost, availability, and result turnaround time were the same, then, the strip tests would be inferior if we were looking for the most sensitive detection of the virus.

But all else was not the same. And for the public health goal of avoiding an out-of-control spread, it was not so much diagnosing the virus's presence that mattered (infections) but isolating those who were *infectious* to others at that specific time. This subtle distinction is crucial. As economist Joshua Gans and subsequent medical studies have outlined, the lower sensitivity of the rapid tests is not as important as you might think for curbing transmission of the virus, because the infections that a less-sensitive rapid test fails to detect will tend to be among people far less likely to be infectious at that time.[11] The test was still sensitive enough, however, to catch potential superspreaders or those who are most likely to be at or near their infectious peak.

In setting the high sensitivity bar, the FDA was, in fact, putting insufficient weight on the two massive advantages of rapid testing that, combined, dwarf any sensitivity problem.[12] First, given they are cheaper, the strip tests could be undertaken more frequently across a wider population for a given testing budget, meaning they would be more likely to identify asymptomatic cases at the time a person is actually infectious than if we relied on people seeking out a PCR test only when they suspected that they might be infected.

Second, because the strip test results are provided rapidly (in 15 to 20 minutes, sometimes at home, compared to one to three days for PCR tests at best), potentially infectious people can isolate themselves immediately and notify those they have been in contact with sooner. These advantages minimize the window of transmission between people becoming infectious and ultimately isolating—the time the person would likely be out spreading the disease.

Of course, it would be safer from a public health perspective if these cheaper rapid tests were more sensitive too. But public health policy should acknowledge real-world tradeoffs. In that regard, many economists and medics concluded early on that COVID-19 tests that give up a bit of sensitivity for speed and frequency would produce a better overall testing regime.

Think about it this way. The absence of mass regular testing through most of 2020 meant we suffered from lots of effective "false negatives" each day anyway, as many people did not know they were actually infected and so did not get tested, at least until they experienced symptoms or were informed that someone they had been in contact with was infected.

As a result, we had to experience many aspects of life as if we were "false positives"—finding our activities severely restricted or being unwilling to engage in them just in case we, or those we come into contact with, were unwittingly infected, even when it was most likely neither were. Without the availability of mass rapid testing, we also faced the continued threat of new lockdowns or restrictions being introduced, chilling activity further. That is the reality our regulators should have been comparing the rapid strip tests to, not some imaginary world where we had population-wide COVID-19 surveillance at PCR test levels of sensitivity.

Economists have realized the potential of widespread regular testing to get the virus under control within weeks and so allow the normalization of much economic activity.[13] In that sense, mass testing would work a bit like a vaccine. We outlined earlier how twice-weekly testing had gotten the spread of the virus under control at Cornell University. University of California economists Ted Bergstrom, Carl Bergstrom, and Haoran Li have shown that, assuming people isolated if they got a positive result, even a rapid test with a 30 percent false negative rate would only require each of us being tested every three days to keep the average reproduction rate of the disease below one (meaning infections would be unlikely to spiral).[14]

The country of Slovakia undertook mass rapid testing of almost its entire population over two weekends in late October, finding 57,500 new COVID-19 infections (the country had previously been identifying one to three thousand cases per day).[15] Combined with a regime mandating 10 days of isolation for those with positive test results or for those not participating in the testing program, the country appeared to reverse its sharply rising COVID-19 infection numbers quickly, with the tests providing clear information about people who needed to isolate who might otherwise have continued to live life as normal and so spread the virus. Slovakia's experience was clear evidence that doing extensive testing could actually reduce COVID-19 caseloads, rather than just identify new cases, by reducing transmission of the disease. As a result of its policy, the Slovakian government felt able to relax some of its COVID-19 restrictions on theaters, cinemas, and churches.

Rapid tests, then, could have potentially been a crucial tool in both getting this virus under control and normalizing more life. This double dividend for economic welfare would, however, have required trust that a positive result was accurate (low numbers of false positives) and need people to be tested regularly. Otherwise, we might have run into problems of people not adhering to isolation even after a positive result because of a lack of confidence in the system. Without regular testing, one-off population tests would merely delay case growth.[16]

Presuming regular, accurate testing was feasible, to test everyone in the United States twice per week for a year using a $10 rapid test would have brought an upfront cost of just over $340 billion (328 million people multiplied by $10 multiplied by 104). Yes, that level of testing would have brought huge administration costs and have required an unimaginable production scale, so it may have been unrealistic for the whole population. But that calculation shows that, relative to the economic welfare losses we have experienced through this pandemic, transformative regular testing would have been a relatively low-cost way of reducing the risks associated with the virus.

There would be major privacy costs if such a surveillance-testing regime was overseen by government, with results submitted to the state. We'd really have wanted the availability and use of this test to be as decentralized as possible. At the very least, however, proactive cheap screening tests held huge promise in institutions with significant socializing and large numbers of potential asymptomatic spreaders, such as schools and universities, or for entry into hospitals, nursing homes, sports stadiums, theaters, or other indoor events. The FDA made another big mistake in allowing its regulations to delay the rollout of this technology, undermining economic welfare and preventing businesses and individuals from safely opening or socializing. Such costs are greater still for any unnecessary delays to effective vaccines being rolled out because of regulatory hurdles.

Regulations Impair Adaptation

Now it would be easy to claim that these examples show that regulation is economically destructive. But that itself would be bad economics. That one regulation fails a basic cost-benefit analysis does not mean that other regulations must too. As a libertarian, I could easily document lots of regulations that do fail to achieve their primary goal or else impose broader net societal costs. But this chapter is not about the wisdom of regulation per se, or whether the FDA regulations here are representative of regulation generally.

Instead, I want to make a simpler point that sometimes get lost amidst focus on a particular rule: economic regulations usually entail a tradeoff between the outcome targeted and economic actors' ability to adjust to new circumstances. That is, regulations invariably restrict the opportunities for businesses and individuals to undertake certain practices, curbing the potential for innovation and adaptation. That much has become painfully obvious during the pandemic. But it is also true in the day-to-day economy, where demand and supply patterns are constantly evolving.

Of course, the introduction of a new regulation can sometimes spur specific innovation—new ideas, products, or technologies—as a consequence of changing the economic incentives. Making it more difficult or expensive to burn coal encourages entrepreneurs to explore and invest in renewable or nuclear energies. To the extent that a new regulation changes the underlying economics of business models, or indeed technologies, it can cause apparent new activity as businesses and consumers adapt to the specific mandates.

This can give the appearance of the sort of creative destruction we see from market-led activity—with new products cannibalizing incumbent businesses through marked changes in the types of goods that are offered. So studies that try to assess the link between innovation and regulation often find mixed results. But the change will be artificially induced—driven by the necessity to meet government demands, rather than customers' demands or the underlying economics of the industry.

In general, regulation, particularly inefficient economic regulation, actively hinders the within-market process of *entrepreneurship*—the process of discovering new means of combining resources, or managing processes, to meet or tap into consumer demands in the pursuit of profit.

As Matt Ridley has shown in his recent book, *How Innovation Works: And Why It Flourishes in Freedom*, innovation is about trial and error and tinkering with existing practices as much as anything else.[17] There is perhaps no time of greater need to tinker with your business model, or products, than when a pandemic hits that fundamentally alters how customers and workers live their lives.

When regulatory rules preclude certain activities, or delay them via the need for tedious form filling or broader compliance, the cost of such responsive and speculative entrepreneurial activity is raised, particularly for new projects. As a result, we end up getting fewer of them. Recent academic work has found that new entry of small firms has crashed as the overall regulatory burden has multiplied in the past 40 years.[18]

In the case of the FDA's testing regulations, Commissioner Stephen Hahn, the head of the FDA, admitted that the agency was trying to "strike the right balance during public health emergencies of ensuring critical independent review by the scientific and public health experts and timely test availability."[19] In other words, the agency always knew that the regulations would slow the ability of labs to develop new tests, but it went ahead with the stringent new rules anyway.

In fact, on February 29, 2020, the FDA ultimately issued a new policy that expedited testing, further admitting that its original approach was mistaken.[20] It relaxed regulations to allow certain private labs to develop and begin to use their own tests for COVID-19 before the FDA had completed their Emergency Use Authorization requests. Even then, however, the FDA was still forcing labs to prepare and submit a vast application within 15 days of beginning testing. This would have deterred some labs, on the margin, from developing tests at all.

Hurdles designed to ensure that products or processes meet certain criteria act as a barrier to within-market innovation. This is not just a clerical issue, either—regulations such as the Emergency Use Authorization require time and effort for form filling and compliance. No, regulatory restrictions, although they can sometimes achieve their primary goal of dealing with some externality problem or trying to ensure a certain product standard is met, actively prevent or deter certain ways of doing business. That can therefore make it less likely that businesses engage in the sort of incremental innovation that branches out into developing better products, finding new ways to produce efficiently, and more.

This might be because a regulatory restriction prevents companies from testing the consumer demand for a variation on a product by, in effect, banning it. It might be because it is costly to go through the process of regulatory approval. The effect might arise because a regulation creates inefficiency by making it more difficult for the business to hire new workers, adapt its premises, or alter its product offering. But in many cases, regulation reduces or deters the set of possibilities for new products, production methods, or services. The pertinent point here is that it harms our ability to adapt to new circumstances.

A good example of this was provided in a paper by economists Philippe Aghion, Antonin Bergeaud, and John Van Reenen.[21] In France, a lot of labor-market regulations only apply when companies hit a threshold of having 50 employees, after which businesses have to establish a work council, health and safety committee, and more.

The economists found that companies below the threshold were far less likely to innovate (as proxied for by holding patents) than those above it when the size of the market for the company's product increased. That's because the payoffs to innovation are much riskier for the firms just below the threshold. The very high cost associated with growing the business acts as a disincentive for the business to engage in research and development.

Regulation does not mean you get no innovation, of course. Even in that paper, the economists found that labor-market regulation does not much affect the degree of radical innovation. Companies still have incentives to swing for the fence in developing new ways to capture large amounts of business, produce game-changing goods, or else find business models that circumvent or replace existing bodies of regulation entirely (think Uber). What regulation does do, however, is prevent or dissuade businesses or entrepreneurs from easily testing things and adjusting as economic conditions change.

Deregulation in a Pandemic

Policymakers' actions during the pandemic have shown that regulations ordinarily harm our ability to adapt to new economic circumstances. You do not get a much bigger change in economic conditions than governments mandating nonessential business closures and banning international travel, and customers who decide or are ordered to stay home. The virus and the lockdowns to curb its spread saw huge shifts in the types of products and services that consumers demanded and how they wanted existing services provided.

Demand collapsed in social industries, such as leisure, entertainment, and hospitality, but soared for home delivery, COVID-related medical safety equipment, and home entertainment. Businesses had to shift their supply of goods—from food to toilet paper—to meet domestic rather than commercial needs. Supply chains had to adapt quickly to disruption. Grocery stores, then retailers, then restaurants had to win consumers' trust by adopting social distancing protocols.

Faced with this disruption, politicians and regulators have had to relax a whole range of regulations on economic activity. They recognized that these would prove a barrier to many newly demanded business activities during the lockdown and beyond.

At the time of writing this chapter, Americans for Tax Reform had catalogued 621 regulations that were waived to help deal with

COVID-19. Some of these were related to increased flexibility in health care: allowing out-of-state doctors to treat patients through telehealth, the FDA giving states more leeway in virus testing, the Transportation Security Administration allowing passengers to take on board larger containers of hand sanitizer in carry-on bags on flights, and allowing seniors on Medicare to consult doctors via smartphone, for example.[22]

But plenty of the waivers were related to granting more flexibility for the operation of businesses and their services too. The Department of Transportation provided regulatory relief to truckers in terms of working hours for transporting emergency goods and services, for example.[23] The Environmental Protection Agency eased enforcement of environmental obligations.[24] The Alcohol and Tobacco Tax and Trade Bureau waived revenue laws to allow distilleries to produce hand sanitizer for sale.[25] State governments waived regulations restricting restaurants from offering delivery and takeout of alcohol. Restrictions on single-use plastic bags were lifted.[26] Certain localities delayed increasing their statutory minimum wage.[27]

After the shock of the virus hit, politicians knew they had to suspend regulations that limited how businesses operated or which products they could sell, lest consumers or businesses find themselves unable to source essential supplies. But this act in itself is an admission that those same regulations prevent businesses' ability to adapt their operations during normal times. We may have only noticed the restrictive effects of regulation because the supply and demand of goods changed so drastically. But a large number of those same regulations prevent businesses adapting to much smaller shocks to supply and demand every single day.

Regulation comes with a cost—often an unseen cost—of reducing our ability to adapt to ever-changing wants, needs, and economic conditions. It often entrenches current ways of doing things, deterring businesses from tinkering or testing a new product line that could better match consumer demands. This can be particularly harmful in periods of profound change, such as during pandemics. A recent paper on how countries fared during the 1918 Spanish flu pandemic found that those with more economic freedom—in particular those with fewer regulatory restrictions or barriers to international trade—saw much better economic outcomes.[28]

The supply and demand conditions for products will change as businesses reopen, tastes and preferences adjust, and work habits shift toward an as-yet unknown "new normal" following the rollout of vaccines.

To give the economy the best chance to adapt to these new conditions, we need as much flexibility and openness as possible to allow adaptation in health care, the food supply, childcare, retail, and many other industries. We want and need entrepreneurs to be founding new businesses, creating new jobs, and finding innovative new ways to serve consumers in safe ways. Regulation—of standards, products, and the labor market, in particular—threaten to thwart that rapid adjustment, just as we saw in the crucial area of COVID-19 testing.

One consequence of these big changes to the economics of product markets, however, is likely to continue to be unusually large fluctuations in prices. Economists have recognized since the 1970s that regulations that seek to control prices have extremely damaging consequences to the efficient allocation of resources. But when crises strike and people are struggling, large jumps in prices can be regarded as unfair. Politicians get put under a lot of pressure to punish businesses and merchants that raise them significantly, which is the topic of our next chapter.

ECONOMIC LESSON

Governments impose regulations with a whole range of aims, from protecting consumers to alleviating environmental damages. Economists often undertake cost-benefit analyses to judge whether such regulations are effective. But one tradeoff that seems common to most regulations is that they restrict businesses' and individuals' adaptability to new conditions—they curb within-market *innovation*, broadly defined. In the case of COVID-19, FDA regulations that were designed to improve the efficacy of diagnostic tests came with the huge cost of deterring and delaying labs from developing them and then holding up the rollout of cheap, rapid strip tests. Policymakers' decisions to waive much business regulation in light of these extraordinary times is further admission that regulation prevents economic adjustment to new conditions, both during crises and during normal times.

ECONOMIC TERMS INTRODUCED

- **market failure:** when free-market activity leads to an inefficient outcome for social economic welfare
- **government failure:** when the cost of a government intervention exceeds the benefits, leading to a less-efficient outcome for economic welfare than a free-market approach or some alternative policy
- **innovation:** the process of devising a new idea, product, or way of doing things
- **permissionless innovation:** a policy framework where the default is that innovation is allowed to occur unhindered by government intervention or regulation
- **entrepreneurship:** the process of discovering new ways of managing, organizing, or combining resources, or of developing new products or services, in the pursuit of profit within markets

10

WHY WAS THERE NO HAND SANITIZER
IN MY PHARMACY FOR MONTHS?
An introduction to the price mechanism

As I rummaged through half-empty shampoo bottles and long-forgotten hotel toothpaste tubes in preparation to move apartments in June 2020, I stumbled on something that back in March 2020 could have made me a nice chunk of money: a tiny container of unused Purell travel-sized hand sanitizer.

At the start of the pandemic, this stuff was like gold dust. A colleague visited five different pharmacies across Washington, DC, to try to track some down but to no avail. Even having a CVS pharmacy directly across the street from me, in full view so that I could see when delivery trucks arrived, I hadn't been able to locate any bottles of sanitizer for three months.

With public health officials emphasizing the importance of hand hygiene to halt the spread of SARS-CoV-2, the shelves of sanitizer had emptied rapidly, alongside most stores' selections of medical facemasks. What was striking, however, was not how quickly the goods became scarce but how long these shortages endured.

At the same time that shelves lay barren, governments and major online platforms took to attacking merchants for selling products online at much higher prices than usual. Some price jumps on online platforms were genuinely breathtaking. A packet of 24 two-ounce Purell hand sanitizers, usually costing around $10, was selling for $400.[1] Facemask prices jumped by 2500 percent in those early weeks of the pandemic.[2]

Policymakers were not amused at what they dubbed "unfair" price rises. The French government slapped price controls on hand sanitizer.[3] The chairman of the UK's competition authority threatened to act against "rip offs" and demanded new powers from the UK government to police prices directly.[4] Companies such as Amazon, recognizing the potential impact on their reputation for hosting sellers profiting from the shortage, condemned "bad actors" for price gouging—the practice of a seller increasing the price of a good or service beyond that considered to be fair or reasonable.[5]

A month later, with shortages still in stores and evidence of persistent high-price markets online, Sens. Kamala Harris (D-CA) and Elizabeth Warren (D-MA) demanded new federal price control powers.[6] Their proposed legislation would have limited price increases to no more than 10 percent during emergencies, right across the whole country. "No one should exploit people who are suffering," said Harris.[7] "Price gouging on household necessities is shameful." Warren added that she wanted to protect families from "companies out to make a quick buck."[8]

The Economics of Emergency Demands

What can economics tell us about these phenomena? What we were observing could be explained by Econ 101—it is a story of *supply* and *demand*. Or, at least, it represents our societal attempts to deny how these forces ordinarily determine prices in a market economy.

Most people don't usually use much hand sanitizer. Yet after public health officials talked of the importance of keeping our hands clean throughout the day, the want and need for it soared. Not just for individuals but for use in business settings too.

People rushed to buy up whatever they could, emptying the shelves over and over again as soon as they were refilled. There was a huge, unexpected expansion in demand. With stores out of the goods and customers' willingness to pay rising sharply, this near-term shortage was leading to sales at higher and higher prices in a smaller market online. People who really want something badly are often willing to pay vast amounts for it.

Now, ordinarily, with more buyers competing to obtain the normal supply of products, prices would start to rise for sanitizer across the economy. These rising prices would be a message, screaming that there is relative scarcity in the market—of supply not satisfying the now higher level of demand. It's the same sort of message that we get in years with sharply rising rents in cities such as New York, or when flight prices spike when a destination becomes more fashionable and desirable during holiday seasons.

That very price rise ordinarily spurs a reaction from companies. With it becoming more profitable for many producers to supply more of a good to the market, they might hire some more workers or offer more overtime to ramp up production to meet demand.

With a rising price, other closed businesses that have large stocks of sanitizer onsite find that they are facing a bigger incentive to unlock their cupboards and sell the sanitizer to people who want or need it. Firms that usually produce other goods might start to think it is more profitable to repurpose their production facilities toward producing sanitizer, too, as we in fact did see over time with alcohol distilleries. Rising prices, then, provide an incentive in their message: manufacturers would expand production, or merchants bring more to market, to fulfill the uplift in demand.

At the same time, as the price rises from that initial demand shock, consumers would start questioning whether they really need a second sanitizer bottle enough to justify paying a higher price. The price rise would serve as an effective rationing device, partially reducing the quantity of sanitizer that would have been demanded had the price remained fixed. Those that placed higher value on obtaining sanitizer, such as businesses where having hand sanitizer is important to assure consumers that they are lowering their risks from the virus, would continue to pay for the amounts they needed. Others who might have picked up a bottle or two might now instead opt for soap.

As these two incentive effects play out, gradually the market would converge to a position where the supply of sanitizer was able to meet a higher demand at a new, higher price. Consumers would be paying higher prices, yes, but more sanitizer would be available than it was before. Pretty soon, there would be no shortages on the shelves.

In fact, the process of market price discovery itself could lead to longer-term benefits too. As entrepreneurs try to find ways of meeting the needs of this lucrative market more cheaply, we'd likely see substantial innovation—increasing the supply of sanitizer substantially while demand remained elevated and, over time, pushing prices down again. At the very least, existing firms might invest in what the economist Tyler Cowen calls "option ready supply"—processes or capacity to capitalize on these sorts of demand spikes should history repeat itself in any future pandemic.

In a market economy, then, prices play a crucial role in coordinating economic activity. Not only do they embody a range of information about the underlying state of the market, but their movements provide signals and incentives for economic actors to adjust their behavior in light of that new reality.

In this case, the rising price of sanitizer would have signaled that it was in short supply relative to the huge demand—encouraging producers and merchants to find ways to bring supply to market in order to profit. Only individuals and businesses have the localized knowledge to decide whether they really value obtaining sanitizer or if they could feasibly produce it cost-effectively. The price mechanism provides the incentive for them to change their actions.

Shooting the Price Messenger

At least, that's the theory. But with shelves barren for so long, theory clearly did not play out in the short-term reality. The main reason for that is that prices were not able to adjust for a range of products.

Every day, fluctuations in prices send out messages to consumers and producers to alter their behavior, as demand and supply conditions change. Yet usually such small changes in prices might not capture our attention.

In fact, fascinating research by the economist Jonathan Hartley, examining Americans' performance on the TV show *The Price Is Right,* suggests that we have gotten worse at knowing the "correct" price of goods over the past few decades.[9] One theory he has for why this is so is that price-comparison websites give us the confidence to compare relative prices among companies so easily that we pay less attention to the absolute price itself.

That's not true, though, when we are at the height of an emergency, when huge shifts in the demand or ability to bring products to market change their in-store availability. Then, in search of the goods we want, we become painfully aware of how prices have changed when we do find the odd seller online.

Think of all the ways the pandemic severely disrupted supply and demand in product markets. On the demand side, we got the unexpected and sudden demand increases for goods perceived as "needed" for COVID-19 (such as facemasks and hand sanitizer). But there was also a demand surge and then ongoing elevated spending at grocery stores and for delivered food, because sit-in restaurants were first closed and then perceived as less safe to dine in (see Figure 10.1). All that was mirrored by the opposite effect of collapsing demand on travel, recreation, and entertainment—industries with higher perceived risks of infection.[10]

Consumers stocked up on some products, such as home toilet paper, out of precaution because they expected shortages. Then, in other sectors, we saw a big demand substitution, such as from movie theaters to home streaming.

But it's not just the demand side. Travel and work restrictions, as well as the virus itself, disrupted supply chains. We saw meat shortages, for example, when meatpacking plants were closed after being found to be prolific virus transmission sites.[11]

In other sectors there was severe disruption because of the nature of the demand shifts. As we were ordered to stay home, demand for domestic toilet paper rose, but demand fell for the commercial-grade toilet paper we use at work. Commercial suppliers initially didn't have relationships with supermarkets and weren't used to selling in quantities demanded by the ordinary consumer, so they took time to adjust to meet the new supply.[12] The same was true of wholesalers who previously sold fresh produce and fish to restaurants pivoting to selling to individual consumers at home.

FIGURE 10.1

U.S. grocery, transportation, and restaurant and hospitality spending, relative to January 2020 levels

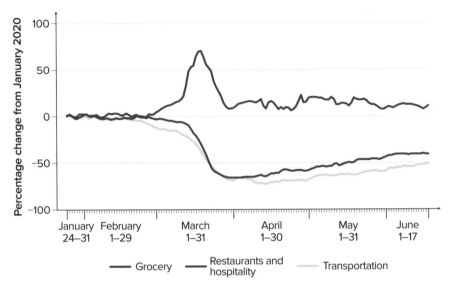

Source: Opportunity Insights Tracker, "Consumer Spending: National," www.tracktherecovery.org.

Businesses might not want to adjust prices much when supply and demand varies within expected ranges. After all, it is costly to adjust prices, and they have to take into account how consumers will react to fluctuating prices in terms of willingness to search for alternative sellers. But these COVID-19 disruptions were so drastic that major price changes might be more likely to occur. What's more, these price changes would be desirable. Price increases in markets with surging demand, for example, would actively incentivize wholesalers to take time to redesign their products and build new relationships to fulfill our new needs. Rising prices would make us think twice as consumers about overbuying and hoarding toilet paper. Elevated prices for scarce goods would encourage those with big stocks of the products to bring them to market. And a bigger payoff for existing manufacturers would incentivize entrepreneurs to reengineer their businesses to the new realities, paying overtime or ramping up production to meet demand.

Yes, these effects would not be instantaneous. Yes, it's regrettable that consumers would have to pay more. Yes, no economist pretends this is good for everyone. But, as a society, we want resources to shift to producing things that consumers want and need.

Yet when such large-scale changes to supply and demand occur as a result of an emergency, such as a pandemic or hurricane, many of us seemingly reject or ignore the underlying economics. Instead, we blame the companies raising prices as being greedy rather than acknowledging the supply-and-demand realities they face.

Whereas market prices before an emergency are deemed good, fair, and reasonable, market prices that rise significantly during an emergency are dubbed bad, unfair, and unreasonable. Firms are accused of profiteering. Where once we understood that supply and demand determines what we pay for things, now we imply that companies have complete discretion to set prices at whatever level they like, irrespective of consumers' willingness to pay or the risk of being undercut by competitors. Hence the charge of price gouging.

We do not apply our complaints consistently or symmetrically, either. People online have slammed sellers of facemasks, sanitizer, Nintendos, and even food delivery companies for supposedly inflating prices during this crisis. One article, with no hint of irony, bemoaned how "gougers have shifted with consumer demand."[13] Having moved on from sanitizer and facemasks, "CNET found Cottonelle toilet paper listed on Amazon for $57.42 (price for the same item on Target: $21.49), and a two-pack of 28-ounce jars of Rao's marinara sauce for $29.04 (an adjacent listing of 24-ounce jars from Amazon-owned Whole Foods would cost you $10.78)."[14]

Of course, news outlets such as CNET were not complaining that prices of flights, restaurant food, sports merchandise, and hotels collapsed due to the very same supply-and-demand forces.[15] Nobody, as far as I'm aware, was suggesting that consumers should be mandated to pay the old higher prices for these goods and services because it would be unfair to sellers to do otherwise. Yet when it comes to higher prices that we must pay for scarce goods in emergencies, we lash out at companies.

This societal economic denialism amounts to trying to shoot the price messenger: a messenger screaming that there is a relative scarcity of certain products, such as hand sanitizer. Instead we hold the price messenger hostage in order to tell a comforting lie about the availability of products by both shaming companies that raised prices and by urging politicians to cap prices. Both these actions prolonged shortages in stores by dampening the market incentives that we would usually see to encourage companies to produce more. It is that which facilitated the extremely high prices online and empty shelves for such a long period.

A Tale of Both Reputation and Law

Evidence of major firms being concerned about their reputations from raising prices was seen in both anecdote and data. A friend of mine sent me a photo from a CVS in New York at the peak of the demand for sanitizer. The store's price stickers were advertising that the products were "Buy 1, Get 1 50% Off." In other words, the company had actually discounted sanitizer to try to show they were being helpful to customers, even as their shelves lay empty.

It is easy to make such a gesture when there is nothing to sell. Yet there is a longer-term economic cost here. The result of this seemingly considerate gesture was prolonged shortages on shelves and many customers walking away empty-handed who would willingly pay much higher prices. This harms economic welfare.

But it was not just CVS. The economist Russ Roberts has quoted the CEO of Flexport, a company that helped people getting access to facemasks.[16] He was clear that one key reason for the shortage of masks was the fear of being accused of price gouging, saying "U.S. distributors can't pass higher prices through to hospitals in the midst of the crisis, for fear of being accused of profiteering. Foreign governments and health care systems have been less encumbered by this, showing a willingness to pay more and pay faster to get first in line."[17]

Nobel Prize–winning economist Richard Thaler has observed that national brands, such as big pharmacy chains, big-box retailers, and major online platforms such as Amazon, face a particularly large reputational risk from raising prices during an emergency. In highly localized emergency situations, such as hurricanes and other natural disasters, established suppliers therefore often take a longer-term view about what's in their brand's best interests to maintain future demand, so avoiding hiking prices during a crisis. Major firms, such as Walmart, can instead move supplies to the affected area from other stores, largely meeting any extra demand without taking the bad publicity of raising prices and being accused of profiteering.

Although COVID-19's impact is anything but localized, major sellers have similarly acted as if it is. Amazon, for example, has tried to prevent price gouging on its platform through fear of the reputational impact of high prices during the crisis. CVS, as we have seen, even discounted prices.

These reputational concerns appear to influence third-party sellers in marketplaces too. The economists Luis Cabral and Lei Xu reviewed facemask prices on Amazon's marketplace during the pandemic.[18] Broadly, prices had risen by a factor of 2.7 in March 2020 compared with 2019. But significantly, sellers who had been selling since 2019 charged just 63 percent of the price of sellers that entered the facemask market after the SARS-CoV-2 outbreak. This suggests that existing sellers couldn't jack up prices due to fears for their reputation. Consumers notice it more when a company they usually buy from raises their retail prices.

Now, such reputational concerns are a natural part of a market economy. Businesses want to keep customers; losing them could be worse for profits. Provided that there are other entrepreneurs and small-scale sellers that have less of a reputation to lose, or indeed more of a reputation to gain from entering the market, we will see some of the price-driven responses to expand supply as discussed earlier, particularly in businesses that can repurpose production.

And we did. Some outlets online served a much smaller sanitizer market with very high prices online. Shadow markets developed as well. A family member of mine told me that she saw a staff member in a Brooklyn pharmacy selling hand sanitizer under the counter at inflated prices. Over longer periods, of course, when it became clear that demand would remain elevated and bottlenecks in supply chains became less problematic, a whole range of new sanitizer suppliers entered the market.[19]

Breweries shifted to producing sanitizer, often for profit, and sometimes just distributed it for free to restaurants, first responders, and other businesses in order to aid the public health effort or for reputational gain. Companies reoriented production to other pandemic-related products—the TV manufacturer Sharp, for example, repurposed a factory to produce facemasks.[20] A Bloomberg investigation found examples of wallet and bag producers pivoting toward face-shield production, pizza restaurants repurposing their ovens to do the same, and a company that previously provided heat shields for cars instead producing medical gowns.[21]

Yet government policy deters this sort of business adjustment through anti-price-gouging laws that restrict large price increases during emergencies. In fact, just 14 states do not have some form of anti-price-gouging law that applies to certain products in emergencies or after natural disasters.[22] These price controls, and the legal uncertainty they create for businesses, undermine the incentive for existing suppliers to ramp up production—risking sustained shortages of products. Unsurprisingly, reducing the payoff to producing more of a product reduces the willingness of businesses and entrepreneurs to do so.

To give a flavor of the laws and the uncertainty they create, let's consider Virginia's anti-price-gouging statute.[23] It prohibits a supplier from charging "unconscionable prices" for "necessary" goods and services in the period following a declared state of emergency.

The degree of discretion in the statute is extraordinary. Whether a good is necessary is determined by whether the Virginia Office of the Attorney General deems the good to be needed as a result of the emergency. Meanwhile, an "unconscionable" price rise is defined as one that "grossly exceeds the price charged for the same or similar goods or services either by the same supplier, or within the same trade area, during the ten days immediately prior to the disaster."[24] What a minefield for businesses.

Other states have much more prescriptive laws. California's, for example, limits price increases to just 10 percent. If sellers are found to be in breach of the law, they can find themselves in jail for a year or faced with paying huge financial penalties.

The problem is that these de facto price controls actively discourage the provision of goods during shortages. Yes, some kind-hearted businesses and individuals might donate sanitizer supplies to those who need them. Or if some companies find that their other business activities have been shuttered, they might turn some resources to providing sanitizer as a new entrant to the market.

But the unwillingness by policymakers to allow the price mechanism to ration the goods means that those who need it most (and are willing to pay more for it) will often not be able to find the sanitizer, while the financial incentive to produce more, particularly for existing suppliers, gets smothered—resulting in empty shelves, at least until demand subsides somewhat. Although we might expect national brands to avoid raising prices out of concern for their reputations, anti-price-gouging laws also prohibit smaller convenience stores and existing online merchants from raising their prices to ensure supply meets demand. This eliminates the market safety valve of sellers who are less concerned with their reputations from providing the more expensive goods to those who really value them highly.

Price controls like this, in fact, have very negative short-, medium-, and long-term consequences. In the near term they encourage buyers to overpurchase and hoard. Those fortunate enough to be in the store when shelves are replenished buy more than they would have if prices reflected the reality of the situation. Meanwhile, these just-in-case purchases worsen shortages for others, who see their demands unmet, given the gap between the amount of the product available and the amount they want to consume at the regulated price.

If prices had risen significantly, those in possession of large amounts of the good would have had much bigger incentive to sell, but this effect is neutered by price caps. In fact, the failure of the prices to rise to clear the market encourages irrational or dangerous behaviors. Hoarders try to play the market, waiting for opportunities to sell in shadow markets. Goods sit at home, as in my cupboard, when they would be valued highly elsewhere. And others take advantage of the shortages by producing fake products.

Then the price controls deter companies from meeting the new higher demand by increasing their production. If it's not financially rewarding, then ramping up production will just not happen as often, especially if it brings extra costs, such as having to pay workers overtime or replace certain machines after running them hot.

Longer-term, the price controls also deter new companies from getting into the market, or making large monetary commitments for investments to serve ongoing elevated demand, or building capacity for a future demand surge. We therefore either see sustained shortages of goods where demand is likely to remain elevated indefinitely, or we are more likely to suffer a similar shortage when a future crisis hits.

Why Do We Think So Differently in an Emergency?

Economists agree that anti-price-gouging laws are destructive in this way. In a 2012 Initiative on Global Markets poll of top economists, 53 percent disagreed with a Connecticut bill to curb price gouging, against just 8 percent who agreed with it.[25] That's because economists think of prices as an outcome of supply and demand, not just something firms can set at their discretion. Firms are limited by customers' willingness to pay and the potential to be undercut by competitors.

In fact, we all understand this in normal times, even if we don't think about it. Uber surge pricing is highly responsive to market conditions, such that when demand rises sharply, ridesharing prices jump on the app. If you're a user, you know that when the surge price is high, you will think twice about hailing a driver. But if you really need to get somewhere, you end up putting up the cash. The system rations the service to those who most value the ride. As a result, economists have found that surge pricing increases overall economic welfare, especially of the riders.[26] Most importantly, the biggest gains to welfare occur in areas underserved by taxis and public transit. Higher prices encourage more transport supply to those who most need it.[27]

This is unsurprising. Prices send signals to drivers about where it is most lucrative to go out and work. Even if it remains difficult to find a ride when the immediate demand surge occurs, the higher price attracts more drivers to stay on the road rather than go home. In the future, it will incentivize them to hit the surging area at peak time. As Russ Roberts says, "you get more stuff when you let the price go up."[28]

Some businesses clearly understand the adverse consequences of keeping prices artificially low. One Danish store charged a relatively low price for a customer buying the first bottle of hand sanitizer but a much higher price for any additional bottles after that.[29] There were all sorts of creative workarounds consumers could have adopted to ensure that they did not ever pay the higher price. But at least the business was acknowledging the large economic costs associated with both hoarding and unmet demands of those who valued the product more highly.

The broader problem, however, is that when crises hit, our tolerance for market pricing seemingly goes out of the window. A particularly tragic example of misguided price controls occurred in San Francisco during this pandemic, when the city capped the fees that UberEats and other delivery apps could charge restaurants at 15 percent in order to "help" the restaurant industry during this difficult time.[30]

Lo and behold, when you cap prices below market rates, you get less of the economic activity. UberEats simply removed services from part of the city. It explained that this was because the price cap was below their operating costs for delivery to the Treasure Island area, making it uneconomical to serve it. But it was the poor communities there who suffered from a reduction in the food delivery service.

Policymakers must pay heed to these negative consequences of suppressing price signals, particularly as this pandemic evolves. In the coming months, pandemic-induced business failures could lead to higher prices for services in the future when demand rebounds by creating near-term shortages of supply. In other sectors, as the rollout of vaccines facilitate reopening, we may see demand for certain services roar back. In order to adjust to our new post-pandemic "normal," we want prices to accurately reflect the underlying conditions that these product markets face. We need to set prices free.

Why then do we feel so unwilling to allow market-set prices during emergencies? One suspects this takes us out of the realm of economics and into psychology and why certain things "feel" wrong. But if we are to take people at their word, there are two reasons why people and politicians think raising prices during a crisis is so abhorrent.

The first is that price rises hit some groups, such as the poor, harder than others. The second is a more primal feeling that it is simply wrong for a business to seek to profit from a time of adversity. Both complaints appear not so much to be the fault of businesses raising prices but a lament at the economic realities that emergency situations bring.

Yes, it would be unfortunate for people who really need hand sanitizer to have to pay more for it in a world where prices were rising. But the alternative, as we have seen, is not plentiful, affordable sanitizer for all. It is empty shelves and a thin online market with even higher prices.

If we do not ration by price, we need another mechanism. If you are lucky enough to be poor and in a pharmacy when they obtain a delivery, then you might indeed be better off with anti-price-gouging laws. But there is no guarantee that a system of rationing in this way is better for the poor than the rich, as we saw with shortages of COVID-19 tests. And it certainly is not better for those unfortunate enough to have conditions where hand sanitizer is an essential part of their daily health care needs. They'd much prefer to pay more to guarantee that the supplies of the product are adequately available to them in-store.

Companies also can't set prices to whatever they like. To sell their products, they must find willing buyers. A rising price would merely reflect that during this pandemic, more people want to purchase sanitizer and are willing to pay higher prices to do so. To deny this reality and act as if business owners should suddenly become charities or serve some higher need to avoid fines or jail time is to guarantee prolonged shortages of sanitizer on store shelves, while some people remain overstocked at home.

The free operation of the price mechanism, then, is an area where lots of us appear to completely lose our economic minds during a crisis, rejecting market mechanisms we ordinarily accept, to our broader detriment. The economist Steven Suranovic even goes as far as saying that the public and political reaction to price rises during emergencies is the true market failure.[31]

ECONOMIC LESSON

Price changes send messages to consumers and sellers about how much of a good to consume or produce. Rising prices highlight a relative scarcity of the product at the current price: that is, demand exceeds supply. When the price rise is driven by higher demand, this encourages producers to ramp up production and consumers to ration what they buy until there are no ongoing shortages. With regards to COVID-19, by deterring major price increases through anti-price-gouging laws during emergencies, politicians ensured that there were prolonged shortages of important products and that they ended up in places where they were not most highly valued.

ECONOMIC TERMS INTRODUCED

- **supply:** the goods and services producers are willing and able to take to market
- **demand:** the goods and services buyers are willing and able to purchase in markets
- **price gouging:** when a seller increases the price of a good or service to a level higher than what is considered reasonable or fair

11

DOES THE PANDEMIC SHOW THAT WE NEED MORE U.S.-BASED MANUFACTURING?

An introduction to trade and specialization

How efficiently do you think you could make your own sandwich? I'm not asking "How quickly could you slap some mayonnaise, meat, salad, cheese, and a pickle between two slices of bread?" but rather, "If you had to produce a sandwich completely from scratch, how cost-effectively do you think you could do it?"

At the time of writing, the Subway closest to where I live sells a six-inch oven-roasted chicken sub for $5.09. That seems a reasonable (perhaps generous) pricing benchmark to which we can compare a solo effort, given that the restaurant service brings with it the option of an array of toppings, somewhere to eat the sandwich, and a markup for profit.

Back in 2015, Andy George, the creator of the YouTube series *How to Make Everything,* decided to try to answer my question. He endeavored to produce a chicken sandwich using all homemade ingredients.[1]

He soon found out that using the labor of just one man for this task was quite an undertaking. George had to build a garden patch before planting, growing, and tending to vegetables. He traveled to the ocean to collect seawater, undertaking thermal distillation at home to extract the salt. Using the vegetables he had grown and the salt he'd extracted, he set about to jar some homemade pickles.

His toil didn't stop there. A farm visit was necessary to milk a cow to home-produce cheese. He harvested wheat, separated it from the chaff, and ground it into flour to produce his own bread. He collected honey from a beehive, built a press to extract oil from sunflower seeds to make mayonnaise, and killed, plucked, and cooked a chicken. Then, after all that, he assembled the sandwich in his kitchen. The whole pursuit ended up costing him a massive $1,500.

Did he value the eventual sandwich highly? "It's not bad," he said on his YouTube video as he tucked into the finished product, clearly disappointed given the huge amount of time and money he'd ploughed in. Even with his efforts over the period of half a year, he'd still been reliant on the input of others. He didn't rear the chickens from hatching, for example. Nor did he extract his own iron ore to produce the steel for the knives that cut his vegetables. Producing a sandwich by yourself is hard.

The Limits of Self-Sufficiency

There's an important lesson from this story about the desirability of self-sufficiency. It turns out to be extremely inefficient to try to produce everything by yourself. George remarked he could have bought an expensive artisan sandwich for just $15 nearby, but his efforts had cost 100 times that, at a massive opportunity cost of lost time. As we've mentioned, economists describe opportunity cost as the value of the best use that we forgo when we use any resource—including the value of the best alternative use of the time that George had put in over six months.

It's for this reason that most of us don't try to be self-sufficient in producing what we consume. We might grow some of our own herbs or produce some personal arts and crafts. But there's no way any one person would ordinarily go about producing his daily sandwich from scratch, let alone building himself a computer or a television.

Mercifully, a market economy where we can trade freely allows us instead to specialize in activities that we are relatively efficient at, earn money from this activity, and then purchase things that others produce relatively more efficiently than us.

In fact, this sort of *specialization* occurs even within your workplace or when deciding to divvy up tasks at home. I study economic policy; my colleagues are expert editors, fundraisers, and event hosts. I do more cooking of meats and cleaning when I am at home with my fiancée; she usually undertakes more day-to-day tidying and preparation of desserts. Economists refer to this as the *division of labor.* By focusing on a few tasks that we can become more proficient at, collectively we can get more done at lower costs of time or money.

But a similar story occurs across the economy too. Companies tend to focus on the production of a small range of products they can produce well. Trade then allows them to sell their products in markets, with the earnings distributed over time to workers and investors such that they all can buy things other businesses or traders are relatively more efficient at producing or providing. I use my income from studying policy to purchase haircuts, smartphones, and, yes, ingredients for sandwiches—goods and services that other individuals or businesses specialize in.

The magic ingredient that facilitates specialization is therefore trade or exchange. Markets where trade can occur as freely as possible help create opportunities for richer and deeper specialization. That allows us to produce more at lower cost, making us wealthier and ultimately granting us more resources to then consume other products.

As my Cato colleague Dan Ikenson never tires of telling people,

The purpose of trade is to enable us to specialize; the purpose of specialization is to enable us to produce more; the purpose of producing more is to enable us to consume more.[2]

As 18th-century Scottish economist Adam Smith recognized, trade is crucial to achieving a high standard of living. Without it, we'd all end up farming the land just to stay alive. Being free to trade goods and services presents us with more opportunities for specialization that ultimately make us more productive. It's the ability to trade that allows the evolution of professional salt processors, chicken farmers, pickle manufacturers, and beekeepers, who find ways to produce their products at scale, allowing us, the consumers, to make sandwiches quickly and cheaply.

These benefits of trade do not just come in the form of sandwiches, however. Trade is even more important to facilitating the specialization of companies building high-tech components of computer equipment than it is your favorite sub. The same logic works when discussing millions of consumers and producers in a complex economy as thinking about buying ingredients for lunch, albeit with a wider array of people at work.

Perhaps most contentiously, the advantages of *free trade* that make us wealthier remain just as true when discussing trade that crosses national borders as when discussing your purchase of a sandwich from your local deli. Enforced or mandated self-sufficiency is costly, whether that be at the individual, local, or even national level.

Just as free trade for goods or services within the United States allows domestic specialization, free international trade represents the expansion of free markets across political borders, encouraging countries in aggregate to produce goods and services that they have a relative efficiency in producing, a situation known as *comparative advantage*.

A lot of noneconomists find this concept difficult to grasp. "What if one country produces everything more efficiently than others?," they ask. Wouldn't that single country end up producing everything in a world of free trade? The answer is no. And the reason why is embedded in why I said *relative* efficiency rather than just efficiency.

It may be that Country A is most efficient at producing both, say, coffee cups and mattresses. In that case, it would be said to have an *absolute advantage* in the production of each. But it cannot have a *comparative advantage* in both.

Suppose the opportunity cost for Country A of producing more coffee cups is higher than the opportunity cost for Country B, meaning that the number of mattresses that Country A would have to give up from diverting workers and capital to coffee cup production was higher than it would be for Country B. By allowing Country B to produce coffee cups, with its *relative efficiency* advantage, and Country A to produce mattresses, with its relative efficiency advantage, we could produce much more overall, making both parties richer.

For a simpler example: it might be that one member of your household is simply more efficient at all cooking, cleaning, and other domestic chores than you—holding absolute advantages in each. But this absolute advantage doesn't mean they can and should do all the work when you are preparing the house for guests. If you have a set amount of time and that person is much, much better at cooking than you but only a tiny bit better at cleaning, then it makes sense for that person to focus on their comparative advantage (cooking) while you clean.

Reducing barriers to international commerce, such as the removal of tariffs, quotas, subsidies to domestic producers, or regulatory barriers, allows the possibility for a more extensive specialization, then, because it allows resources across deeper markets to be diverted toward countries' comparative advantages through finding companies'—and ultimately countries'—relative efficiencies. This raises the capacity for us to produce yet more goods overall, making us richer still.

Now that doesn't mean the gains are instantaneous or seamless when we make trade freer. Insulating American businesses in specific industries from competition from foreign products through tariffs, subsidies, or industrial privileges can bring acute localized pain when those barriers are removed. Although it may grow the economic pie, freeing trade has distributional consequences—not everybody wins.[3] These job losses and industry failures can create interest groups opposed to free trade.

But freer trade enriches the economy more broadly in less discernible ways. Yes, consumers do indeed benefit from cheaper goods as trade is freed up among countries—that is the most obvious effect.[4] But we become broadly richer, too, through the less visible process of that specialization—of resources being shifted into sectors where U.S. companies are relatively efficient at producing goods and services, given the economic realities that face them.[5]

There is good evidence, for example, that China's integration into the global trading system accelerated this process in the United States, with net job losses in manufacturing more than offset by massive job gains in services, which the United States is relatively more efficient at providing.[6]

A debate has been bubbling in recent years over just how great the enriching impacts of international trade are, and a similar debate exists about the size of the economic costs of disruption associated with the freeing of trade. But economists still overwhelmingly agree that freer trade makes a country richer, and they tend to be the biggest supporters of removing trade barriers.

A survey of leading economists in 2012, for example, found a weighted average of 96 percent of them agreed or strongly agreed with the statement "freer trade improves productive efficiency and offers consumers better choices, and in the long run these gains are much larger than any effects on employment."[7] Economists have also overwhelmingly opposed Trump's trade war with China and new tariffs he imposed on goods imported from other countries.

The Pandemic-Induced Critique of Free Trade

This pandemic, however, has led to a very different critique of free trade policies. Rather than challenge the free trade consensus of economists on distributional or efficiency grounds, critics now claim the pandemic itself proves that the efficiency free trade brings creates a different tradeoff than we usually consider—that the specialization free trade encourages itself sacrifices the *resilience* of the United States as a country.

Open markets might encourage the most cost-efficient supply chains for goods and countries operating according to their comparative advantages, Florida Senator Marco Rubio has argued, but that often means Americans importing lots of medical supplies, including facemasks, personal protective equipment, and respirators from abroad.[8] When emergencies such as the pandemic hit, Rubio believes this puts Americans at the mercy of trade disruptions and foreign governments, who in this pandemic moved to ban exports of medical products to ensure a supply for their own citizens. The result, Rubio wagers, is a shortage of essential medical products and more pain from COVID-19 for Americans.

Too little self-sufficiency in the production of medical goods or manufacturing capacity, in Rubio's view, has therefore undermined the public health effort, with devastating economic consequences. U.S. Trade

Representative Robert Lighthizer has similarly condemned U.S. supply chains for their "lemming-like" desire for efficiency that has left them exposed to unacceptable levels of risk from things such as business interruptions and pandemics.[9] He believes this crisis has proven the case for repatriating extensive manufacturing capacity more broadly.[10]

The policy conclusion of both Rubio and Lighthizer is that the federal government should use trade and industrial policy to encourage the re-shoring of important medical and manufacturing capacity. Contrary to the traditional case for free trade, they argue that more national self-sufficiency in these areas would raise Americans' economic welfare, despite it harming efficiency.

Some people even want to mandate local content requirements to require that certain goods or supply chains *must* be produced or based in the United States.[11] Not only would that supposedly free us from being beholden to countries such as China for facemasks or respirators, but it would encourage the manufacturing capacity that would make us self-reliant and resilient to other shocks. Crises, in short, are believed to prove that a higher degree of self-sufficiency, or national economic independence, is more desirable than free traders suggest.

Throughout history, pandemics have tended to be followed by a reversal of economic integration, so such calls are perhaps unsurprising.[12] Restrictions on the ability to trade or travel because of pandemic-induced disruption is always going to reduce opportunities for (or the profitability of) international trade, thus encouraging domestic production. These changes then tend to stick somewhat.

What's more, it's perfectly rational for merchants and businesses to reassess their sourcing and production decisions after a shock like this. If the particular unexpected disruptions from this pandemic cause them to sit up and reassess risks, from business interruptions in their supply chain through to foreign government interference with their product, they may decide to re-shore some activity closer to the U.S. market irrespective of any change in government policy.

Already we hear talk of less emphasis on just-in-time supply chains and more emphasis on just-in-case supply chains as profit-seeking companies adjust to this new world. The pandemic will naturally cause businesses to revise what they believe to be efficient practice for them in the long term, which might suggest they were over-optimized in the short term.

But Rubio clearly wants to go beyond what private businesses will choose to do voluntarily. What's more, he will likely find receptive ears for going further than businesses decide. Government-led protectionism was already on the rise in the United States before this virus, exhibited by Trump's trade war with China. Think tanks pushing for manufacturing re-shoring and industrial policies have been founded. Politicians will use the pandemic to make the case for policy to target greater domestic self-reliance. The virus penetrating the United States from overseas will only add to this feeling that dependence on suppliers in foreign nations threatens American prosperity.

The Flaws in the Resilience Argument

There are big problems with Rubio's assumption of such a clear trade-off between efficiency and national resilience, and conservatives such as him shouldn't be so quick to dismiss what they used to know about free trade.

A high degree of interconnectivity of people and goods may well spread viruses more rapidly during a pandemic and lead to some disruption of supply chains that cross national boundaries. But that same process of specialization that comes from the free movements of goods and services also makes us richer because of improved efficiency. This greater prosperity gives us more resources to invest in health care and other relief efforts when crises do actually hit. In that sense, free trade improves a country's resilience.

Indeed, efficiency is not some small-fry second-order issue to be scoffed at. Re-shoring a large chunk of industrial production back to the United States just in case another pandemic hits would be an extraordinarily expensive and wasteful endeavor in normal times (not to mention incredibly complex.)

The Healthcare Supply Chain Association estimated in April that health care providers would use 500 million N-95 respiratory masks in 2020, compared with just 25 million in 2019.[13] A survey of American hospitals found "17 times the typical burn rate for N-95 respirators,

8.6 times for face shields, 6 times for swabs, 5 times for isolation gowns and 3.3 times for surgical masks."[14]

Deliberately using policy to create the domestic production capacity to meet all this emergency demand on a permanent basis would either result in a whole load of excess unused capacity in normal times, or else create a complete glut of unneeded products if such high production levels were maintained.[15]

Investment in that sort of unneeded capacity has real economic costs, removing workers and capital from other possibly more productive endeavors. And for what? There's no guarantee it will be effective for the next crisis, especially because we have scant knowledge of what future pandemics or crises will look like.

Building more facemask manufacturing factories might not help much if we are faced with a very different threat next time—say, the prospect of nuclear war, a bacterial pathogen in the water supply, a massive West Coast earthquake, or a nonrespiratory virus. So is the logic here that we'd preserve domestic capacity to produce goods to meet the needs of any possible threat? It would be extraordinarily inefficient to be startled into preparing for every single improbable risk, however minor. As the *Financial Times*'s Martin Sandbu has written, "being self-sufficient for every eventuality is prohibitively expensive."[16]

"Self-sufficiency" is also dangerous. One benefit of open trade is diversification. Freeing up trade allows businesses and consumers more options on where to source their supplies or sell their goods. The old adage of not putting all your eggs in one basket applies to trade as much as anything else. It's all very well, then, to say that we should produce what we might need domestically—a national economic independence that economists usually dub *autarky*. But what happens if a pathogen or some other unexpected shock hits the United States first, necessitating widespread business closures here? How would local content requirements help then?

We've seen in this crisis how COVID-19 disrupted the domestic meat supply following outbreaks in meatpacking plants. In a scenario where we became self-dependent on producing a medical good, and a shock shut down most domestic factories, we would quickly find severe shortages. In that sense, we'd clearly be less resilient as a country, not more.

Indeed, one analysis by economists Barthélémy Bonadio, Zhen Huo, Andrei A. Levchenko, and Nitya Pandalai-Nayar examined whether renationalization of global supply chains would have improved the resilience of U.S. GDP during the pandemic.[17] They found that the downturn would have been almost exactly the same in magnitude under that hypothetical scenario.

Isn't this obvious? Becoming less reliant on foreign inputs means becoming fully reliant on domestic inputs. Yet lockdowns, business closures, and sick workers have affected domestic businesses too, and would have done so no matter what industrial policies the United States had in place. Economists have found in normal times that trade diversification actually tends to reduce the volatility of GDP because "it reduces exposure to domestic shocks and allows countries to diversify the sources of demand and supply across countries."[18]

Some of the East Asian economies that dealt better with the virus were able to restart clothing production quickly, for example. It was the lack of demand from importing countries that took longer to contain the virus, such as the United States and the UK, which prolonged a depression of activity in those industries. If all that manufacturing activity had been re-shored through policy efforts or mandates, taking resources outside of service industries where people can work more easily from home, the downturn here may well have been sharper than the already massive contraction we actually saw in Q2 2020 (reference to the second quarter of the year—April, May, and June 2020).

A great example of how protectionism makes us less resilient was seen in early May 2020, with widespread reports of U.S. auto dealers worrying about a shortage of pickup trucks due to SARS-CoV-2 induced plant closures.[19] At that time German and East Asian car manufacturers had already restarted production. But because of long-term protectionism in the form of a 25 percent tariff on imported trucks, these would-be suppliers were not oriented for selling in the U.S. market after finding themselves being priced out it for years. Compare that to Apple and other high-tech firms, which have been rolling out new products produced overseas even during the pandemic, and it's obvious that re-shoring encouraged through government policy is neither necessary nor sufficient for resilience.

The idea that re-shoring critical supply chains within national borders somehow makes them safe from interdiction or disruption is therefore a complete illusion.[20] Future shocks are uncertain and could well affect the domestic economy more than international supply chains. Consider the scalability of the logic: Did the SARS-CoV-2–induced disruption in meat packing plants prove that it would be better for your personal resilience to source your own sandwich fillers at home, as Andy George did? No? So why do Marco Rubio and others assume that disruption to ventilator availability necessitates repatriating ventilator production to the United States?

In fact, there's little evidence from the protectionist policies that the United States already adopts that policies designed to improve resilience achieve their goals. Insulating industries from foreign competition in the past has instead tended to make them inefficient, expensive, lazy, and less likely to adopt innovative new procedures and technologies, rather than being on the cutting edge and adaptive to unexpected shocks.

We see this with the U.S. steel industry and the shipping industry, which is protected by the Jones Act.[21] So why would we expect different results in the medical or manufacturing sectors? If this whole episode has shown us anything, it has surely emphasized the limits of the idea of having experts manage complex systems to improve outcomes, particularly in conditions of uncertainty. And that's important: a recent McKinsey report showed how incredibly complicated modern supply chains are. The room for error in politicians seeking to rebuild them domestically is therefore incredibly high.[22] Interestingly, that report concluded that industries such as medical devices and pharmaceuticals would be relatively unaffected by disruptions such as pandemics and other external shocks. It claimed politicians' trade policies posed a much bigger risk to those industries.

A Better Way?

Yet if policy-led re-shoring or trade protectionism would likely undermine economic efficiency with no guarantee of improving resilience to future shocks, then is there anything government policy could change for the better?

We shouldn't pretend the status quo is perfect. Rubio and others exaggerate how much free and open trade has been a problem in this pandemic, not least because they exaggerate both how dependent the United States is on imports of medical supplies and how disrupted the global pharmaceutical supply chains have actually been.[23]

But there clearly have been difficulties, not least in how governments have responded. Even where there have been pinch-points, however, there are alternative, more cost-effective solutions than re-shoring industries. Paradoxically, the efficiency-enhancing free trade approach that Rubio laments could help.

One more-efficient approach to better resilience to public health might, in some cases, be to have private companies and public health authorities buy up and stockpile the needed goods in advance when they are cheap.

Switzerland famously has a national stockpile for essential foods and medicines in case of crises.[24] The United States already has a Strategic National Stockpile of "antibiotics, medical supplies, equipment, antidotes, antitoxins, antivirals, vaccines, and other pharmaceuticals that are strategically located throughout the United States and its territories."[25]

If it is so obvious that these stockpiles were inadequate, then the U.S. government could simply build up and broaden the composition of stockpiles to prepare for possible future shocks. If it were not obvious what would be needed in the future, in contrast, then it's difficult to see why we should gamble on a vast re-shoring of activity that purports to second-guess what we will need.

Free trade and specialization, of course, makes it cheaper to purchase these stockpiles, which could be stored relatively inexpensively in normal times. Combined with our insights from chapter 7, high uncertainty about what precisely we might need should instead mean that we desire a flexible economy that adapts quickly when stockpiles or international supplies prove inadequate, rather than betting the house that the government can plan our industrial needs.

One way to achieve this is to actually broaden our free trade horizons. If the United States had expansive trade agreements with, or lower trade barriers on, other countries with producers of facemasks, personal protective equipment, and other medical products, then Americans could import these important goods more cheaply from a wide array of sources when other governments decide to close off supplies from being exported.

A lighter-touch regulatory system could also facilitate swifter adaptation of existing production capacity to producing emergency supplies too. We shouldn't underestimate just how much American-consumed medical supplies are produced domestically already.[26] But, on the margins, we can acquire more resilience through adaptation. For example, the regulatory relaxations that allowed distilleries to produce hand sanitizer could be a model for reorienting production capabilities elsewhere. We already read in chapter 10 about pizza and car heat film suppliers repurposing to provide personal protective equipment during this crisis, showing the capacity for businesses to adjust, particularly when the regulatory burdens are light and prices are freely set.

Perhaps a better way than having stockpiles to deal with unexpected future shocks and the needs they might create could be the use of *options*. These are contracts that are very prevalent in commodity and asset markets, where the buyer pays an ongoing sum to a seller (called a premium) for the right to buy a certain amount of products, such as facemasks or medical supplies, at any given time.

Under this type of arrangement, governments or coalitions of private groups, such as insurers or hospitals, could buy an option for facemasks or other medical products from domestic or foreign producers. This would, as with insurance, give the producers ongoing premium income, which could be used to maintain some surplus capacity. And it would give governments and private groups the opportunity (but not the obligation) to purchase a given amount of what they require when the next crisis hits.

If there were still shortages during crises, ramping up production at home can be encouraged further by having the federal government make purchasing guarantees at high fixed prices in order to give companies a clear profit incentive to shift production to much-needed medical and personal protective equipment.[27] As we learned in chapter 10, price signals matter, and high prices would encourage production. This, again, will be much more efficient than maintaining excess capacity in a whole range of goods forever.

Finally, we must acknowledge that the problem of what economist Alex Tabarrok calls "sicken-thy-neighbor" trade policy has been real in this crisis.[28] Lots of countries did institute export controls on medical products such as ventilators as a knee-jerk reaction to the pandemic, making health care more difficult and leading to needless deaths worldwide. India restricted exports of paracetamol, for example. Romania banned the export of a critical input to ventilator production. A French requisition order prevented a company fulfilling a facemask contract with the UK health service. The U.S. Federal Emergency Management Agency banned the export of certain facemasks, respirators, respirator parts, and gloves.

Now, there should be obvious incentives that deter countries from going down this path again. If other countries respond to your export bans with their own, we've found out that not only are you likely to not get access to some products you don't produce, but you may also struggle to source inputs for the products you want to produce more of at home. As Tabarrok argues, denying companies the ability to export also disincentivizes them from making big investments to ramp up production at home because there's less profit opportunity that comes from serving a smaller market.

Governments do daft things when the fog of war descends, however. Avoiding a repeat of this sorry episode, though, will not be achieved by trade wars or by declaring that it should be every country for itself, producing for itself. No, the only way this problem can be avoided in the future is through multilateral cooperation on medical supplies and commitments not to use these sorts of export controls, perhaps mediated through a body such as the World Trade Organization or through clauses in trade deals. A protectionist arms race through local content requirements or punitive tariffs on foreign medical imports will make achieving such cooperation more difficult.

It turns out, then, that any tradeoff between national resilience and the efficiency that free trade produces is much, much weaker in theory and practice than Rubio alleges. While it may seem common sense to strive for self-sufficiency after encountering a foreign-born crisis, diverting policy to achieve that will be extremely costly, maybe even undermining our resilience in a number of ways.

ECONOMIC LESSON

Free and open trade makes us richer by facilitating specialization that improves economic efficiency. We see this in our everyday lives, but it is just as true for trade occurring over national borders as it is for trade within a country. In regards to COVID-19, it is increasingly popular to say that the crisis proves the need for more self-sufficiency—that there is a tradeoff between the efficiency that free trade delivers and national resilience. But overt policies to re-shore supply chains risk severely reducing efficiency with no guarantee of actually improving resilience and perhaps even worsening it.

ECONOMIC TERMS INTRODUCED

- **specialization:** the process of an individual or business choosing to focus on a specific task
- **division of labor:** the separation of tasks to allow that specialization
- **free trade:** exchange unhindered by taxes, regulations, or controls; at an international level, trade without tariffs, quotas, or other restrictions
- **comparative advantage:** in international trade, when one country has a relative efficiency advantage in producing a good or service compared to another country (i.e., it can produce the good at a lower opportunity cost)
- **absolute advantage:** in international trade, when one country can produce a good or service more efficiently than another (i.e., it can produce the good at a lower absolute cost)

12

WHY IS THAT GUY IN THE MASK GETTING SO CLOSE?
An introduction to moral hazard

I t was mid-May 2020, six weeks after the District of Columbia had issued its stay-at-home order and a seeming age since the recommendation to stay six feet away from people while outside your home had been issued. I was shopping for groceries on Washington, DC's 14th Street in the vegetable section of a grocery store when another guy got very close to me to grab an onion.

A few seconds later, he did the same for a packet of tomatoes. A minute later in the next aisle, it turned out the pasta he wanted was right next to me too. After the third time he'd invaded my personal space, I reminded him that the six feet distancing guidance was still in place, at least the last time I'd checked.

His response would have made economists laugh. "Yes," he acknowledged, "but now we've been told to wear masks."

In his understanding, facemasks reduced the risk of him getting infected or infecting others with COVID-19. But rather than seeing that as a marginal reduction in risks, on top of social distancing, he thought that meant he could afford to get closer to other people than if he wasn't wearing one. The facemask was considered a substitute to physical distancing for him, in other words, rather than a complement to it.

Economists would have immediately recognized his behavior as an example of the famous *Peltzman effect*. Looking at automobile safety back in 1975, University of Chicago economist Sam Peltzman posited that certain regulations that were intended to improve safety were often undermined by the behavioral change they induced.[1]

It might be, for example, that mandating a large airbag in automobiles makes it less likely that the drivers will be hurt in an accident. But having that extra security may cause them to drive more recklessly than they otherwise would—thus putting others in more danger from collisions. As a result, the regulation may well fail on its own terms of seeking to produce a net improvement in safety outcomes across society. At the very least, the overall direct safety benefits might be reduced a lot by the offsetting impact on people's behavior.

The correct takeaway from Peltzman's work is that, when devising regulatory policies, we have to always remember that we are applying the rules to human beings. Human beings adapt their behavior to the inherent risks of an activity. If a government mandate alters the risks, it alters their behavior. Indeed, Peltzman's thinking can be applied to all sorts of regulations on driving, from anti-lock brakes through to seatbelts or cycling helmets.

Acknowledging these behavioral responses does not necessarily mean that a regulation imposes net costs on society—that it would fail a cost-benefit test. *Freakonomics* author Steven Levitt has provided evidence suggesting that there are large net benefits to mandating seatbelts in cars, for example.[2] But it's important that we consider the potential unintended consequences that the Peltzman effect implies when devising regulatory policy. People who think they are protected from risks might have a propensity to engage in riskier activity.

It's not just in economic regulation that we see this effect. The economist Michael Munger has written extensively about how mandates to wear helmets in the National Football League (NFL) may inadvertently make football less safe. In an article for the *New York Times* in 2017, Munger compared the number of concussions to another high-impact sport, rugby union—which does not require helmets.[3] Despite rugby having a longer match than American football, a more open field, a greater number of players, and more tackles per match, the number of concussions is almost three times higher in the NFL.

Why might this be? Having the safety of a mandated helmet in the NFL appears to mean that football players adjust their play to tackle in ways that otherwise would not be safe for their heads, Munger argues. This paradoxically makes certain forms of injury more likely. It's the Peltzman effect again, but for sports. The safety of the helmet changes players' behavior to make them tackle in more risky ways.

Masking the Truth?

Was the Peltzman effect a meaningful and valid concern when it came to facemasks and COVID-19, as my grocery store encounter suggested? Journalists did worry after some states and stores mandated mask wearing that there were noticeable changes in behavior, including a greater willingness to sit closely in parks and, yes, get closer to others in grocery stores.[4]

Harder evidence suggested an effect too: a Yale study tracking smartphone data appeared to find that as state and local governments mandated mask wearing in public places, Americans governed under those laws spent up to 30 minutes more time per day outside the home, including at stores and restaurants.[5]

That research concluded that "mask orders provide a sense of protection, leading people to substitute face mask wearing for other non-pharmaceutical interventions like avoiding time in public. The net effect of these behaviors on public health outcomes depends on the relative effectiveness of masks and other behaviors in reducing transmission."[6]

Theoretically then, yes, everyone wearing facemasks should lower the risks of transmission of a virus such as SARS-CoV-2, at least if everything else about our behavior remains the same. But everything else may not remain the same. There was a stated fear that the use of facemasks might lead some people to feel invincible and so engage in behaviors that increased the risks of transmitting the virus.[7] Of course, governments, in part, recommended widespread mask wearing precisely because they thought it would mitigate risks and allow people to engage in more activity safely. But there was a risk that people would take this too far, engaging in prolonged indoor contact, touching their faces more often to adjust their masks, or even not fitting their masks properly. If masks got people out and about more often, and these ventures then led people, on the margin, to also engage in other maskless activity, such as indoor dining after an afternoon's shopping, then the overall effect of mask-wearing on disease transmission was ambiguous.

These fears were initially heightened by reviews of existing trials and observational studies of viral respiratory infections that were equivocal about masks being effective when worn community-wide.[8] True, some previous studies on their use during the SARS outbreak had found them to be highly effective, but the overall pre–COVID-19 evidence base was certainly mixed.[9] As a result, some governments took an absence of strong evidence as evidence that masks might not help much for COVID-19, creating confusion over whether they were worth wearing even as a low-cost, low-risk precautionary measure.[10]

It is certainly welcome that policymakers acknowledged the possibility of Peltzman effects in regard to facemasks. But ultimately whether a safety measure brings net benefits or not is an empirical question. Highlighting a behavioral response alone tells us little about the desirability of the measure. In the case of facemasks, the latest best evidence now suggests that authorities' fears were overblown and that their reluctance to provide guidance for people to wear surgical facemasks when indoors in public cost lives. It was a potentially low-cost recommendation, in other words, that could have had large benefits if it had been implemented as guidance earlier.

One economic study in Germany examined the variation in timing of towns and cities adopting mask-wearing mandates in shops and on public transport. It estimated that these policies reduced the growth of daily new cases by as much as 40 percent.[11] Surveys of the population of the USS *Theodore Roosevelt*—an aircraft carrier affected by a major COVID-19 outbreak—similarly found that reports of individuals wearing facemasks appeared to substantially reduce their risk of getting infected.[12] More recently, an economic study that exploited the different timing of indoor mask mandates across the public health regions of Ontario, Canada, found they were associated with a 25 percent fall in COVID-19 cases after a few weeks.[13]

This appears to be corroborated by an anecdote about two Missouri hair stylists who were COVID-19 positive but who did not pass on the virus to 140 clients or 7 coworkers in their salon, which had mandated mask wearing.[14] Increasingly, scientists suspect that airborne indoor transmission may be the dominant means of spreading the virus and that mask wearing could be "the most effective means to prevent interhuman transmission," at least if one must meet only for very short periods of time indoors.[15]

True, none of these results above were from the gold-standard randomized control trials that scientists usually prefer to confirm their intuitions. But the laboratory setting evidence has found surgical facemasks highly effective in preventing the transmission of respiratory droplets, at least. Other studies have found cloth masks partially effective.[16] What's more, statistical evidence examining the impact of facemask mandates across the United States appears to suggest they help reduce daily transmission by 1 to 2 percent.[17] A more recent *Lancet* meta-analysis of observational studies agreed that high-quality masks could be important in reducing virus transmission.[18] Some experts have even speculated that, even if you do catch the virus while wearing a mask, it may reduce the severity of your experience by reducing your viral load. Hence, mask wearing, by reducing the likelihood of your spreading the disease, and the potential severity should you catch it, reduces the virus externality associated with socializing.[19]

Given all of these signals, public health officials' early mixed messages on facemasks appear to have proven, in retrospect, costly to U.S. public health. As mathematician Nassim Nicholas Taleb has written, given that we have strong indicative evidence that masks might help, given that they are a very low-cost measure for the wearer, and given that any benefits compound when all people interacting wear them (mask-wearing is a clear example of the collective action problem we discussed in chapter 2), it's bizarre that public health guidance took so long to at least recommend wearing them. Even if masks only bring a small reduction in risk, the fact that they are so low cost for the wearer suggests that wearing them has potential social benefits that vastly the exceed the social costs.

Yet, as was the case with Anthony Fauci and Surgeon General Jerome Adams, some public health officials actively downplayed the effectiveness of masks early in the pandemic, telling people not to wear them. They have since admitted that these public statements were not primarily about the expected efficacy of face coverings, although at that time public health experts believed that the virus was primarily spread by those exhibiting symptoms, meaning that community-wide face coverings for everyone else was not considered important for disease control. No, Fauci and Adams advised the public not to wear masks because, even though there was a chance they reduced COVID-19 transmission risks, the pair wanted to avoid a surge in demand that they worried might crowd out the availability of masks for health care professionals, who really did need them.[20]

This line of thinking proved a costly mistake, on two levels. In terms of public health, the risks associated with mask wearing were extremely asymmetric in favor of wearing them. Fauci and Adams provided guidance suggesting otherwise, predicated on uncertain science about asymptomatic transmission being unlikely (which now seems incorrect). As such, they likely deterred mask wearing during that period and reduced faith in future public health pronouncements when they then reversed their advice. But more pertinently, the pair wrongly considered mask markets to be zero-sum. They ignored that people could have easily made face coverings at home and that markets would have ramped up production of surgical masks quickly if more people had demanded them. The bad economic reasoning exhibited by these health officials has almost certainly done more to damage compliance with public health advice by undermining its credibility than the impacts of shortages or Peltzman effects. As one *New York Magazine* article headline put it: "People don't trust public-health experts because public-health experts don't trust people."[21]

The culture war politicization of mask wearing after this U-turn ultimately undermined compliance with a relatively low-cost and potentially highly beneficial piece of guidance to wear masks indoors. Eventually rates of self-reported mask wearing in the United States caught up with East Asian countries such as Taiwan. But it took a long time coming and by that stage other behaviors of socializing without them in certain settings were well entrenched.

This does not mean the Peltzman effect identified earlier was not a real concern. Clearly, for the guy in my grocery store, the mandate to wear a mask did lead him to take more risks in terms of social distancing. A lack of guidance on the nature of airborne transmission may have led to many people spending too long socializing indoors while wearing masks, too, increasing exposure. But, with effective information about this, they could surely have helped on the margin.

In fact, masks may well have countervailing behavioral impacts that aid the public health effort. Although the perceived security of wearing a mask may lead an individual to go outside more, other people may see his or her mask as a visible reminder of the pandemic, deterring them from getting too close to the wearer. Indeed, this is precisely the effect Italian computer scientist Massimo Marchiori found in an experiment when he developed a sensor for how close people got to other people who were wearing and not wearing masks.[22]

None of this discussion should be taken as implying that a *government mandate* to wear masks is necessarily preferable to mere guidance, or to social norms developing for voluntary mask wearing. To assess the wisdom of a government mandate, we'd have to take the approach outlined in chapter 6 and compare the marginal benefits and costs of a law above and beyond what could be achieved with less-coercive means, such as recommending that retailers, private residence blocks, and other organizations institute their own policies. Such a marginal analysis would mean assessing how many additional people would wear facemasks if it were mandated as opposed to being guidance and how this would affect transmission of the virus. These benefits would then be weighed against the costs (social and fiscal) of the compulsion, such as the policing of the law, including enforcement of the requirements and penalties for non-compliance.[23] But what does appear clear is that, given the balance of probabilities and the low costs to individuals of wearing masks relative to the potential benefits, especially for indoor activities, a social norm or guidance toward mask-wearing would have been prudent.

What I hope this chapter has shown so far, however, is that by adjusting risks, policy can elicit a behavioral response, which must be taken into consideration when examining policy questions such as whether mask mandates are a good idea. Any potential adverse behavioral impacts that are identified, such as the Peltzman effect, however, must be put into the broader context of the full costs and benefits of the guidance or regulation.

A Passport to Immunity?

A Peltzman effect describes a scenario where a regulation designed to ensure safety induces an increase in risky behaviors. But this is a subset of a broader economic concept known as *moral hazard.*

In economic terms, moral hazard refers to instances where an individual or group has an incentive to engage in riskier behavior because they do not bear the full costs of the risk they are taking, or because others insulate them from the consequences. In the case of the mask wearing, it's because, as we've seen, at least part of the cost of acting irresponsibly will be borne by other people who are at greater risk of the health consequences.

But there are other more obvious examples. Think about how the belief that a government would always bail out a major bank might affect the institution's willingness to engage in a risky high-return activity. Or whether, in the future, airlines would be more or less likely to take out business interruption insurance that covers pandemics, given that the federal government has bailed them out this time.

Another example of a policy idea discussed during this pandemic highlights the concept of moral hazard perhaps better still—the proposal batted around in the early stages for so-called "immunity passports."

The idea was this: someone who had recovered from COVID-19 and whose body contained antibodies exemplified by testing positive in an antibody test would be immune to the virus. Once we had become confident in the accuracy of this form of testing, those with positive results for antibodies could have been given a certificate or passport that allowed them to participate in as ordinary a life as possible, bringing economic benefits to others at no risk.

Now, the potential moral hazard problem here should have been obvious. An immunity passport would have been a potential pathway to an individual's freedom. Its mere existence might have changed the balance of costs and benefits of desirable behavior for many individuals, particularly if the passport meant not having to abide by public health regulations upon receipt.

For those young or lonely people who faced lower mortality risks from the virus, the possibility of the passport would increase their incentive to deliberately contract the disease, recover, and have their life return to some semblance of normality—even more so, given that immune workers would have been highly valued in the labor market.[24]

An immunity passport might therefore have encouraged cavalier behavior or even more occurrences of the otherwise rare COVID-19 infection parties, where attendees tried to catch the disease from those who were infected.[25]

The problem is, because of the externalities highlighted in chapter 2, this type of reaction would have imposed risks and so costs on others. A low-risk person deliberately trying to contract the disease would have risked spreading it to other people who would not have sought infection. If lots of people quickly changed their behavior to win their freedom, then we would have risked more transmission of the virus and possibly the eventual congestion externalities in hospitals discussed earlier too.

If these behavioral reactions to immunity passports really did just affect those making them, such free choices would be good for society. But those who had contracted the virus would be imposing a share of the costs of their risky behaviors on others. This is a clear example of moral hazard.

Putting aside the obvious civil libertarian objections to differentiating what people can do according to their medical history, this particular moral-hazard problem was not insurmountable. As the economist Alex Tabarrok has explained, the government could have eliminated the lion's share of the costs of moral hazard by having government-run centers for a COVID-19 variant of the historic practice of variolation used against smallpox.[26]

These would have been places where those who wanted to get deliberately infected with COVID-19 could have done so in a highly controlled medical environment. If they were contained there for the duration of their infection, the risk of spillovers to others beyond health care professionals would have been minimized, meaning the costs to society of those risk-seekers looking for immunity would have been significantly reduced, while the benefits to the risk-seekers of fulfilling their preferences would have remained. As such, the centers would have enhanced economic welfare.

Moral Hazard, Testing, and Vaccines

As it happens, we never had to have this thorny ethical debate that immunity passports and a COVID-19 version of variolation would have thrown up. Immunity passports turned out to be dead on arrival, not least because provisional research on antibody testing suggests that those who had the virus may only test positive for antibodies for a few months.[27] There have been several reports about people suffering COVID-19 reinfections, too, albeit this is still thought to be rare, suggesting some form of immunity is sustained beyond the time during which antibodies can be identified.[28]

That means the value of antibody tests to determine who is immune and eligible for a passport would have been extremely limited in the longer run. In fact, it turned out that the idea of immunity passports had limited potential benefit even in the early stages of the pandemic.[29] When not many people have had the disease, even an antibody test with a low false positive rate could wrongly inform millions of people that they were immune to the virus. The existence of immunity passports, of course, would have raised the demand for these tests, given that people would have seen them as an opportunity to try to claim their freedom. With huge numbers of people coming forward for tests, these false positives would have risked giving millions of people the confidence to engage in risky behavior, however much policymakers cautioned against it. Immunity passports therefore proved to be an unhelpful idea in practice.

Just because this immunity passport idea has disappeared, however, does not mean that the issue of moral hazard is not important in this pandemic. Immunity passports might have been a particularly acute example, but in truth moral hazard exists whenever there is a big variance in the risks of the virus across demographic groups.

In the case of COVID-19, youth appears to provide a form of security against the worst pain, suffering, and possibilities of death from the disease. Public health interventions mandating social distancing arguably impose much higher costs on the young (by more fundamentally changing their lifestyles) and the financially insecure (by making their work unviable).

This causes two types of moral hazard. Young people have an incentive to engage in insufficient precaution, with the worst costs of the virus being borne by others. Those who are more financially insecure, meanwhile, have an incentive to engage in more risky work behaviors to continue to earn incomes. Again, other more vulnerable groups and health care workers would bear some of the costs of their actions.

The incentives that immunity passports exemplified still exist, then, albeit to a lesser degree. In this case, they would manifest themselves as people failing to engage in sufficient precaution, rather than actively trying to catch the disease. That's one reason why policymakers around the world provided huge income support to those who had lost their jobs or been placed on furlough—to reduce the likelihood of laid-off workers throwing off precautions during lockdowns in order to obtain income.

Widespread infection testing, however, was an alternative policy framework that again had big advantages.[30] If fast and reliable tests had been available early, they would have helped to overcome the moral-hazard problem by going a long way to solving the informational problem of determining who is infected or likely to be contagious.

Rapid and regular tests at an early stage, with quarantine for those testing positive and their relevant contacts, would have alleviated the need for costly lockdowns, as we have seen. Rather than incentivizing people to catch the disease to gain immunity by offering them passports, such a test-and-quarantine regime would have flipped the incentives the other way: now the costs of isolation that would have come with quarantine, relative to going about the "new normal" life, would have been imposed on those infected or meeting with the infected. Although this might create some perverse incentives to try to avoid being tested, such a regime provides an incentive for people to be more cautious about their interactions to avoid risking quarantine.[31]

Although this type of regime would have still required good compliance on testing and quarantining to be effective, this would likely have been achieved more easily than through lockdowns or ongoing regulation, given that quarantine would be a clearly temporary constraint on people's freedoms. If the system had been extremely effective, then it would have also facilitated a far greater normalization of activity.

Another advantage would have been that retained information on those who had tested positive could then have been applied to future contact tracing attempts, avoiding restrictions on those who had already recovered and were highly likely to be immune. Some of the benefits of immunity passports would therefore have remained but without the risks of encouraging people to seek infection or subjecting more people than necessary to the costs of lockdown.

Sadly, as noted earlier, we still have not yet got to a widespread, regular, and rapid testing regime. But it's worth bearing in mind as we begin to think about the next potential moral-hazard problem: vaccines.

In theory, immunization programs can increase individual risk-taking by reducing the likely cost of risky behaviors. Particularly after such long periods of social distancing and being extremely careful about hygiene, a vaccine for COVID-19 may create a sudden desire to be bolder in returning to sporting events and crowded parties, and lead to the reduced wearing of facemasks and less frequent hand washing. We might see a COVID-19 vaccine moral hazard. Indeed, we have sought a vaccination cure to this pandemic precisely so that we can go back to normal.

Now this would not be a problem if there were universal take-up and the vaccine was almost 100 percent effective against the virus. But as previous modeling on flu vaccinations has shown, at low levels of take-up or high failure rates, the benefits of such a vaccine program can actually be outweighed by the costs if moral hazard occurs.[32]

A study of a flu vaccination in Ecuador, for example, found strong evidence of moral hazard effects.[33] If, as some believe, the initial vaccines might not provide full immunity to COVID-19 but instead reduce the symptoms and duration of infection, then we may still need very high compliance rates for vaccine take-up to pass the immunity threshold so that the normalization of behavior that results does not put significant numbers of people who cannot be vaccinated, or whose vaccines were not effective, at risk.

True, it will likely be the case that many of those most willing to receive a novel vaccination early will also be those who engage in more precautionary behaviors anyway. Presumably, they will get vaccinated because they will be worried about the risks to themselves and others of spreading the disease. Evidence on human papillomavirus immunization suggests that women who have been vaccinated against this virus are also more likely to get a Pap test, for example, perhaps because they are just more aware of the risks of the disease.[34]

But it could well be the case that many others, desperate to escape the tedium of the COVID-19 lifestyle, will rush to get any vaccine, precisely to resume normal life. The immunization program will therefore require a clear and accurate information campaign on the vaccine's believed effectiveness, especially against mutations, as well as guidance on how this changes the risks associated with certain activities or behaviors when the vaccination program is ongoing.

Fortunately, early trials of COVID-19 vaccines suggest that their efficacy might be very high indeed. As of December 2020, Pfizer-BioNTech's trials implied that their vaccine had "95% efficacy in preventing COVID-19" and Moderna's vaccine was believed to have a 94.1 percent efficacy in preventing symptomatic COVID-19, both of which are much higher than the 40–50 percent rate associated with most flu vaccines.[35] This means that the balance of risks in regard to the dangers of moral hazard, assuming high take-up, are likely to be more favorable, although for how long this immunity holds and what proportion of the population is willing to be vaccinated remains to be seen.

But policymakers will still have to carefully consider the likely behavioral consequences that will result from people obtaining the shot. If the vaccine only reduces symptoms or is less effective against certain virus mutations, then the vaccines could still create a large moral-hazard problem. Weighing up efficacy and moral hazard concerns will also be important in deciding who should be prioritized to obtain the vaccine until it is widely available. A lot of people will assume that those at the highest personal risk of mortality from the disease should be first in line for the vaccine. But if the vaccine is high efficacy, reduces susceptibility to the virus, and a large number of doses could be administered quickly, it could have conceivably been best for overall economic welfare to vaccinate people who were most likely to transmit the virus to end the pandemic sooner.

Unfortunately, some moral hazard problems have deep roots in the messy world of politics; as we shall see in the next chapter, such problems can be more difficult to solve. The important takeaway here, though, is that regulations, policies, or actions that seek to insulate people from risks can actually encourage risky behavior, sometimes to the detriment of society as a whole. At the very least these behavioral responses may attenuate the benefits of a given policy or action, requiring careful assessment of the policy's overall impact.

ECONOMIC LESSON

Rules and regulations sometimes inadvertently encourage risky behavior by providing individuals with a sense of security or by incentivizing them to change their behavior in a way that imposes costs on others. When designing rules or policies, it's important for policymakers to consider these behavioral responses and the risk of moral hazard. In regard to COVID-19, policymakers have had to grapple with these issues when considering policies on facemasks, immunity passports, and vaccines.

ECONOMIC TERMS INTRODUCED

- **Peltzman effect:** a theory (originally devised in consideration of automobile safety regulation) that people are more likely to engage in risky behavior when safety measures are mandated to reduce the risks to them of an activity
- **moral hazard:** instances where individuals have an incentive to engage in riskier behavior because they will not bear the full costs of that risk

13

WHY DID AIRLINES GET A SPECIAL BAILOUT BUT NOT MY INDUSTRY?

An introduction to public choice economics

The greatest financial bailout of all time is underway. It's 2008 on steroids. Yet where is the outrage? The silence is deafening. Remember the Tea Party and Occupy Wall Street? "Never again" they said in 2008. . . . The federal government just bailed out the airlines—or more precisely airline stockholders, bondholders, unions, airplane leaseholders and other creditors who would lose in bankruptcy.[1]

The quotation above is the opening of a blog post by Hoover Institution economist John Cochrane from April 2020, entitled "Bailout Redux." At the time of the financial crisis and its fallout in 2008 through 2010, economists such as Cochrane warned that one consequence of bailing out ailing companies was precisely the moral hazard problem discussed in the last chapter.[2]

Economists and financiers can quibble about what is or isn't a *bailout*. Some differentiate between grants and loans, because loans have to be repaid. When I discuss bailouts in the policy sphere, I'm referring to any financial assistance from government for distressed companies or industries. This can be explicit, through grants, subsidies, or direct loans from taxpayers. Other times it is implicit, in the form of guarantees from the government, which might enable the companies to borrow more cheaply elsewhere.

Anyway, the point is that firing off taxpayer assistance of one form or another toward banks and automobile companies, free market economists warned, would create the impression that Uncle Sam would step in whenever large businesses suffered from an economy-wide shock. Perversely, that would encourage companies to take greater risks. The expectation of a bailout might lead businesses to load up on more debt ahead of downturns, for example, in turn risking greater financial distress when an unexpected shock did hit. The demand and need for taxpayer support tomorrow risked being driven, in part, by government relief today.

The worry then was that bailouts would deter behaviors that make a business more resilient. *Precautionary savings*—putting aside money to self-insure against uncertainty of future income—would become less likely if businesses expected government efforts to alleviate their distress. So when major private sector bailouts took place again during this pandemic through the $2.2 trillion Coronavirus Aid, Relief, and Economic Security (CARES) Act, just a decade after the financial crash, free market economists could be forgiven for saying, "Hate to say I told you so!" In fact, there have been other forms of bailout in this pandemic occurring through the wizardry of the Federal Reserve, but those are beyond the scope of this book.[3]

What if we are caught in a spiral of moral hazard encouraging more bailouts and then more moral hazard? Unprecedented relief efforts this time around will no doubt alter expectations about what might and should happen when the next "ordinary" recession hits, too, however much policymakers claim, as they did in 2008, that "this time is different." Since no recession has the same causes or consequences as previous ones, people can always claim that this particular crisis is exceptional.

Is This Time Different?

In the Great Recession, the bailout of the financial sector was justified on the grounds that it was systemically important, with the companies being deemed "too big to fail." If banks were allowed to go under, so it was said, the broader economy would suffer, both because of *contagion* to other banks and the reduction of banking services to nonfinancial sectors. In other words, there was believed to be a large negative externality to any major bank's failure—the financial shock would spread to other industries.

The financial crisis, it was therefore believed, was not a normal recession—the term economists use to describe a significant downturn in economic activity across the economy.[4] Usually a downturn might accelerate some *creative destruction*—a term coined by economist Joseph Schumpeter to describe the "process of industrial mutation that incessantly revolutionizes the economic structure from within, incessantly destroying the old one, incessantly creating a new one."[5] But a full-blown financial meltdown threatened to pull down viable businesses, too, not least through the mechanism of bank failures begetting more bank failures and so bringing a freeze in the availability of credit. Hence, the government supposedly had to step in to stem the contagion.

It's beyond the ambitions of this book to fully critique that view. My colleague Jeffrey Miron has written a compelling case against the financial sector bailouts, arguing that managed bankruptcy would have been preferable from both a distributional and economic efficiency perspective.[6] He believes that evidence for the sort of externality effects that policymakers claimed were present was weak.

What's more, the bailouts and the resulting view of government as a savior shifted focus away from an obvious truth: government policies themselves were a key cause of that crisis. The Great Recession was not some *exogenous* shock—the result of some outside force hitting the economy. It was *endogenous*—a product of policies and behavior within the economy itself.

In that way, this year's pandemic-induced downturn really is exceptional. Yes, governments made mistakes, both before and after the virus hit. As earlier chapters on testing (9) and the lack of marginal thinking in regard to lockdowns (6) showed, policy errors worsened both the death toll and the economic consequences of this crisis. But the ultimate source of the disruption—the virus—was still akin to an act of God. It clearly was an exogenous shock.

The justifications for bailouts this time were therefore somewhat different. Rather than certain companies' failures threatening broader negative externalities, this time financial assistance to businesses got justified as a form of emergency insurance to keep them afloat because of the manifestation of a risk they couldn't have foreseen. There was barely a pandemic insurance market for businesses to have tapped into prior to the virus hitting. Even if there had been, as UK economist Jonathan Portes put it, "it's hardly reasonable to suggest that your local Thai restaurant should have made a business plan that took into account the risk of a three month pandemic-induced shutdown."[7]

Governments were ordering businesses closed too. The pandemic was affecting whole sectors, with scant regard to which were "good" and "bad" businesses in regard their viability once the virus passed. So this time, plenty of economists across the spectrum argued for more extensive financial support across the private sector and, in particular, to businesses shuttered by government mandates. Even libertarian commentator Megan McArdle wrote a column entitled "A Libertarian's Unlikely Pandemic Plea: Subsidize Everything."[8]

The basic idea behind this sentiment, which ultimately resulted in the $2.2 trillion CARES Act, was that the welfare of society as a whole demanded we pause activity across major sectors for public health reasons. To encourage this, governments needed to insulate households and businesses from suffering during this pause and ensure there were businesses to go back to when things were restarted. Although throwing taxpayer cash at households and businesses would inevitably keep some businesses alive that would be unviable in any future upswing, this risk was deemed preferable to risking vast numbers of otherwise viable companies going under, and the costly process of rebuilding companies from scratch.

The potential loss of businesses—these unique bundles of contracts, employment relationships, and supply chains—would, many economists wagered, drag on economic well-being for some time if no relief packages were forthcoming. In fact, when asked whether *additional* federal spending, structured the same as the CARES Act, would be less costly to the economy than not doing more, 60 percent of the expert

Initiative on Global Markets (IGM) Forum panel of top economists agreed that more funds would "avoid long-term economic damage and promote a stronger recovery."[9] Just 2 percent disagreed, with 38 percent uncertain.

Now I have significant reservations about the measures that seek to preserve the economy in its March 2020 form as a route to recovery, as will be discussed in chapter 16. In those days, a lot of economists appeared to think this was just a pause in activity for a few months, rather than disruption for a year or more. For me, the signals that come from free activity—prices, profits, and losses—are the best way to allocate resources, especially coming out of crises, when we have no idea how such a profound shock will affect preferences and working habits. We want to make sure that economic actors adjust to new realities quickly, which is one reason why we must remove the regulatory impediments to that adjustment, as detailed at length in chapter 9. As it happens, it now seems likely there will be significant changes to people's consumption habits and the way businesses operate even beyond the pandemic, the length of which is determined by how quickly companies are able to manufacture and distribute the vaccines.

But one noteworthy detail in the responses of economists to that IGM survey was just how many thought the initial CARES Act was not particularly well-targeted to protect against business failure. In fact, one criticism across the political spectrum was that the initial balance of funds was too heavily weighted to large companies rather than small businesses, who, at least initially, found themselves having to compete for a relatively small $349 billion pot (relative to the downturn) dubbed the "Paycheck Protection Program."

Coming back to the John Cochrane quotation at the start, this raises an obvious question: At a time when there was demand for huge bailouts everywhere, why did the passenger airline industry receive a special, industry-specific bailout from Congress, while small businesses similarly affected by the pandemic in the leisure, hospitality, restaurant, and retail sectors had to scramble over each other applying for the Paycheck Protection Program? What made airlines so different or deserving?

Why the Airlines?

The passenger airline industry was initially allocated $25 billion in direct financial assistance (notionally to support payrolls for six months) and a further $25 billion in loans. True, after negotiations with the Trump administration, 30 percent of the direct financial assistance was subsequently converted to loans to be repaid over 10 years. There were conditions as well, such as having to maintain staffing levels for six months, a mandate to continue running the scaled-back services they'd instituted by that time, and the federal government being given a right to purchase shares in the companies at a set price at a later date.

But ultimately, the industry got a huge, distinct financial package on the scale that it was demanding. Although the federal government can argue that it was just supporting jobs, any bailout of this kind was relaxing the financial pressure on the businesses. As Cochrane stated, this is akin to bailing out the "airline stockholders, bondholders, unions, airplane leaseholders and other creditors who would lose in bankruptcy."[10]

So what explains why the airlines were thought worthy of their own special package? The answer might be found in what's known as *public choice* analysis.[11]

Public choice applies the methods of economics to the theory and practice of government. It analyzes political players and problems in the same way that we consider behavior in markets. Rather than assuming that benevolent social planners determine political decisions to enhance the welfare of society as a whole, public choice analysis examines the role of incentives and the pursuit of self-interested goals, not least those of politicians and interest groups, in shaping collective choices through politics.

The economic method applied to politics is particularly interesting, because unlike in most private sector transactions, the people enjoying the benefits of a political decision are not usually those who bear its costs.

When we start to apply public choice reasoning to the airlines question, we find there are good economic reasons why the industry might have found that obtaining a bailout from politicians was much easier than it was for other sectors. In many ways, airlines represent the perfect lobby group to obtain special treatment from government.

Now, if you really were a disinterested social planner, there is not much *economically* special about the airline industry that makes it obvious that it should be at the front of the line for government assistance. Yes, airlines were struggling with travel bans, other countries' quarantine policies, and, of course, the reluctance of customers to fly in the presence of the virus. With new bookings cratering, high levels of debt, certain fixed costs of operating, and the need to dish out refunds for canceled flights, it was understandable that airlines would be plunged into financial trouble without support.

But as a *Boston Globe* editorial pointed out, other American businesses and industries were suffering similarly, from casinos and coffee shops through to water-rafting businesses and wellness centers.[12] In fact, lots of these did not enjoy the boom years prior to the pandemic that airlines did. And other sectors had far less reason to be aware of the risks of full-scale business interruptions from a global shock like a pandemic than the passenger airline sector.

If the aim of government is to support viable businesses to bridge to a world after social distancing, other sectors might have looked more viable than airlines. Behavioral change and worry about the spread of viruses might depress demand for flights for some time, particularly as the pandemic smolders on around the world. We don't yet know either whether the greater use of internet-based communications for business meetings and conferences during lockdowns will stick, thus lowering demand for business flights permanently.

Nor could we argue that the most likely alternative path—bankruptcy of individual airlines—posed a systemic risk to the economy, as was claimed with financial sector bailouts in the Great Recession. In fact, as the Mercatus Center's Veronique de Rugy and Gary Leff have explained, major airlines have gone through bankruptcy procedures before and lived to fight another day.[13]

While the bankruptcy of any given company would certainly have spillovers into downstream businesses, these effects would have been similar to the sorts of knock-on effects likely felt in other sectors.

At an aggregate level, the bankruptcy or even liquidation of any given airline business, while bringing near-term pain, would not mean pilot skills or planes being lost. Other sectors, say live entertainment or design teams, might suffer catastrophic productivity losses if relationships among employees are lost forever. But the planes and worker know-how in the airline sector would still be available for new entrants to buy up when air travel is viable again.

So what explains why politicians decided to prioritize bailing out airlines? To understand this, we need to think both about the features of the industry and the political interests at play.

The Demand for an Airline Bailout

There are good reasons to believe the airline sector might be a particularly effective lobbying force in these circumstances. First is the sheer size of the companies and so the stakeholder power that the industry can harness—that is, the wide reach of people affected by its prospects.

In theory, the size of the companies should make bailouts to the industry less necessary than for small businesses, given that major airlines have much better access to capital and equity markets, which are well-placed to judge their ongoing viability. The experience with major players in the sector going through bankruptcy procedures, too, points to a presumption that bailouts should not be needed.

Yet, in public choice terms, the size of the industry matters to the possibility of getting a bailout, even if the sector's difficulties do not pose a systemic risk. Politicians do not have time to meet every small business and industry trade body to hear their pitch for funds. But very large companies, especially in industries dominated by a small number of players, are much more likely to get an audience with members of Congress and other government officials.

A second, related, feature is the concentration of the industry. According to a preliminary *Forbes* analysis soon after negotiations with the Trump administration were complete, 75 percent of the payroll funds would be going to just four firms—American Airlines, Delta, United, and Southwest.[14]

Ramping up coordinated lobbying efforts and mobilizing to overcome a *collective action problem* (situations where individual businesses would be better off cooperating but have incentives not to) is much more straightforward with a limited number of major players, such as this, than in other sectors with more disparate concentrations. (Note that forming this combination of firms to lobby for favors isn't economically optimal for society. In this case, the collective action problem merely refers to maximizing the interests of the airlines in question through their combined activity.)

Third, we have the nature of the shock. All these airlines operate across the whole of the United States, so they will be affected by the downturns in demand for air travel and ongoing pandemic-related policies, such as lockdowns and state-level quarantines.

They have a much clearer collective interest than, say, the hotel industry or retailers. These sectors might be similarly affected in aggregate. But many individual businesses operate locally, facing different local policies and conditions through the pandemic. Some will be able to reorientate their customer base or what activities they engage in; others will see opportunities to take business away from competitors in other states. In the airline sector, in other words, the nature of the shock is much more common—again, a reason that helps overcome the collective action problem.

Finally, the industry already had a major lobbying operation and there was a clear economic incentive to expand it when the crisis hit. According to Statista, air transport was already the ninth-largest industry by lobbying expenditures in 2019.[15] The website OpenSecrets estimates that this broader industry spent $106.4 million on lobbying that year, with 70 percent of the lobbyists being former government employees.[16] Airlines themselves spent $24.5 million on lobbying in 2019 but had an even larger proportion of lobbyists (83 percent) who were "revolvers"—people that had previously worked in Congress or the executive branch.[17]

Interestingly, analysis from the Center for Responsive Politics for the 2018 election cycle shows that players in the airline industry made campaign contributions to individuals and through political action committees right across the aisle.[18] The two biggest recipients of funds from the industry as Senate candidates were Republicans Ted Cruz and Beto O'Rourke, who were running against each other in Texas.

Academic research suggests these campaign contributions and longer-term lobbying efforts matter. Analysis by economist Salvatore Nunnari has suggested that campaign contributions from the Big Three automakers (Ford, Fiat Chrysler, and General Motors) made House members more likely to favor the 2008 bailout of auto companies.[19] Another paper by political economist Michael Dorsch found that campaign contributions from banks positively affected the likelihood that a member of Congress would vote for the bank bailout.[20]

None of this would surprise the late economist Gordon Tullock. He documented how it was rational for companies to spend money on lobbying if their efforts led to them capturing privileges from lawmakers that brought net gains above the costs of the lobbying.[21] But this *rent seeking*—the attempt to capture economic payoffs through politics— was wasteful at a societal level. Perhaps the one positive from recognizing this is that, given the potentially huge payoffs across industries to securing such privileges, companies do less of it than we might expect.

In the case of airlines, the structure and size of the industry made ramping up and coordinating lobbying efforts easier when the crisis did hit. *Roll Call* has documented how many airlines increased their lobbying expenditure in the first quarter of the year.[22] Quickly, the 11 major companies got together to sign an open letter to lawmakers on March 21, talking up the urgent need for the bailout for the "750,000 airline professionals and our nation's airlines."[23] As the pandemic rolled on, and with the grants expiring, airlines lobbied for another bailout and seem to have been rewarded. In late December 2020, Congress passed another stimulus bill containing a further $15 billion for passenger air carriers.

The Supply of an Airline Bailout

But so far we've only explained the airlines' demand for funds. This side of the public choice equation doesn't explain the supply of funds—that is, why politicians were willing to provide them.

Some governments around the world, most famously former prime minister John Howard's Australian government, have previously resisted calls to assist major airlines. The particular features of the airline industry may improve the chances of successful lobbying for funds, but they do not guarantee it. We also have to account for the preferences and interests of politicians themselves, who are primarily in the market for votes and delivering for their supporters.

Doctoral research has shown how, historically, free market conservative politicians are less likely to deliver bailouts.[24] Election years often reduce the incentive for politicians to engage in them, too, because of the blowback that comes if voters perceive that a politician is giving favors to special interests. A poll of Americans before the bailout found a plurality of American voters opposed to one.[25] Post-bailout, airlines saw the biggest decline of any industry in public approval compared with the start of the pandemic.[26]

So what explains why politicians were willing to bailout airlines—something for which there was overall public opposition?

The first explanation is the idea that the bailout had concentrated benefits and diffuse costs. Politicians are in the market for votes and 2020 was an election year. The vast majority of the 750,000 airline workers' jobs that the companies suggested were at risk if no bailout was forthcoming are voters too. For these workers and others in downstream industries who felt their livelihoods were dependent on the bailout, opposition to the assistance by either of the major parties could have swung how they voted.

Although the broader public opposed the bailouts, it is unlikely, with everything else going on, that this would be at the forefront of their minds in influencing their voting decision. In electoral terms, then, there was a strong incentive for politicians to back the bailout. Those workers benefiting from it could be appeased, while the costs would be broadly spread across taxpayers for whom (as voters) the issue was of limited importance. On balance, it likely had an overwhelming electoral upside.

A second potential explanation is that the airlines presented their demand for support in language that appealed to both political parties' current philosophies—giving each a "win."

The Republican party at the time, led by Trump, had broken with free-market orthodoxy and seemed less concerned with the downsides of special interest favoritism. Instead, it appeared more interested in economic nationalism and returning whole industry supply chains to the United States. The appeal from the industry to support our nation's airlines was not a coincidence—they were seeking to chime with the new ideology of the right. Of course, Boeing, the major supplier of planes, is the closest thing the United States has to a national champion.

The airlines' pitch for funds was carefully tailored to suit the sensibilities of today's Democratic party too. The industry body worked with unions to emphasize that the funds would be used to support payroll and workers directly—a deliberate strategy.[27] Left-of-center politicians will always be sensitive to the prospect of large job losses in the short term if bankruptcy goes ahead, particularly if their union allies support the terms of the deal.

The airlines also promised to not pay out to shareholders or buyback stock over the lifetime of any loans and to avoid increasing compensation of executives if they borrowed funds. Again, these could be chalked up as ideological wins for left-of-center critics of major corporations. Given the bailout arose in a package with other progressive wins, such as checks to most families and a huge increase in the generosity of unemployment insurance, politicians were also less likely to face blowback about this being an extraordinary payout to special interests.

Third, and finally, the outlook for airlines was perhaps more salient for politicians personally than the fortunes of other sectors. Not only do many politicians themselves fly extensively, often between their constituencies and Washington, DC, but the failure of an airline could potentially have generated secondary local impacts from what would have been a huge national story.

Most congressional seats could have been threatened with a critical flight route facing the chop if the airlines entered bankruptcy. And the concentrated hubs of activity in Texas, California, Georgia, and Illinois would have meant a huge observable loss of jobs and investment in influential states. Although other industries crushed by COVID-19 have larger workforces overall, and perhaps a better claim to require support, this combination of very concentrated hubs and dispersed links means that airline failure could have brought larger political costs for incumbent politicians.

If You Bring Out the Buffet . . .

Airlines got funds quickly, while other businesses struggled, in other words, because of these dynamics of political economy. Not only did the size and composition of the industry give airlines a seat at the table with national politicians and lessen the industry-level costs of lobbying efforts, but the ideological and electoral interests of policymakers aligned with the companies' near-term goals.

Even when it came to the broader Paycheck Protection Program for smaller businesses, however, which was administered by banks, economic analysis has found that because of larger businesses' greater ability to access information and the first-come, first-served approach of the program, payouts were skewed toward relatively bigger companies.[28]

Although very small companies were less aware of the program and so less likely to apply in the first place, even when they did they faced longer processing times and higher rejection rates for funds—probably because banks were more likely to approve relatively larger businesses with whom they had relationships already. And this matters in distorting competition: studies found that the program meaningfully changed a company's likelihood of survival and expectations of future performance.[29]

When governments dish out subsidies or advantages, it's invariably bigger interests that find it easiest to benefit. Unfortunately, decisions get made this way through the political process fairly often, even in normal times. Well-connected large firms with big Washington, DC, lobbying capabilities will always be more likely to get privileges from lawmakers, even if they do not make economic sense. Meanwhile, politicians have incentives to engage in *crony capitalism*—working with certain businesses to help their constituents or supporters and so enhancing their electoral prospects.

The biggest losers when decisions do get made in this way are taxpayers. Taxpayers' interests are more diverse and so difficult to represent in a strong political voice. While those who benefit from government largesse or privilege become assiduous defenders of their prioritization, taxpayers may not notice the relatively small uplift in their lifetime taxes to pay for these programs, or the slightly less efficient economy, or indeed that they pay marginally more as consumers to fund companies' lobbying costs. Other industries, too, may not ever realize that government support for certain sectors makes life marginally more difficult for them in hiring workers or attracting capital. This, again, is another example of the concentrated benefits and diffuse costs problem.

Rather than a free market, where companies invest in the best products or services to attract customers, financial buffets such as the CARES Act grant opportunities for rent seeking and actively encourage companies to invest in lobbyists to extract their share of the assistance. As my colleague David Boaz wrote upon reading of an increase in lobbying activity before the emergency pandemic relief package, "When you lay out a picnic, you get ants. When you lay out taxpayers' dollars, you get lobbyists."[30]

We can debate whether, in this emergency scenario, it was wise to care less about these rent-seeking distortions, as well as the problem of moral hazard, given that the alternative might have been widespread bankruptcies induced by lockdowns and the virus. A lot of economists seem to believe so. In the case of the Paycheck Protection Program, for example, the decision to operate the scheme through banks might have been made because it allowed a more rapid dispersal of funds.

But libertarian economists would argue that we should at least strictly limit the size and scope of government's role in the economy in ordinary times. Perhaps if the government had a smaller footprint in economic life, the payoff to lobbying and cronyism would be that much smaller. In that world, we would get far less cronyism and its destructive consequences.

Cronyism and rent-seeking behavior, however, are not the only problems arising from the politicization of economic decisionmaking. Often policymakers just take insufficient account of basic economic considerations, such as the role of incentives in changing behavior.

ECONOMIC LESSON

Political decisions are not made by benevolent social planners attempting to maximize social welfare. They are shaped in part by incentives and the political or electoral goals of politicians and interest groups, just as private sector activities are driven by the interests and incentives faced by businesses and customers. Businesses weigh up decisions to invest in political lobbying or rent-seeking behavior by comparing the cost against the likely returns, with some industries better suited to these efforts than others. Politicians' actions in office are influenced by their own electoral and ideological concerns. When it comes to COVID-19, the priority for lawmakers in dishing out a tailored bailout for airlines highlights the role of these sorts of public choice considerations in political decisionmaking.

ECONOMIC TERMS INTRODUCED

- **bailout:** government actions, with recourse to taxpayer funds or guarantees, that aim to help a distressed industry or company survive
- **precautionary savings:** saving that occurs as protection against uncertainty in regard to future income
- **creative destruction:** the process within a capitalist economy of new companies or ideas cannibalizing existing industries by producing new products, services, or ways of operating that improve efficiency or better meet consumers' demands

- **exogenous shock:** an event or development coming from outside of the economic system itself, such as a war, natural disaster, or virus
- **endogenous shock:** an event or development coming from within the economic system itself, such as a financial crisis caused by bad policy or a period of overexuberance
- **public choice economics:** the application of the methods of economics to the theory and practice of politics and government
- **rent seeking:** the practice of businesses or individuals seeking to manipulate the social and political environment to obtain returns without producing new wealth, including lobbying for special privileges
- **crony capitalism:** an economic system where business success is determined not by providing value to customers but by having close relationships to government

14

WHY DIDN'T MY WORKERS WANT TO BE REHIRED?
An introduction to incentives

Spa owner Jamie Black-Lewis was not expecting that reaction from her workers. Back in April 2020, the businesswoman had applied for loans from the federal government's Paycheck Protection Program (PPP) to help her cover the costs of running two spas in Washington State.

Faced with the virus and the state's order to close so-called nonessential businesses, her company was facing financial ruin. She had had to suspend pay for her 35 employees and was relying on this government loan (that potentially became a grant) to help cover payroll costs.

So, she was relieved to eventually hear that she had been granted the funds. Yet when Black-Lewis told her staff the supposed good news, CNBC reports her claiming that she faced a "firestorm of hatred."[1]

The reason was simple: *financial incentives*. Some of her employees had realized that they would be financially better off, at least in the short term, receiving emergency pandemic-related unemployment insurance payments rather than remaining on her company's payroll. Perversely, they were disappointed that her business obtaining the PPP loans meant that they would keep their jobs.

No doubt most of these workers valued the greater likelihood of se-cure employment in the longer term. But the immediate consequence of the financial reprieve for the company was to make the would-be laid-off employees worse off in terms of dollars and cents. That is what explained their anger and disappointment. People care about their ma-terial well-being—which is only to say that financial incentives matter.

When Federal Programs Collide

In fact, this particular tension between employer and employee was a direct consequence of financial incentives instituted by two different emergency congressional policies. With a tidal wave of economic de-struction caused by social distancing and lockdowns, policymakers were trying to get money out the door as quickly as possible to provide relief for households and businesses. The result was the massive $2.2 trillion Coronavirus Aid, Relief, and Economic Security (CARES) Act, which was signed into law at the end of March 2020.

Lawmakers wanted dollars to flow rapidly to businesses through loans and payroll support and to households through checks and more gener-ous unemployment insurance benefits. Given that time was perceived to be of the essence in ensuring this relief did not leave gaping holes in family and business budgets, thus risking broader defaults, the provisions of this large stimulus bill were put together much more quickly than usual.

The changes to unemployment insurance, in particular, were huge. The act included provisions that waived job-search requirements and massively expanded eligibility, including to the self-employed.

Crucially, in order to ensure that nobody earning average wages was made worse off as a result of the pandemic and to circumvent admin-istrative problems in state unemployment systems, Congress agreed to just pay anybody eligible for unemployment benefits $600 more per week for up to four months, in addition to any state unemployment benefits they might ordinarily have been able to access.

The impact was a huge financial payoff to being unemployed. Whereas traditionally unemployment benefits replaced about 30 to 50 percent of a worker's wages (varying by state), University of Chicago economists' revised estimates suggested that these higher benefits replaced 145 percent of previous wages for the median recipient.[2] In fact, a full 76 percent of those eligible for the program could receive more in unemployment benefits than from their previous earnings, with a typical worker in the bottom fifth of the income distribution likely to receive double their prior work earnings.

To show the scale of the changes, a low-income worker in Massachusetts previously earning $535 per week faced a pre-pandemic replacement rate of unemployment insurance benefits to earnings of 48 percent ($257). Yet during this period of pandemic unemployment insurance, the same worker would obtain benefits worth 160 percent of their pre-recession earnings ($857). In New Mexico, someone in the same relative position in the income scale previously earning $342 per week pre-pandemic would see a replacement rate of 229 percent from the expanded benefits ($783).

Given that we'd usually expect market wages for new hires to fall in industries ravaged by huge downturns in demand, these unemployment benefits as a proportion of *potential earnings* in employment (the true measure of the incentive to work) would likely have been higher still for many unemployed people, as the Congressional Budget Office has indicated.[3]

There was therefore an extremely strong short-term financial incentive for workers to prefer to remain unemployed or take longer to search for work while these benefits existed. That financial incentive was especially strong when you consider that laid-off workers were often obtaining higher incomes than those having to physically go into their businesses as janitors or food-service workers—jobs with an elevated risk of contracting COVID-19.

On the margin then, the unemployment insurance was providing an incentive both not to take up any new available job vacancies and to resist being kept on or rehired. It explains the disgruntlement Black-Lewis heard.

Now think about the financial incentives Black-Lewis herself faced. At the time, her federally guaranteed loans under the Paycheck Protection Program would be forgiven only if her business avoided cuts to headcount and wages by June 30. Meanwhile, 75 percent of the loan her business received had to be spent on payroll costs over eight weeks. Her company then had a very strong incentive to rehire or retain workers it would have otherwise have laid off or furloughed to ensure that the loan got written off and became a grant. The financial incentives embedded within the PPP were designed to encourage employee retention—to "save jobs," which is what politicians usually like to say that they are doing.

The financial incentives from the two programs were therefore working directly against each other. The PPP loans were incentivizing re-hiring or payroll retention. The unemployment insurance benefits were incentivizing unemployment. And if there's one thing economists have drummed into them, it's this: incentives matter.

Some employees no doubt would have looked through the temporary disruption and prized the longer-term job security of their company living to fight another day thanks to the loans. Some employers who were were confident of a return to robust business post-lockdowns may well have similarly decided that it was better for staffing relations to look out for their workers' financial interest, allowing them to obtain the unemployment insurance.

But on the margin, these financial incentives will have changed the preferred behavior of employers and employees in conflicting ways, especially because, with the chaos of the pandemic, the safeguards that are supposed to prevent voluntary unemployment or gaming had been relaxed.

The CARES Act, for example, loosened eligibility for this unemployment insurance expansion, confirming that it would cover those who provided self-certification that their employment situation had been altered for COVID-19 related reasons. Meanwhile, although in theory employers could have reported former employees who refused to be rehired, thus ending their eligibility for unemployment benefits, there were big risks to companies of using this nuclear option. Not only were there big gray areas, with employees being able to argue that their role had changed drastically owing to the pandemic, but struggling employers would also have found it difficult to find willing replacement workers at the old wage rate given the generosity of the unemployment benefits, making bridge-burning with formerly valuable employees risky.

It's little surprise, then, that at the same time we read both stories about employees urging their employers to lay them off, as well as tales of businesses finding it difficult to rehire workers.[4] Financial incentives mattered in producing conflict between employers and employees.

Short-term versus Long-term Incentives

Just because short-term financial incentives matter does not mean they alone explain economic outcomes, of course. Nobody believes that the unprecedented spike we saw in unemployment was *caused* by the increase in generosity of unemployment insurance benefits, for example. The initial sharp downturn in activity, as outlined through chapters 3 and 5, was overwhelmingly due to a steep decline in social spending as behavior changed, worsened by the lockdowns.

In fact, the unemployment benefits were introduced, in part, to stop this downturn chilling demand across other sectors if unemployed workers cut their spending sharply after being laid off. Much of the economy was locked down or highly regulated then anyway, so there were relatively few new job opportunities, at least initially. The net impact of the extended unemployment benefits on jobs and GDP therefore depended on how the expanding benefits impacted demand for other products and services, not just the impact on people's willingness to supply their own labor. The balance of these two effects would no doubt change over time—the former dominating in lockdown but getting weaker over time.

Economists therefore became involved in a heated debate about whether the expanded benefits held back the jobs recovery in mid-May and June, after the lockdowns were first lifted. This was an important discussion, because the expanded benefits expired on July 31, and Congress had to decide what to replace them with, if anything. The labor market conditions in the second half of 2020 were expected to be very different than they were during the lockdown period.

Some initial studies assessed whether states where the expanded benefits were relatively higher compared to previous wages saw slower employment growth in May and June than states with smaller uplifts. They found little evidence to suggest so.[5] Supporters of the expanded unemployment payments jumped on these findings to say that the expanded benefits were not having the deleterious impacts on employment that the financial incentives would suggest. This was cause, they claimed, to extend the benefits until at least the end of 2020.

But this sort of aggregate analysis potentially hid more than it revealed for the purposes of formulating policy. It could be, for example, that particular industries were finding it difficult to attract low-wage workers across all states given how generous the benefits were, but this was being hidden by simple comparisons between states.

Evidence from the *Beige Book* of the Federal Reserve (a summary of commentary on current economic conditions) for August did report disincentive effects, even after the initial $600 per week benefits had expired and were replaced for four to five weeks by a $400 per week supplement through a presidential executive order. The Federal Reserve's national summary for August stated: "Firms continued to experience difficulty finding necessary labor, a matter compounded by day care availability, as well as uncertainty over the coming school year and jobless benefits."[6]

Regional Federal Reserve Banks reported more evidence from their contacts that the elevated unemployment benefits undermined work incentives. The Federal Reserve Bank of Boston said "The majority of contacts reported difficulty finding candidates who were willing to work, especially for pay rates that might be lower than pandemic-augmented unemployment benefits."[7]

The Federal Reserve Bank of Atlanta highlighted the particular impact on low-wage employment, saying "Among those hiring, most indicated that the pool of available workers was ample, although there were reports that unemployment insurance benefits continued to present challenges attracting low-wage workers."[8] Similar concerns about the impacts of the unemployment benefits on these groups were expressed in the reports of the Federal Reserve Banks of Richmond and Chicago.

After the $600 benefits expired on July 31, the Federal Reserve Bank of New York's explained that "Some businesses have noted less trouble bringing back furloughed workers and hiring new ones in recent weeks, as unemployment benefits were scaled back."[9] This supports the idea that the previously higher unemployment benefits were reducing employment levels. The Federal Reserve Bank of Philadelphia echoed that sentiment about the falling benefits easing pressure on employers.

Is there a way to square the circle of these reports with the state evidence and the fairly robust bounce-back in employment in April through July, when elevated unemployment benefits were still in effect?

One obvious explanation is that although some laid-off workers would have sought to pocket the wage-busting benefits for June and July, many would have been more forward-looking. Without the knowledge that Trump would ultimately extend benefits at a lower level by executive order, many unemployed folk faced a risky decision at some stage in June and July: take the security of an immediate job, or gamble on high benefits that were only guaranteed for a month or so.

Many of those unemployed would have been aware that benefits were set to expire on July 31, with the possibility that they would not be replaced. If the option in rejecting returns to employment was perceived as receipt of 140–220 percent of past earnings in unemployment benefits for July but then falling to 30–50 percent of previous earnings while facing the uncertainty of unemployment, it's perhaps unsurprising that many accepted recalls or took up new roles.[10] Even for those unemployed in August, Trump's supplement only came with guaranteed funding for four to five weeks.

In fact, I heard precisely this story on a trip to a hotel on the West Virginia border in August. One worker told me that he simply ignored his employers' calls by turning his phone off for several weeks in May and June, such was the uplift in his income on pandemic-related unemployment insurance benefits. He ultimately decided to take up the offer to return after this time because he recognized the threat that the expanded benefits might expire.

A very large component of the fall in employment over these months was the return to work of people who were temporarily laid off or furloughed. We'd imagine the financial incentive effect would have been weaker for this group, given that the Department of Labor made clear that workers must accept recalls from their former bosses or face being stripped of benefits.

A second explanation for what we saw is that employers changed their behaviors based around expectations of what unemployed workers would do. The expanded unemployment insurance did reduce job applications from affected workers.[11] The sentiment from businesses that was expressed in the Federal Reserve reports may have reflected that they were unable to find workers at the pay rates they thought reasonable and so gave up.[12]

Indeed, if companies perceived that they would have difficulty filling some low-wage roles, they may not have even advertised for them, waiting until it looked as if benefits were set to expire before advertising those roles. Trade associations and regional commerce institutions were widely quoted in the press as saying that it was extremely difficult to find people at $11 to $13 hourly pay rates before July.[13] Honda asked its office employees to work on assembly lines because they found it difficult to hire temporary workers to run its plant in Ohio.[14] So businesses may simply have stopped looking for certain types of labor across many sectors in the early months of the expanded benefits, explaining why differences across states were so small.

If these sorts of effects are in any way generalizable, then the advocates of extending the $600 benefits beyond July may have had it backward. The early jobs bounce-back would, in very small part, reflect the expectation of expanded unemployment benefits ending, rather than the absence of a financial disincentive. If the benefits had been extended at that high level through the end of the year, unemployed workers might have reacted as if they were more permanent and we'd have heard louder complaints about worker shortages as outlined in the *Beige Book*.

In any case, the debate here not need have been all or nothing. Nor is what happened before always a good guide to how to set policy in the future.[15] Remember what we said in chapter 6? Good economics happens on the margin.

Economists Kurt Mitman and Stanislav Rabinovich examined how unemployment insurance benefits might optimally change over time. They found that although the $600 uplift may have been good policy during lockdowns, extending it through the second half of 2020 when fuller reopenings had occurred would hurt the recovery and economic welfare.[16]

A good economist then would have recognized that finding a balance between maintaining financial incentives and avoiding huge crashes in income for unemployed households was important in that nascent recovery. Abolishing the expanded benefits entirely would really have caused big sudden drops in income for millions of people. But, likewise, it's not clear why $600 per week is thought to be some magical figure. The marginal benefit of moving from $400 to $600 per week in terms of additional unemployment payments to maintain consumer spending power is much smaller than the uplift from $0 to $200 but a lot more costly in terms of the financial incentive effect. When the $600 unemployment benefits expired there was little evidence of a major decline in overall consumer spending, suggesting that those payments allowed people to accumulate a large buildup of savings that were then drawn down afterward. Of course, this undermines the idea that the $600 benefits had a big stimulus effect in those initial months.

Some economists proposed a pathway to lowering the benefits over the second half of 2020 but with reductions in their generosity triggered by improvements in the labor market situation at the state level.

The problem with this idea, though, was one we encountered in chapter 8. If high unemployment benefits really do cause elevated unemployment levels, then linking those benefit levels to unemployment rates is silly. High benefits would keep unemployment high, which, in turn, will incentivize the continuation of high unemployment benefits. To a certain extent, we would risk getting caught in an endogeneity doom loop, as George Washington University economist Steven Hamilton has called it, thus slowing the recovery.[17]

Ultimately, of course, Trump intervened with an initial executive order that provided (for four to five weeks) funds for $300 per week in additional federal payments to those unemployed workers receiving at least $100 in unemployment benefits from their state. This reduced the disincentive effect of the previous $600 regime, while not crashing incomes as abruptly as abolishing expanded benefits entirely would have done. As of the end of December 2020, Congress has just passed a bill that would add $300 a week to unemployment benefits for 11 weeks.

Given states' antiquated benefit systems, it perhaps would have been much better for Congress to have just reduced the unemployment benefit levels gradually over time, allowing the economy to adjust to the huge shock that the pandemic has been. Now, with a vaccine being rolled out, policymakers should want to facilitate as rapid a jobs recovery as possible. That requires people moving into new jobs. As news story after news story on unemployment insurance has shown, financial incentives do matter in terms of people's individual decisions to take on these new positions, and high unemployment insurance, if sustained, will be a barrier to that adjustment.[18]

Are Financial Incentives All That Matter?

Of course, financial incentives aren't the only thing that determines whether people take jobs. Having a job can give purpose to our lives, while with unemployment comes uncertainty. Perhaps an individual was highly specialized in the role they've been rehired for, or has good camaraderie with colleagues, or has an affinity for the business that transcends financial rewards. As we saw in chapter 1, there are a whole multitude of factors that might mean, on balance, that someone would forgo the option of what looks to be in their financial interest.

While incentives *matter* in influencing outcomes, then, they are clearly not the only determinant. In their book *Good Economics for Hard Times,* Nobel Prize–winning economists Abhijit V. Banerjee and Esther Duflo write about this beautifully in regards to immigration.[19]

Given the payoffs to the world's poorest of moving to wealthier, more productive economies, an analysis predicated on financial incentives alone would suggest that the demand to migrate to the United States would be limitless. Yet the authors present extensive evidence that the overwhelming majority of people choose not to move, even when they can. Important support networks, family ties, language barriers, and more, can all offset the financial incentives to move to a new country.

Banerjee and Duflo extrapolate from this to conclude that economists have put too much weight on financial incentives in policy debates. But just as with swings of a pendulum, one wonders whether the debate on unemployment insurance shows that things have now swung too far in the opposite direction. In recent years it has become fashionable for commentators to stop thinking about financial incentives and instead to use the absence of clear evidence of their effects as evidence that financial incentives do not matter much at all. This risks very bad decisionmaking.

The most obvious example of this is in regard to marginal income tax rates on top earners. These days, left-leaning thinkers and economists use crude analysis across countries to simply deny that higher income tax rates reduce the incentive for people to work hard and engage in the entrepreneurial activity that drives the high income in the first place. This is likely to be an important debate in the aftermath of the pandemic, when the desire to reduce the federal government budget deficit will lead to calls for higher taxes on the rich.

While it's true that financial payoffs are only one consideration in human decisionmaking, including for entrepreneurs and top talent, we still have lots of evidence that incentives matter in terms of shaping economic activity and people's willingness to report taxable income.

A couple of examples suffice to show that tax rates do really affect behavior of the very rich and mobile. A 2010 study by economists Henrik Kleven, Emmanuel Saez, and Camille Landais, for example, found that an income tax reform in Spain that lowered the income tax rate of foreign professional soccer players led to a dramatic expansion of foreign players moving to the Spanish league.[20]

What's more, this increased talent in the Spanish league (as measured by representation at national team level), while improving the performance of Spanish teams in pan-European competitions. In this case then, financial incentives both led to a behavioral response and appeared to improve the quality of the output of the industry.

But it's not just soccer. Those same authors found that a preferential tax scheme in Demark was similarly successful in attracting rich and successful foreigners.[21] In a 2016 Cato research brief, economists Ufuk Akcigit, Salomé Baslandze, and Stefanie Stantcheva likewise showed that the top 1 percent of inventors are heavily influenced by top tax rates when deciding where to physically locate.[22]

Financial incentives do appear to matter when it comes to international mobility then, particularly for highly successful individuals. Although it is beyond this chapter to assess the full literature on taxes, it therefore stands to reason that financial incentives are likely to affect other things that determine one's tax burden, including work and entrepreneurial endeavor. Economist Charles Jones has shown that if we think entrepreneurs' willingness to engage in innovation is even marginally affected by the incentive to receive a top income, then high taxes can make everyone worse off by deterring wealth-creating activity.[23] If we react to the sharp uplift in public debt from this crisis with a dramatic increase in marginal tax rates, then we could pay a large price later in terms of less transformative innovation.

Financial incentives, of course, underpin the whole capitalist system we live in. The system of profit and loss is crucial in providing incentives to encourage the reassignment of resources to where they are most valued by consumers. Profit provides a key incentive for new entrepreneurs to enter and compete in a given market. We have already seen how this encourages the supply of new goods when rising demand raises prices and how a bigger financial reward could be used to encourage more investment in vaccine development.

Again, monetary payoffs aren't everything. But whenever examining government policy, it's always worth asking: What behavior does this policy incentivize? Too often politicians do not pay sufficient attention to this and put too little weight on the role that incentives play in decisionmaking.

And, who knows? Such are the dramatic costs of this ongoing pandemic that, now a safe COVID-19 vaccine is available, it might behoove policymakers to find a way to encourage vaccination less coercively and controversially than via a mandate. At this stage, using financial payoffs to encourage immunization might become appealing, given their strong track record of changing behavior via incentives. High vaccine efficacies mean fewer vaccinations are needed to achieve herd immunity. But generous reimbursement to health care providers, vaccine manufacturers, and maybe even payouts to patients could speed up the process.[24]

If you don't think financial incentives will affect health behavior around COVID-19, then you probably missed the story about Brigham Young University–Idaho. There, administrators had to threaten students with suspension from school if they deliberately contracted COVID-19, after evidence that some students were seeking infection so that, having recovered, they could be paid for their plasma, which would contain COVID-19 antibodies that could be used as a treatment.[25]

Who Should Pay the Price When You Get Infected?

Financial incentives might not always be about direct cash payoffs but may be indirect too—an incentive may come from a potential risk to a business, such as potential fines for breaches of regulations or having financial liability for certain eventualities.

A funny example of this came in post-lockdown New York, after Governor Andrew Cuomo banned bars from opening unless they sold food alongside any drinks sold. Faced with the risk of forgone drinks revenue if customers were deterred by this regulation, bars got innovative. Many introduced menus with tiny food portions, including The Lafayette in Buffalo, which offered "A Piece of Meat," the "Smallest Piece of Cheesecake in Buffalo," and "Nine French Fries," all for $1 each.

Upset that businesses were not abiding by the spirit of the law, Cuomo held a hilarious press conference where he outlined what he considered reasonable food that constituted a proper meal. "To be a bar, you had to have food available—soups, sandwiches, etc.," he said. "More than just hors d'oeuvres, chicken wings, you had to have some *substantive* food. The lowest level of substantive food were sandwiches."[26]

Aside from the absurd micromanagement this constituted for a regulation that was really designed just to encourage people to remain at tables and so socially distance, the incident highlights well how businesses react to incentives from regulations. These bars sought out ways to revive their business without the huge costs of developing full meal menus.

Another COVID-19 example is pertinent here. As the original lockdowns began to be eased, Senate Republicans made clear that their primary aim from the next stage of COVID-19 legislation was to provide coronavirus-related liability protections for businesses.

The thinking behind this was that businesses would have a financial disincentive to reopen if they could potentially have been held liable for consumers or workers becoming sick on their premises, something that would be difficult to prove. The risk of liability for someone catching the disease, and the potential for court action and devastating financial consequences, it was thought, would have kept many businesses shuttered.

Now, we might expect that in a world with completely free and enforceable contracts, these liability risks could have been dealt with through free market activity alone. Businesses have strong reputational reasons to not want to be known as infection vectors—especially if they are dealing face-to-face with consumers. A bad reputation is bad business. Businesses could, in this world, also use liability waivers or specify worker contracts to compensate workers for the COVID-19 risk, too, thus insulating themselves from potential lawsuits.

The problem is that businesses have learned from experience that courts often will not enforce liability waivers. Nor have businesses been able to find they can save themselves by saying that they were adopting the best practices of their competitors.

Due to these realities, it might have been prudent for them to behave as if they faced strict liability anyway. Republicans worried this would have led to excess risk aversion and high levels of economic damage from sustained business closures. In fact, George Mason University economist Tyler Cowen argued that not putting liability limits on businesses would have been a "recipe for never reopening again."[27]

Other economists thought that giving liability waivers to businesses would itself be dangerous during a pandemic. From a public health perspective, they argued that it was a good thing if businesses acted as if they had strict liability, because they would then have an incentive to ensure offices, venues, vehicles, and shops were as safe for employees and customers as possible.

Economist Justin Wolfers wrote of the Republican proposal, supported by many businesses, that "the whole point of making employers liable for risking the lives of their staff is to prevent them from exposing their staff to undue risk. Businesses are asking for the right to expose their workers to fatal risks with no consequences. It's bad economics and bad policy."[28]

Given there could have been a financial penalty should a company have been found liable for a COVID-19 case, Wolfers believed businesses would have had strong financial incentives to take precautions—

to test employees, ensure regular sanitizing of shared spaces, screen people's body temperatures, or ensure that whatever work could be done from home would have been. The threat of liability would therefore have helped the public health effort.

This debate brings us back to the externalities of the virus. In chapter 2, I mentioned how one way of dealing with an externality like this efficiently might be to assign liability to one party in particular—the party who can bear the imposition at the least cost.

Wolfers was essentially arguing that because businesses often have deeper pockets than individuals, they would be the least-cost avoider of bearing the liability of the virus spreading on their premises. Cowen believed the opposite. Since businesses have far less information than individual workers and customers have about their own health status, and it would be extremely costly to get such information through daily testing or temperature screening, Cowen believes the worker or customer might actually be the least-cost avoider in many instances. It's easier to stay at home when you have a fever, for example, than for businesses you decide to enter to test you.

Yet putting full liability on workers or customers clearly wasn't a good idea either. We did want businesses to take some safety precautions. The messy reality of this particular virus, including the lack of clarity about who might have spread the disease, meant that neither of these simple liability solutions was the best we could do.

We wanted, in other words, to both incentivize businesses to provide safe environments and ensure that employees and consumers behaved responsibly. Cowen thought that policy required a variety of components to achieve this—strict liability for businesses for evidence of clear recklessness, direct regulation of particularly dangerous actions or practices, and capped liability for certain entities.[29]

These answers might not have been precisely optimal, but at least they would have recognized that the financial incentives from unlimited liability were far from ideal. This is one of those cases where we cannot follow the textbook of just applying a liability and assuming everything will work out.

But there would have been another problem with the sort of unlimited liability on businesses that Democrats considered. That is, that a business facing unlimited liability would have had *time inconsistent preferences* for whether to take actions that improve public health.

As law professors Daniel Hemel and Daniel Rodriguez pointed out, although the fear of financial liability may cause businesses to take precautions to improve safety, once a potential exposure has been identified, an unlimited liability world would have created strong financial *disincentives* for the business to honestly inform people about the incident.[30]

At that stage, a system where businesses are liable for what happens on their premises may have become actively harmful for the public health effort of tracking the spread of the virus, at least if the business could have kept it secret. These professors therefore proposed a safe harbor—a reduction or elimination of liability—for businesses that rapidly let employees and customers know about an outbreak.

This brings us full circle to our original story about the spa owner and unemployment insurance. When Sen. Lindsey Graham (R-SC) first identified the incentive problem from the $600 per week extra in unemployment benefits, a lot of left-leaning commentators dismissed his complaints. Given we were in the grips of a pandemic, they said, paying people highly for being at home and not out spreading the virus was a feature of the policy, not a bug.

Yet those same incentives, as we have seen, undercut the success of the Paycheck Protection Program and, on the margin, elevated unemployment benefits made it less likely for unemployed workers to seek out jobs for the benefits' duration. Just as with the messy solutions to the liability issue, policymakers had to then find another workaround to ensure that their support for laid off workers both didn't harm the economic recovery and also didn't create perverse public health incentives.

Why don't politicians often fully consider the role of financial incentives when devising their original legislation? What is it about the political process that means economic incentives often get ignored? One answer is the very different incentives politicians themselves face. Those same incentives can help explain why many governments were simply not ready for the pandemic itself.

ECONOMIC LESSON

Financial incentives matter. Yes, they are not the only consideration when we make decisions as individuals. But policies that raise the financial payoff for individuals or companies to take a course of action will encourage more of that action on the margin. When it comes to COVID-19, it is important that policymakers assess how the financial incentives incumbent within their policies affect the propensity to engage in actions that enhance public health or economic activity.

ECONOMIC TERMS INTRODUCED

- **incentive:** a payoff or reward that encourages a particular behavior
- **disincentive:** a penalty or punishment that discourages a particular behavior
- **financial incentive/disincentive:** a monetary reward/penalty to encourage/dissuade some particular action
- **time inconsistency:** instances where incentives, policies, or behaviors that looked optimal in one period become suboptimal in a later period and are therefore abandoned

15

WHY WEREN'T WE WELL PREPARED FOR THE PANDEMIC?

An introduction to political incentives

W hy did nobody notice it?" At a London School of Economics briefing at the height of the financial crisis in November 2008, Queen Elizabeth II flummoxed academics by directly asking economists and financiers why so many experts failed to spot the ongoing financial disaster.

Professor Luis Garicano, the research director of the school at the time, had the unenviable task of trying to cobble together an answer for Her Majesty. "At every stage," he mused, "someone was relying on somebody else and everyone thought they were doing the right thing."[1] The crisis, in his view, sounds much like the basic externality problem we discussed in chapter 2. In a letter to the *The Guardian*, he confirmed that he thought everyone, from mortgage agents, to banks, to ratings agencies, to asset managers, were doing what they thought was rational and in their own best interests, but with consequences that were devastating for society more broadly.

If true, it is a comforting thought. If we believe that the financial crash really was just a case of a failure to deal with an externality problem that was obvious, or a lack of anyone taking responsibility for it, then that allows us to convince ourselves that lessons have been learned and that the same thing will never happen again. With the benefit of hindsight, scores of academics and pundits duly stepped forward after the event to explain why the financial crisis was inevitable, offering up policy ideas to prevent a repeat.

World-renowned mathematician Nassim Nicholas Taleb would have given the queen a less soothing answer. In his 2007 book *Black Swan*, Taleb instead laid out a framework for thinking about how some highly improbable events will always take us by surprise, no matter how much we delude ourselves that we understand their origins.[2]

These so-called black swans are not the result of activities generating obvious and correctable externalities that we could mitigate but which incompetent governments choose to ignore. No, certain events are just far beyond the comprehension of our normal expectations. So rare are they like to occur that we just fail to compute their probability. Our psychological biases mean we take insufficient account of these types of rare events' impacts on our historical direction.

Taleb even went as far as outlining the three conditions that satisfied an event constituting his definition of a black swan. First, he said, it is something that lies outside of past events, such that people could not point to its possibility. Second, the impact of the event itself is huge. Third, our human nature means that, after the event, we rationalize why it happened and so fool ourselves that it was, in fact, predictable. Taleb, of course, shot to fame after the financial crisis hit, because the events proved to be an obvious example of something that fulfilled all of these conditions. Although many people warned about problems in the financial system, nobody fully outlined how a confluence of complex activities would have such damaging consequences.

I rerun this history here because during the early stages of this pandemic, politicians and businesses found it convenient to conclude, similarly, that the spread of SARS-CoV-2 was a completely unexpected occurrence. The pandemic itself has been described as a black swan multiple times on broadcast media and online.[3]

It suits both CEOs and politicians to believe this and convince us that it is true. If nobody could have possibly foreseen the pandemic, then it absolves politicians and businesses from many of their failures in preparing or reacting to the eventuality. Businesses, because of the absence of insurance or widespread precautionary behavior by them in anticipating a pandemic, can use such an argument to justify the provision of widespread relief from taxpayers. Politicians, meanwhile, can paint this virus as something entirely unexpected and which we should discount when considering their reelection prospects.

A Pandemic Was Predicted and Predictable

Yet far from being a black swan, a viral pandemic was, in fact, both predicted and predictable. In the 20th century alone the world struggled with the Spanish flu of 1918–1920, the 1957–1958 Asian flu, the 1968 Hong Kong flu, and human immunodeficiency viruses. In the 21st century, countries have had to react quickly to Ebola, severe acute respiratory syndrome (SARS), and H1N1 influenza outbreaks. Humanity has to deal with viral outbreaks with unnerving regularity, and those risks were heightened in a world bound by deeper interconnections and cheap air travel.

Public figures, including Bill Gates, had been warning about the global threat of a viral pandemic for some time.[4] Yes, the precise form that it would take was always highly uncertain and perhaps unknowable, but we cannot use the black swan analogy as "a cliché for any bad thing that surprises us," as Taleb says, especially when we knew the broader risk.[5]

In fact, although there was certainly not a salient insurance market— one reason why governments bailed out business—some institutions had been aware of the risks. In 2018, the Gies College of Business and the Grainger College of Engineering at the University of Illinois, for example, took out a prophetic three-year insurance contract in case of a large drop in revenue from Chinese students owing to visa restrictions, a trade war, or a pandemic.[6]

Governments were well aware of the risks of a pandemic too. Former U.S. Health and Human Services secretary Michael Leavitt, who served under then president George W. Bush, was concerned enough about the threat of bird flu in 2005 that he told the American public to stock up on canned goods.[7] In November 2005, his Health and Human Services Department published an almost 400-page report dubbed a

"Pandemic Influenza Plan," albeit for dealing with a flu pandemic.[8] Before becoming president, Barack Obama similarly wrote in an op-ed for the *New York Times* that "these exotic killer diseases are not isolated health problems half a world away, but direct and immediate threats to security and prosperity here at home."[9] Awareness of the pandemic threat was there, and partially lived through, with the warnings of swine flu and then Ebola. Health and Human Services Secretary Alex Azar wrote about the risks of a global pandemic in 2018.[10]

At various times in the past two decades, the country's preparedness for a pandemic has been heavily criticized. A Health and Human Services assessment of the 2009 swine flu outbreak, while overall deeming that response as successful, highlighted both the potential for delays on the side of medical innovation and the difficulties of obtaining good information at a national level.[11]

A 2014 report for the Department for Homeland Security was damning on the United States' readiness, particularly in regard to the country's stockpiles.[12] It found that "tons of expired hand sanitizer and more than 80 percent of medications they had invested in are already set to expire next year [2015]," while explaining that it was often difficult to know where personal protective equipment was, how much of it the department had, or its usability.

The problems with decisions taken in Trump's administration are well documented elsewhere, including (but not limited to) rebuffing a budget proposal to replenish the national stockpile and significant problems in the delay of COVID-19 testing. There were reportedly numerous distracting bureaucratic battles, too, that worsened the preparedness for the pandemic.

The president famously abolished the White House's dedicated office on global health security in 2018, a measure described by administration insiders as more akin to streamlining of personnel and activities.[13] While it would be tempting to just blame the country's poor response on Trump administration incompetence, however, a deep-dive *Politico* report suggests that focus on the pandemic threat has waxed and waned under previous presidents too.[14]

As the pandemic's impact has been felt, it is clear as well that the East Asian countries that experienced SARS and Middle East respiratory syndrome (MERS) seemed to cope with the initial phases of the pandemic much better than most governments in the West. While politicians can rightly say that the majority of their plans focused on influenza and not a coronavirus, it is baffling that such little apparent attempt was made by the federal government to learn from other countries' experiences with similar diseases.

What's clear is that despite being predicted and predictable, few would argue that the United States was well prepared when this pandemic did hit. When one observes the huge economic and social costs the pandemic has wrought, it is surely clear that more time and preparation was required to ensure that regulations and institutions were responsive to a crisis situation like this.

True, nobody could have foreseen exactly the features or effects of this particular virus in advance, including its transmissibility, infection rate, deadliness, differential impact on demographic groups, or even much of its medical effects. Any government was going to face difficulties in responding to SARS-CoV-2 (COVID-19). The countries that have done better bear little relation to those identified by the Global Health Security Index as being best prepared for a pandemic.[15]

Yet that same index highlights the general problem of underpreparedness across most countries. Clearly the experts misjudged some countries' preparations, too, mistaking checking boxes and approving processes for a readiness to deal with actual shocks.

Yes, it may be that more coercive forms of government are better versed in using power after public health crises hit. But the evident difference in performance across countries and the speed of efforts in some East Asian democracies does suggest that certain forms of preparedness might have been crucially important.

A Public Choice Explanation for Unpreparedness

What explains why the United States might have been unprepared for this pandemic?

The intellectually lazy explanation is just to imply this is solely about resources and budgets. It is common to hear that the United States underinvests generally in its *public goods* and that pandemic planning teams being starved of resources are just an example of this. Indeed, that was a view pushed around the internet in early March, notably from Bloomberg columnist and economist Noah Smith, who appeared to imply that the poor response was a consequence of years of libertarians calling for budget cuts that were then made to the civil service.[16]

Now, it may well be that the federal government should have been spending more in preparing for pandemics. There's a strong case for funding genuine public goods, given they might be underprovided in a free market. Robert Kadlec, then assistant secretary for preparedness and response at Health and Human Services, certainly appeared to think funding was inadequate when he testified to the Senate in 2018. He bemoaned not having a budget line item for pandemic influenza, as an example.[17]

But the federal government has hardly been undergoing a period of austerity. Overall, real government outlays have risen in recent years, and the United States entered this crisis with nearly a 5 percent budget deficit, showing politicians' willingness to borrow vast amounts more than would have been demanded for pandemic preparation. Even within relevant agencies, the Centers for Disease Control and Prevention's budget has been fairly flat since 2010, but the National Institutes of Health budget rebounded under Trump, having been cut under Obama. Broader spending on health care today is, of course, massive.[18] Even if a lack of spending on pandemic-related areas or within the relevant agencies was a problem, it doesn't explain this choice—why too little is spent relative to other programs, where money is being spent incredibly liberally.

Others suggest that there is a unique lack of U.S. "state capacity" relative to other countries—that American institutions of government just aren't as effective in their ability to deliver policies or raise taxes in response to crises. Economist Bryan Caplan has noted, however, that any government with the power to close down much of its economy and push through $2.2 trillion in relief spending at great speed does not appear to be lacking either power or capacity.[19]

In fact, international indices of state capacity, proxied for by government effectiveness, usually show the United States above countries such as South Korea, which is widely held up as having performed much better during this crisis.[20] Elsewhere, I have noted that there appears to be no correlation whatsoever between recognized measures of state capacity and COVID-19 country performance in terms of deaths relative to population.[21]

No, what both the spending and state capacity data seem to suggest is that what we are seeing here is not the U.S. government being starved of resources, or suffering from some pre-pandemic general ineffectiveness, but (as Caplan writes) politicians having the wrong state *priorities*. Policymakers have been actively choosing to forgo preparing for pandemics in pursuit of other policy goals.

The key question is: Why? What causes politicians to let core functions of government wither, such as preparation for genuine public health threats, while other functions of government are lavished with cash or expanded? And what explains why some other countries' governments appear to have bucked this trend in relation to COVID-19?

The most likely answer is *political incentives*. Public choice economists—those who study political decisions by analyzing political behavior using economic tools—have long recognized that politicians are in the market for votes. That incentive means that, on the margin, politicians prioritize types of spending or tax cuts that are readily observable to voters rather than those that might merely enhance long-term welfare. The former tend to bring with them more obvious electoral rewards.

A classic paper by Neil Malhotra and Andrew Healy analyzed how voters responded to politicians in regard to their handling of natural disasters such as hurricanes, earthquakes, and tornadoes.[22] They found that spending on disaster prevention was highly cost-effective, often returning payoffs of 15-to-1.

Yet when they examined how voters cast their ballots in presidential elections, they found that candidates engaging in that type of spending saw no apparent electoral benefit at the county level. Increases in relief spending in reaction to disasters, on the other hand, significantly increased the incumbents' vote share. Voters tend to reward those who react to crises by dishing out relief, in other words, but do not reward those who prevent the worst outcomes from crises by preparing.

Preparation is, of course, largely unobservable to the ordinary voter, especially if it is not utilized because a crisis does not occur. Even hearing about preparation provides voters with little information about how effective it would be when the next crisis hits, so there is likely little political benefit from it. In fact, given how infrequent crises are, politicians may find that their preparatory work actually ends up benefiting those who come long after them.

There are therefore strong electoral incentives that point toward spending money on observable, day-to-day programs in good times, and then providing extensive and rapid relief when crises do hit. As Malhotra concludes, it is perfectly rational for politicians to "kick the can down the road" because that is what, on most occasions, is in their electoral interests.

This behavior of voters is a variant of what economists call *hyperbolic discounting*. The basic idea, emanating from behavioral economics, is that human beings sometimes exhibit irrational preferences for small immediate rewards rather than larger rewards at a later date, at least in the very short term. Often we make choices today that our future selves would prefer not to have made.

In this case, voters prefer the relatively tiny payoffs of small uplifts of immediate spending on them rather than the much, much larger payoffs of pandemic preparedness and medical investments. Yet when a pandemic hits, they'd have preferred the preparatory activity and wish they could go back and vote for candidates who'd have delivered it.

Malhotra and Healy's insight explains, too, why politicians are so willing to engage in extraordinary relief efforts when crises do hit. Again, the overwhelming majority of their spending so far has been on huge programs that fling observable government transfers to their voters and constituents.

Given the ongoing economic costs, first of lockdowns and then of adjustments to our lifestyles, the payoff to a solution that would allow us to go back to full normality is massive.

Yet policymakers seem much more animated by developing new ideas for relief spending, rather than identifying the bottlenecks and resource constraints that are delaying or preventing medical innovations (vaccines, treatments, contact tracing) from ending the crisis or severely mitigating it. Although spending on medical innovation is much cheaper than expensive relief programs, with vastly higher possible returns in terms of higher economic welfare, it is less visible to voters, and its impact more difficult for them to discern. In an election year especially, that makes relief spending all the more attractive.

Why Were Some Countries Better Prepared Than Others?

Malhotra and Healy's insight might explain to us why politicians underprepare for these types of crises in a democracy. But it doesn't get us any closer to identifying why some countries, particularly in East Asia, appeared much better prepared for this pandemic than the United States. What was it about South Korea, for example, that meant they were able to mobilize to contain the virus so effectively early on in the pandemic?

It is beyond this book to do a comprehensive analysis across countries. Different demographics, degrees of luck, where the virus first hit, variance in the flexibility of health care systems, the health of the population, population density, the protection afforded to those in nursing homes, culture, and different exposure or underlying immunity to this virus all no doubt partly explain some of the major differences in performance across countries. We are also still living through a pandemic for a disease that looks as if it could be seasonal, of course, so we should be careful not to jump to firm conclusions.

However, there is one major difference between the United States and, say, South Korea that may explain why the latter responded better early: South Korea suffered a similar and credible threat of an infectious disease in the form of MERS as recently as 2015.

When crises like this do hit, political incentives change. The threat of a pandemic becomes salient in electoral terms in a way that it wasn't before. As a detailed write-up for *The Atlantic* explained, the South Korean government was heavily criticized for how it handled that outbreak, including for failures on testing and a lack of transparency in regard to the spread of the infection.[23]

The leader of South Korea's opposition harshly criticized the government of the day, saying that it had lost the people's trust. That critic is now the president of South Korea, Moon Jai-in. In response to that crisis, the country completely rewrote its infectious disease prevention legislation. The country learned from its mistakes, and politicians reacted because suddenly there was a political imperative to do so. The crisis was a short time enough ago that it was still a pertinent political issue in 2020, so the South Korean government was better prepared than others to deal with the COVID-19 outbreak.

As 9/11 shows in the United States, in the aftermath of major crises there may well be a political reward for major policy change. Often, this type of reactive lawmaking can amount to fighting the last war, which can be an overcorrection that leads to inflexibility or wrong priorities for different future threats. Science journalist Ed Yong has talked about how some hospitals' plans for pandemics prior to COVID-19 were based on isolated units suitable for treating lethal but less contagious diseases such as Ebola, for example.[24] So we must be cognizant that the next threat will be different from this one.

But, in this case, the prior experience for South Korea was similar enough to the COVID-19 crisis that it served the country well. It meant fast testing, expansive tracing technology, and a mandatory isolation regime of the most severe cases were ready to roll out quickly, providing both crucial information and early containment.

Once a pandemic hits a country with force, in other words, the political incentives can change. Malhotra and Healy's model explains why we underprepare and why relief is so appealing when a crisis does hit. But unlike a hurricane or an earthquake—whose impact is usually heavily localized—a viral outbreak tends to change the public's risk appetite for that type of threat. That brings with it the strong political incentive for being seen to dramatically change policy early and to prepare to avoid the same mistakes in the future.

Yes, voters appear to reward relief efforts even during crises like this, but they also tend to judge their governments for unnecessary losses of life. Whatever you think of their wisdom, it should not surprise us that, faced with an explosion in deaths in places such as New York, politicians decided to engage in strong lockdowns once it was too late for prior pandemic preparedness to make a difference.

As economist Robert E. Wright has written, when potentially devastating consequences seem possible, the usually dominant strategy for politicians early on is "action," because of the political incentives.[25] If things go well, they can do a victory lap; if things go badly, they can say "imagine how much worse things would have been without our action." We have seen this with how the press has quickly rewritten the narrative to hold up New York as an exemplar of good policy, despite a catastrophic early death toll. Whatever the actual results, the best thing for politicians to do once a crisis hits is to take tough action—hence the broad political consensus for lockdowns early on.

After a while, however, the electoral incentives become less clear. Voters don't tend to reward preparation. They do tend to reward early action, relief, and promises to clean up preparation for next time. But unlike with a natural disaster, which happens suddenly and then requires dealing with the consequences, there is an intervening long period in pandemics where there are a whole range of economic and health tradeoffs that pit interest groups against each other as the pandemic continues.

The massive economic downturn associated with social distancing and forced closures really does affect political decisionmaking too. One cross-country study has found that in countries where an incumbent leader or government is up for a second term very soon, public health restrictions have been weaker.[26] Even in the United States, the president and Republican governors were keener to reopen earlier, citing the economic impact of lockdowns. Republicans were understandably willing to bet on a sharp GDP rebound going into the 2020 presidential election; Democrats, less so.

Over time, voters tend to lose their enthusiasm for constraints on their life, reassessing the threat to their families based on evidence of demographic or localized risks and becoming tired of restrictions on their civil liberties.[27] We began seeing this seep into politics once the initial economic consequences of social distancing became clear, with different interest groups either pressing for economic reopening, or more relief, or indeed ongoing sustained closures. It is now unclear what the favorable electoral strategy is, and politicians are still trying to figure it out, flitting between hawkishness and concerns for business viability as public opinion changes.

The sad general truth though is that although voters clearly dislike governments that fail in emergencies, electoral politics tends not to reward behaviors that create good institutional resilience to crises until we've had to suffer one. The old saying might go "a stitch in time saves nine," but often that stitch, if it comes at the expense of day-to-day spending, costs politicians votes. As Taleb puts it, because taxpayers "did not want to spend pennies . . . now they are going to spend trillions."[28] Electoral incentives often clash with dealing with very-high-cost risks that have low probability.

The result is that when the pandemic hit, unlike countries such as South Korea where the pandemic threat was previously salient, America was not ready. So extreme reactions in the form of extraordinary relief and lockdowns were thought needed, at least in the initial weeks. In delivering that combination, much of the political class sought to insulate the economy of March 2020 while closing things down to try to reduce the spread of the virus. The thinking was that the federal government could step in to make people whole during a necessary economic pause, before stepping out again. But this strategy has proven hopelessly optimistic.

ECONOMIC LESSON

Politicians are in the market for votes. They have little incentive to invest sufficiently in preparation for improbable yet highly damaging risks such as pandemics because this does not tend to be electorally advantageous, unlike providing relief when crises occur. Failures in emergencies can see voters punish incumbents, enforcing better preparation for future crises of a similar nature. But the incentive to set aside resources that could benefit taxpayers and interest groups today, in order to insure against threats tomorrow, is weak. In regards to COVID-19, we have seen this clearly, with inadequate institutional preparation going into the crisis and the huge explosion of relief after the crisis hit. Electoral incentives can also explain the initial extreme measures taken to contain the virus and why some politicians were so keen for early reopenings.

ECONOMIC TERMS INTRODUCED

- **public goods:** goods that are non-rivalrous in consumption (one person's use does not reduce availability for others) and non-excludable (it is very difficult to prevent someone using it once it's been produced). These characteristics suggest there might be under-provision in free markets.
- **hyperbolic discounting:** an identified cognitive bias where people prefer small and immediate rewards rather than larger, later rewards in the short term but are more patient in the longer term

16

CAN WE REALLY JUST TURN AN ECONOMY OFF AND BACK ON AGAIN?

An introduction to the nature of an economy

Those of you who have had problems with computers will know that the first thing the experts ask when you call for advice is "Have you tried turning it off and back on again?"

This can be infuriating to hear. But what's remarkable is how often this advice works. Despite our assuming that we'll need a more complex solution, everything from a power surge to static in the air to a programming glitch can require us to simply reboot our machines.

Shutting down a device for a 5–10 minute period not only wipes clean all the temporarily stored data, it also allows some capacitors and other components in a computer to reset to their factory settings. Most of the time, when we turn it back on, the computer works just fine.

Now few people these days would admit to thinking about the economy as if it were a machine. The works of F. A. Hayek, mentioned in chapter 7, have not all been in vain. But when it came to the partial shutdown of formal economic activity to deal with the early months of COVID-19, a lot of well-versed commentators did appear to think that the "off and on" model had some application to economic activity during this pandemic.

True, the analogies used varied somewhat. Some talked about "freezing" the economy with a lockdown and then thawing it more slowly. Others suggested that the economy was more like a bear that could be put into hibernation and then woken up once we felt that the initial threat of the virus had passed.

But what united all these analogies was the idea that the economy—what they really meant was "formal market activity"—could, in effect, be paused during the period we suppressed the virus and then restarted relatively seamlessly afterwards. Hence why, in the initial phase of the pandemic at least, there was much discussion of a strong "V-shaped recovery."

This outlook wasn't entirely crazy, at least conceptually. For when you think about it, there are regularly partial shut downs in formal market activity that restart just fine a bit later. We call it a "weekend." In some European countries, extensive vacation time sees huge numbers of locals depart their home cities to go off to second homes or other countries for travel at the height of summer, probably depressing formal activity during that time by 10–20 percent.

Nobody thinks vacations will prevent the economy bouncing back to normal afterward. In fact, it is merely considered part of the normal. GDP and employment figures get seasonally adjusted to account for this annual decline and rebound in activity. We give neither a weekend nor vacations so much as a second thought in terms of their impact on economic welfare more broadly.

The Great Pause?

The COVID-19 shock to the economy was clearly not part of the ordinary weekly or annual economic cycle. As we have seen, it brought with it a huge unexpected shock to market activity.

Nevertheless, several high-profile commentators considered that it might have similar effects on economic trends to a normal pause. Former Treasury secretary Larry Summers, for example, was initially optimistic, saying that he suspected the pandemic downturn and rebound to have "the character of the recovery from the total depression that hits a Cape Cod economy every winter or the recovery in American GDP that takes place every Monday morning."[1]

Admittedly, Summers couched these projections as contingent on dealing with the public health threat. And, indeed, there are reasons for optimism in the longer term, after the pandemic passes. We shouldn't expect the pandemic to significantly affect our long-term growth potential, unless, as some economists fear, this episode has "scarring" consequences through heightening our beliefs about the possibility of extreme negative events.[2]

History, however, suggests grounds for optimism on that front. The Roaring '20s followed the Spanish flu of 1918–1919, after all. And as former chair of Trump's Council of Economic Advisers Kevin Hassett said in late May, the virus itself doesn't alter our economic fundamentals much.[3] Despite the constant analogizing to war, the pandemic won't destroy physical capital, for example, such as factories, offices, or machines. Although we face the loss of life and uncertainties around the physiological consequences for those who've had the disease, for most of us it will not eliminate human capital, either—the stuff between our ears. Human ingenuity will live on. The bigger threat then will be any policy mistakes we make as a result of this crisis. Previous emergencies have permanently grown the size and scope of government, for example, which can drag on economic growth.

But that's the long run—once the pandemic itself is a distant memory. In the near term, we have seen much more disruption. Even South Korea, which had both limited COVID-19 deaths and gripped the virus hard without a government lockdown in those early months, nevertheless found its economy contracting for a time, albeit far less so than other developed nations, such as the United States. Although, yes, countries that have dealt with the public health threat well have been rewarded with better economic performance relative to others, all have seen downturns relative to what might have been expected before the pandemic. And in countries with large outbreaks of the virus, the GDP cost of getting the pandemic under control can be huge in the short term.

Too many economists in that early stage, though, appeared to apply Summers's model of economic activity to the lockdowns, rather than to the pandemic. It was widely discussed that we were facing a shutdown of eight weeks to three months before returning to something akin to normal life. Policymakers around the world followed suit, at first acting as if the lockdowns were a simple interlude to our usual economic activity.

As a result, governments appeared to see their role as needing to bridge activity into a robust recovery. They used direct job subsidies, welfare payments, bailouts, loans, and explicit takeovers of businesses to try to protect the existence of as many businesses as possible and to "make people whole" during the mandated period of closure and beyond.

The logic behind this was as follows. The lockdowns were thought to represent a temporary necessary aberration to normal economic life. This would undoubtedly lead to a sharp downturn in GDP, given the closure of businesses that required physical proximity. Yet that was considered necessary to get to grips with the virus.

Governments wanted to ensure that the near-term damage of the lockdowns didn't destroy too many businesses or result in sharp cuts to spending in other markets that were unaffected by the mandated closures. Their tools to prevent this entailed pumping money into households and businesses. By preventing permanent mass layoffs, business failures, or sharp spending cuts, policymakers thought they could stem the economic contagion by providing extensive relief.

This relief came in two broad forms. First were attempts to protect the *supply side* of the economy. That meant relief measures aiming to maintain the economy's potential for producing goods and services. This occurred through loans and grants to businesses in order to try to prevent business failures, to support payrolls, to avoid relationships between employers and employees being lost, and to avoid having whole supply chains disintegrating as key suppliers went bust. The rationale was to protect producers so they could get going quickly again after reopening.

Second were policies to protect the *demand side* of the economy. That was through relief transfers—sending cash to people—to maintain spending levels as far as possible. The aim here was to prevent the decline in spending on services that were closed due to the need for physical exposure thus leading to secondary spending declines throughout the economy, as people held on to their money because they feared for their jobs and wages. The tools governments around the world used included stimulus checks, tax cuts, and expansions in unemployment benefits.

By doing both these things, it was said, policymakers could essentially pause a lot of economic activity and allow it to rapidly resume once lockdowns were lifted. John Springford, deputy director at the Centre for European Reform, was a typical voice in writing about a V-shaped recovery when he said "It's in the government's gift, surely? If they do enough to keep workers attached to firms, keep firms solvent, and then stimulate a recovery when the virus is contained, then why not?"[4]

Different countries used a different balance between these two broad approaches. European countries generally subsidized employment relationships in order to try to avoid mass layoffs. In the United States, the federal government put a lot more focus on providing income support through expanded unemployment benefits and stimulus checks, although there were also effective subsidies for employment through the Paycheck Protection Program (PPP). The result was higher initial unemployment but a lesser contraction in GDP than what was observed in many European economies.

Which approach turns out to produce better outcomes over the medium term will largely depend on how much the pandemic has permanently changed the economy. If, after the population is vaccinated, consumers truly want to go back to normal, then it might have proven more efficient to try to keep workers attached to their old firms. Relief policies that protected economic capacity that then becomes viable again would avoid the permanent loss of healthy employment relationships and the *transaction costs* associated with founding new businesses to enter markets (the costs of searching for new employees, renegotiating supplier contracts, and so on).

If, on the other hand, there is a widespread permanent change in how people work or what they consume even after the pandemic ends, the European model will have protected industries and jobs that prove to be no longer viable. This will prove to be a longer-term economic drag, with workers and resources in the wrong jobs and industries, thus making the economy less productive. In that situation, the United States' focus on incomes would look prudent.

The problem with this overall mental model of the economy, however, is that it does, ultimately, end up treating the economy like a machine. It presumes policymakers can turn things on and off seamlessly or keep the overall level of demand in the economy stable, if only they ensure that businesses and jobs still exist, or that incomes are kept high enough.

As we saw in chapter 7, however, "the economy" is really just us—a complex, dynamic system of networks and relationships. It's an aggregate manifestation of the raft of links among employers and employees, businesses and suppliers, and individual consumers and firms, themselves shaped by ever-changing demand and supply patterns, the entry and exit of new firms, and policies in America and abroad.

The pandemic hugely disrupted these relationships because it fundamentally altered the supply and demand for goods, services, and workers. The policy response may have tried, in various ways, to keep the economy of old on ice or at its prior level of activity, but it's clear that these sorts of changes to demands, tastes, work behavior, and business practices—things that constantly fluctuate at the best of times—have been exacerbated by the pandemic.

While we might always have expected a relatively robust bounceback from the initial sharp shock of the virus and lockdowns, a rebound to where we would have been without having endured either was highly unlikely. By the end of the third quarter of 2020, GDP was still estimated to have been 5 percent below where it would have been had the pandemic never happened. Markets are imperfect, so the crisis might induce some positive creative changes that enhance economic prospects in certain sectors. But overall, the near-term hope of a full V-shaped recovery always looked naively optimistic.

Before delineating the evidence and reasons why, perhaps an example of an industry struggling to come to terms with this crisis is in order.

Case Study: The Premier League

UK Premier League football (soccer) is the most popular sporting league in the world—the crown jewel of the broader English football pyramid. Yet on March 13, 2020, the Premier League season, which usually runs August through May, was suspended indefinitely due to

SARS-CoV-2. As with most sporting and entertainment industries, having large numbers of supporters packing into a stadium and the players themselves grappling, shouting, and spitting on the field was thought to provide potential vectors for the spread of the virus. Some famous players and coaches tested positive for COVID-19 early on. The industry was closed down.

Unsurprisingly, however, there was a big pent-up demand to see soccer resume and a strong will among clubs to complete the season. Supporters of many teams were heavily invested in its conclusion. Certain sides had historic victories within their sights, including Liverpool, which ultimately won its first championship in 30 years. Clubs had contracts to fulfill with suppliers and TV broadcasters, too, and reneging on those would have significantly affected the financial viability of some clubs. The Premier League said that it could have lost up to $1.6 billion if it failed to complete the season.[5]

As a result, talks dubbed "Project Restart" eventually led to the season resuming on June 17. But that brought huge challenges. The first and most obvious was handling the virus. Players could be regularly tested easily enough to mitigate risks, but if a player in one team contracted COVID-19 post-restart, it would probably lead to that team being unable to compete for a few weeks, disrupting the restarted season further. Certain on-field guidance was also thought necessary to try to mitigate against spreading the disease, too—with players told to somehow avoid face-to-face contact and turn their faces away when getting up following a tackle.[6]

The need for ongoing social distancing precluded fans from entering stadiums, meaning the clubs found they would not recoup lost match-day ticket and merchandise revenue. Some offsetting funds could be raised through televising additional matches, but those were unlikely to fully compensate for the losses, especially given the large fixed costs associated with operating the empty stadiums.

The disruption did not start and end with the virus, however. There were impacts of the suspension on the Premier League's labor market. Some players, without the discipline of regular training during the pause, came back in worse shape than they had been before the pandemic. Certainly no one expected after a break of three months that any player would be in top form upon their return. The quality of the early matches after the restart was somewhat reduced, with the slower pace giving them an off-season feel. To avoid players becoming injured, the Premier League also had to adjust its rules to allow more in-game substitutions and additional water breaks.

There were difficulties in regard to players' contracts too. Sixty-eight player contracts were set to officially end on June 30.[7] Given the season was extended far beyond this, clubs faced the prospect of having to complete matches without important players. To counter this, the league had to allow clubs to temporarily extend contracts until the end of the revised season. But in some cases players were not willing to take these up, perhaps through fear of getting injured and jeopardizing signing for a new club for the next season.

On top of all this, there were question marks over whether the outlook for Premier League football might be altered semi-permanently. Until a vaccine is widely available, and all supporters feel comfortable attending matches again, there is likely to be an ongoing depressed revenue stream—estimated by experts to be down anywhere between 13 and 28 percent—not least through regulatory bans on fans entering stadiums. That uncertainty will affect how all clubs plan financially for next season, player salaries, and transfer fees.

Taking the extra time to complete the season resulted in having to delay the current season, too, reducing the preparation time for some clubs to adjust their playing or management staff for the new start. That in itself could lead to clubs signing more players who are ill-suited to the team's needs. The clubs also face difficult decisions on customer management, with season ticket holders from last season owed compensation now that limited numbers of spectators are allowed back into certain stadiums. Determining which fans are prioritized and how ticketing is managed and priced will no doubt prove to be a real headache.

Who knows what further impacts there might be? After nearly a year of severely curtailed social contact and restrictions on travel, the pandemic may result in broader changes in spectators' priorities. The implications for sport are, at this stage, unclear—perhaps it will be a boon, but maybe the pandemic period will have led people to reassess what is important in life. Certainly, when travel restrictions are lifted, many fans may decide to take vacations, so missing matches.

Now nobody thinks that Premier League football is going to be a nonviable industry after this virus is gone. Nor is it a particularly representative sector of the UK economy, let alone the United States, although all major sports leagues have faced similar struggles. But as a case study, its problems do highlight that the idea of switching off and switching on the economy is a lot easier said than done.

With contractual relationships, impacts on workers' productivity, changes to how businesses can operate, deadlines for suppliers, and ongoing changed behavior or enforced regulations on customers, simply picking up where you left off is not an option in soccer, any more than it is elsewhere. While we were right to expect a fairly robust rebound across many sectors after lockdowns, it was always unlikely that the economy would return to where it would have been without the crisis because of these disruptive effects. We cannot return back to the future we would have seen absent a pandemic, however much policymakers will it.

Headwinds against Recovery

The Premier League example highlights three broad reasons why it was always impossible to shut down and restart economies without major headwinds against a full and complete recovery.

1. Ongoing disruption within large sectors

It takes time for a vaccine or effective treatment to materialize or for stable herd immunity to (potentially) be acquired. Until then, consumer and business behavior will be cautious, with social distancing meaning certain industries, such as travel, events and hospitality, entertainment, and sports remaining depressed. The end of lockdowns did not mean the end of the pandemic.

Consumer demand for services that require physical interaction remained much lower even after most initial restrictions were lifted. In light of the virus, businesses had to undertake social distancing and safety protocols that harm efficiency, too, proving a second drag on an economic recovery.

Indeed, a full V-shaped recovery just did not happen. Despite a strong pick-up in retail sales after reopening, overall U.S. consumer spending was still down 5 percent on August 31, 2020, relative to January 2020, after falling to below 32 percent of January's level on March 30.[8] In other words, despite bouncing back sharply, overall spending was still below the pre-pandemic level by a significant *recession*-like magnitude, and nowhere near back to where it would have been had the pandemic never occurred.

In more granular spending categories, there were relatively sharp rebounds in spending on clothing and merchandise after reopenings, as well as health care. But transportation use, restaurant, and hotel spending remained very depressed, while grocery spending stayed elevated. All of these data are suggestive of people having continued to stay home more than usual even after lockdowns were lifted (see Figure 16.1).

These trends are unsurprising given that people were avoiding economic activities that required physical interaction. Indeed, a detailed examination of spending patterns from Raj Chetty's Opportunity Insights Team found that spending on luxuries such as landscaping services—that do not require much physical interaction—held up well among higher-income households, while spending on salons remained depressed.[9]

This is one of numerous pieces of evidence suggesting that the post-lockdown depression in activity arose not from fears households had about their *financial* prospects but from fears over health risks making people reluctant to engage in "social" spending. Reversing lockdown measures or providing federal relief, unsurprisingly, did not alleviate that particular problem, although over time households reassessed the balance of risks and started engaging in more activity. There is only so long that many people are willing to tolerate not using grooming services, for example.

One difficulty of examining any data on spending is that we can't disentangle fully whether the depressed spending is due to consumers being unwilling to spend (demand) or unable to spend on things they want to

FIGURE 16.1

Percentage change in consumer spending categories from January 2020

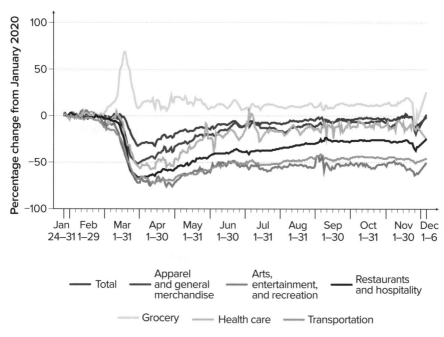

Source: Opportunity Insights Tracker, "Percent Change in All Consumer Spending," www.track
therecovery.org.

(supply). There's likely a bit of both going on. But data from the Transportation Security Administration on flight passenger numbers (see
Figure 16.2) does suggest that elevated health fears continue to depress
demand significantly in certain industries far beyond the impacts of
government regulations (remember, airlines had to maintain their remaining skeleton schedule as a condition of the bailout).

Over time, of course, we'd expect consumers to continue shifting
what they would have spent on these activities to other pursuits. Yet
when lockdowns were lifted, they maintained elevated saving levels—
deciding that if they were unwilling or unable to spend on things
that they would usually like, they would rather just keep the funds.
Bureau of Economic Analysis data show that the personal savings rate
was below 10 percent in January and February but then jumped to

FIGURE 16.2

Passenger throughput, Transportation Security Administration travel numbers 2019 versus 2020

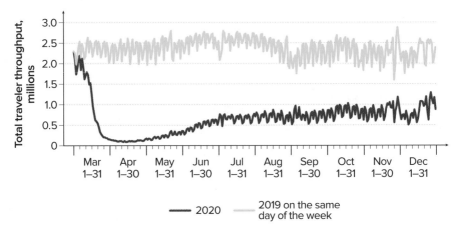

Source: Transportation Security Administration, "TSA Checkpoint Travel Numbers for 2020 and 2019," tsa.gov/coronavirus/passenger-throughput.

33.7 percent in April and remained elevated at 18.5 percent even after lockdown mandates were lifted by July (see Figure 16.3).[10]

Until the vaccine is rolled out and consumers have confidence that the virus isn't a threat, we are unlikely to see a full recovery of consumer demand in these particular industries and, given their size, this is likely to drag on economic activity overall. This is particularly the case given that an ongoing depression of these industries will generate substantial uncertainty for many low-wage employees about their jobs and wage prospects.

But it's not just the demand-side impacts that will contribute to weaker economic activity. Supply-side factors will prove a drag too. Most obviously, some industries still remain partially closed, especially big sports or concerts. Winning trust from customers and workers in other sectors has required businesses to invest in what would ordinarily be considered inefficiency.

Restaurants, movie theaters, and airlines already face regulations imposing social distancing through spacing of customers, thus making their operations less efficient. Other companies have had to install

FIGURE 16.3

Personal saving as a percentage of disposable personal income

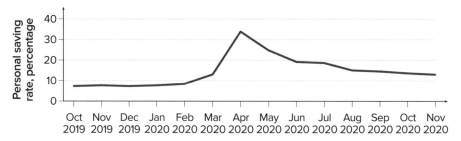

Source: Personal saving data from "Personal Income and Outlays, August 2020," Bureau of Economic Analysis.

more personal protective equipment, finance additional cleanings to sanitize workspaces, engage in temperature testing, or allow ongoing working from home.

Although this might not hit efficiency much in industries where full remote working is feasible, labor-intensive industries and those requiring some degree of seller-buyer interaction are likely to face a significant decline in their productivity.[11] The raised cost of doing business will mean less business will be done. So this will prove a further drag on the economic rebound.

On top of this, businesses have had to deal with a lot of ongoing uncertainty.[12] Workers could be absent for two weeks if they or their families contract the virus at any time, or report being in contact with someone affected, or face difficulties coming in if their kids' schools get closed.

There is the possibility of a repeat of partial lockdowns or other social distancing mandates, or even having to close your business because of an outbreak, as we saw in Florida and California during the summer of 2020. There's the risk that your suppliers or those you supply will be affected by disruption or a forced shutdown, too, either in the United States or abroad. This itself will deter risky investments: Why replace those inefficient industrial dryers in your dry cleaning business without knowing when or if your key local hotel customers might reopen and use your services?

Yes, the ongoing industry-specific depression of demand will constrain economic activity. But even among businesses that do reopen, the virus and its effects put a whole lot of sand in the gears to the efficient operation of businesses, compounding the GDP hit and proving a drag against a full V-shaped recovery after lockdowns were lifted.

2. Many businesses will fail, and jobs will be lost

A second reason that a "back to the future" recovery was unlikely is because, despite the best efforts of programs such as the Paycheck Protection Program to mothball businesses and keep employment relationships alive, many nevertheless failed, and many jobs were lost. This is, sadly, an inevitable consequence of a shock of this magnitude and the catastrophic failure of the public health efforts.

Small businesses in the most affected sectors, in particular, will have found it difficult to survive in an ongoing virus-depressed economy, and these failures will continue the longer the pandemic endures. There was a record-breaking 15 percent decline in the number of business owners between February and May 2020.[13]

Although the PPP loans were designed to prevent these failures or job losses, and there is some evidence that they did, Raj Chetty's team suggests they were less effective in maintaining employment in certain industries. That team's analysis finds that "professional, scientific, and technical services received a greater share of the PPP loans than accommodation and food services," despite the latter accounting for ten times the former's share of the total employment decline in February and March, before the PPP loans were introduced.[14]

Of course, the problem is not just that existing businesses failed. The lockdown, social distancing, and uncertainty also made it more difficult to found and open new businesses. If we compare this year's total level of new business formation against last year's then we can see that there were more than 57,000 cumulative "missing" new businesses overall by June 14, 2020, compared to the previous year. This quickly bounced back when the economy reopened, with a cumulatively higher number of business registrations compared with 2019 by mid-July 2020. However, the number of new businesses opening was

FIGURE 16.4

Percentage change in number of small businesses open, national figures, compared with January 2020

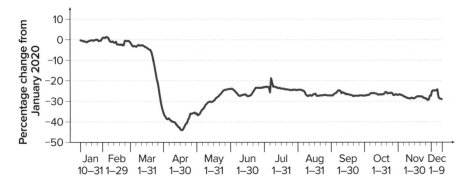

Source: Opportunity Insights Tracker, "Percent Change in Number of Small Businesses Open," www.tracktherecovery.org.

not enough to offset old businesses closing. As Figure 16.4 shows, overall the number of small businesses open as of mid-December was still down by 29 percent compared with January.

This is important, because while we would expect the economy to ultimately adjust to the virus, new businesses take time to open to replace old ones. Entrepreneurs cannot instantaneously build up resources and relationships with suppliers and workers to create an effective enterprise, especially in this disrupted economy. The loss of previously effective relationships and processes is real and will therefore continue to prove to be a drag on economic activity.

There will be a similar problem in labor markets. The United States has relatively flexible hire and fire laws, so when major shocks hit, unemployment spikes sharply (see Figure 16.5). Although these same relatively flexible labor market policies enable low unemployment rates in the long term, it takes some time for workers to reallocate efficiently across the economy into new roles. As you can see from the charts, with ongoing social distancing, although unemployment has seen a sharp fall following reopenings, there is still a long way to go before the economy gets near anything close to full employment.

FIGURE 16.5
U.S. unemployment rates

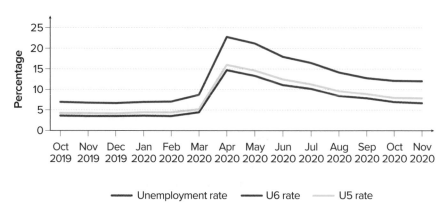

Source: "Employment Situation," U.S. Bureau of Labor Statistics.

Note: The U6 rate is total unemployed, plus all persons marginally attached to the labor force, plus total employed part time for economic reasons, as a percentage of the civilian labor force plus all persons marginally attached to the labor force. The U5 rate is total unemployed, plus discouraged workers, plus all other persons marginally attached to the labor force, as a percentage of the civilian labor force plus all persons marginally attached to the labor force. All rates are seasonally adjusted.

Lots of people well suited, specialized, or experienced in their old roles will therefore find themselves out of work as a result of the shock of the virus or lockdowns. Finding new positions that fit well with their skills takes time, as does being adequately trained to competently undertake the new role. This can mean productive job creation sometimes lags job destruction by a year or more.

The shock of the pandemic has disrupted a lot of work patterns and ways of doing business too. It seems likely a portion of the elevated numbers of people currently working at home will continue to do so even after the pandemic ends. Surveys of employers project that the share of people working remotely could triple compared with those working remotely pre-pandemic, for example.[15]

Yet if we really do see even a modest portion of workers change their working or residency locations, this can have big disruptive impacts on activity. Major modern cities have businesses that seek to attract young, well-educated professionals who then spend significant sums on inner-city transport, entertainment, and restaurants and bars. A combination of more teleworking and fewer people residing in cities could fundamentally change inner-city economies, with big reductions in demands for cleaning, security, hospitality services, ride-hailing services, and dining services.[16]

There's nothing inherently wrong with this. When circumstances change, people's choices change, as we saw in chapter 1. Over time, new services catering to people's revised demands would crop up. But this process of adjustment is not instantaneous, and there are significant search costs for laid-off workers in finding new employers.

We are therefore likely to see elevated unemployment caused by poorer job matching and business failures for some time, producing another headwind against a full, near-term V-shaped recovery.

3. Governments' policies may delay this reallocation process

Finally, while one can argue that the federal government's relief helped avert a greater immediate crisis of business failures and job losses, there will inevitably be tradeoffs between the extensive relief Congress provided and efficiency in recovery over the coming years.

Policymakers might really have tried to freeze bits of the economy of March 2020 to bridge to the recovery. But the economy is an ever-changing system of relationships based on supply and demand, as the Premier League example showed. This is true ordinarily; just under 3 percent of businesses and 6 percent of jobs disappeared every quarter last year, slightly less than the new enterprises and roles they were replaced with.[17]

The pandemic itself has hugely exacerbated this churn, as companies change their work patterns and demands change as a result of the virus. We know there has been huge substitution in spending from nonessential to essential activity, for example, especially from restaurants and bars toward groceries and other food sellers.[18] Economists at the University of Chicago found that, in April 2020, the rate of reallocation of jobs was 2.4 times higher than usual, with 3 new hires for every 10 layoffs.[19]

The problem with trying to preserve the economy of March 2020 is that if the virus has brought substantial permanent or semi-permanent alterations in behavior or tastes, then subsidizing businesses to protect existing jobs could have proved to be a drag on some aspects of the recovery. As the economy woke up to new realities in a changed world, we'd want workers and capital to be reallocated to where they are most productive as quickly as possible. Programs that delayed or disincentivized this reallocation—from subsidies to regulations—would then become extremely costly.

Think about the airline industry again. As economist Chad Syverson has pointed out, if we don't fly as often post-pandemic, then the capital value of aircraft will plunge, irrespective of any government bailout. Hotels in certain locations might not be viable, even with government support. We will no doubt see a raft of companies that tried to cling on in the hope that consumer demand would come roaring back, or that a vaccine would save the day, but which nevertheless just don't survive. Government programs will have kept a large number of "zombie" companies alive that will not be viable in the socially distanced world.

Using historical evidence of layoffs relating to recalls, those same University of Chicago economists believe that "32–42% of COVID-induced layoffs will be permanent, and that one-tenth of all work days (one-fifth for office workers) will shift from business premises to residences in the post-pandemic world relative to the pre-pandemic situation."[20]

These changes to the underlying structure of the economy, the full extent of which we cannot yet predict, are likely to mean there will be a painful efficiency hangover from this crisis. This will inevitably get blamed on governments not doing enough, but in part government relief will have delayed the recovery by prolonging employment relationships that turn out not to be viable post-pandemic.

Much like we saw in chapter 9, to get the best chance of a robust employment recovery we want as flexible a labor market as possible to avoid putting barriers between would-be employees and new vacancies.

That means making sure unemployment benefits do not disincentivize employment reentry, winding down employment retention subsidies, and repealing or suspending important labor market regulations that may have become more of a barrier to job creation in this new environment, such as occupational licensing laws and high minimum wage rates.[21]

The stay of execution that relief provided for certain sectors might have seemed worthy at the height of the lockdown, and there were of course no obvious metrics by which governments could have judged which companies would be viable and which would not. Recent news of delivering vaccines changes the calculus somewhat, of course; businesses and jobs that are able to survive in the coming months are more likely to survive beyond the pandemic. But at the very least we should remove or reduce any barriers that exist now to allow as rapid a possible an economic adjustment to new realities when the pandemic is over. Policies that delay or deter workers and capital from being allocated across sectors and locations to where they are best suited are another headwind against the most robust long-term recovery.

Back to the Old Future?

An economy, quite simply, is not a machine that you can turn off and turn on and expect it to resume unchanged. Yes, in terms of formal market activity, if the initial shutdown had been brief, and if the pandemic had ended quickly with a medical innovation, then tastes and business practices might have changed little. In that case, preserving the old industrial structure of the economy and "making people whole"—pausing the economy as far as possible—would likely have been efficient, and a sharp rebound would surely have followed.

But after some duration, the change induced by a prolonged pandemic makes it much more difficult to try to preserve the industrial structure of March 2020 and brings growing costs of doing so. There is now good reason to expect that the formal economy that emerges post-lockdown will look very different from that seen before, with the virus and the response to it dragging on economic activity for some time. The longer the pandemic, the greater the initial attempts to preserve the economy through the initial lockdown become costly relative to that approach's benefits. An economy is a living set of relationships, characterized by ongoing churn, business failures, and new ventures and jobs. It cannot be paused for long periods of time.

Most importantly, however, we must remember the lesson of the very first chapter. Economic welfare, that concept that should concern us most, is not just about market activity, or even employment, but our broader well-being. Even if we could attempt to preserve in aspic the structure of formal market relationships from the pre-pandemic era, stoppages in relationships such as friendships, jobs, and personal lives can have enduring social and economic effects that are not picked up in these formal indicators. The economy is us. We cannot simply forget the pandemic ever happened.

ECONOMIC LESSON

Formal market activity, commonly referred to as "the economy," is, in reality, a complex set of relationships among different actors that determine the consumption and production of goods and services. Since these are shaped by policies, tastes, and work practices, which change all the time, we cannot easily shut down an economy and reopen it in the same form sometime later. In the case of COVID-19, the virus and the policy response to it will change those relationships and where resources are ideally allocated, despite government efforts to protect the economy of March 2020. There are good reasons to suspect that expecting a full V-shaped rebound was always vastly over-optimistic. Instead, the economy is likely to remain below its pre-pandemic potential for some time, particularly while the public health threat remains and activity adjusts to new tastes and business practices.

ECONOMIC TERMS INTRODUCED

- **supply-side policies**: in the context of this chapter, referring to policies designed to enhance or protect the "productive potential" of the economy—that is, the maximum capacity for the economy to produce goods and services
- **demand-side policies**: in the context of this chapter, referring to policies to enhance or protect the desire and ability to spend on goods and services

- **transaction costs:** the added costs of engaging in a market transaction, including search costs, bargaining costs, enforcement costs, oversight costs, and similar costs
- **recession:** a significant decline in economic activity spread across the economy, lasting more than a few months, normally visible in real GDP, real income, employment, industrial production, and wholesale-retail sales data
- **reallocation shock:** when an unexpected event hits the economy, causing a large unforeseen change in the allocation of resources or workers into new activities or sectors

CONCLUSION

What Is Economics Good For?

COVID-19 is, first and foremost, a public health crisis. Even so, I hope that—in introducing economic concepts to you through the case study of the pandemic—you will finish this book convinced that economists were well placed to weigh in on the implications of, and policy responses to, this extraordinary crisis.

When the debate about what to do about COVID-19 really got going, there were calls to just listen to the experts. By this, commentators seemed to believe that policy should simply act on the advice of the virologists, epidemiologists, and public health officials.

Yet while the expertise of scientists is invaluable in providing ongoing scientific guidance and information, particularly as the knowledge base on COVID-19 evolves, setting policy necessarily requires considering broader tradeoffs, the impacts on human behavior of changes to laws, and the role of the political process in shaping outcomes. In other words, it needs economic analysis.

I began this text by defining economics as the study of choices under constraints. Although noneconomists often think of economics as synonymous with finance, or associate it with forecasting GDP or analyzing stock markets, at its most basic, economics is about analyzing human behavior in a world of scarcity and tradeoffs.

Economic insights were therefore critically important in a situation where we had to weigh up the benefits of saving lives against our liberties and commercial interests, consider how behavior might change with new knowledge or policy, and decide how to make decisions in a world of uncertainty.

Policymakers have been accused on occasion of being too worried about the economy during this pandemic. Supposedly many of them have, at times, prioritized it over public health efforts. But actual economists recognize that "the economy" should really just be a synonym for our well-being. When we talk about economic health, we should be referring to a broader conception of how we are faring overall rather than only what is happening to GDP. Far from too much focus being put on economics, a lot of the policy mistakes that were made throughout this crisis have occurred precisely because politicians have failed to think about human welfare in the more complete way that a good economist would.

The regulatory framework for the approval of new diagnostic tests early on, for example, failed to accurately consider the costs and benefits of a more permissive regime, resulting in too few tests, the rapid spread of the virus, and unnecessary damage to market activity.

Crude early lockdowns eschewed marginal thinking and were justified by epidemiological models that failed to sufficiently incorporate how human behavior would adjust to the presence of the virus. Attempts to fine-tune our behavior by turning regulations on and off to control the path of the virus have proven ineffective, in part because the changing regulations affected our own perceptions of risks, creating waves of unjustified risk-taking followed by overly cautious behavior.

Politicians have paid insufficient attention to the need for timely, accurate, localized data in informing populations about these risks, or to mechanisms that could provide ongoing feedback on the effectiveness of public health measures. The lack of public guidance on how the virus is transmitted and low-cost ways to reduce the risks, such as through better ventilation, has been astounding. At the state government level, anti-price-gouging laws worsened near-term shortages of certain goods too.

Federal regulators, who made mistakes that enabled the virus to spread quickly, making meaningful contact tracing impossible, set high barriers against the approval of fast, cheap, less-sensitive tests. In doing so, they undermined economic welfare and public health by delaying the possibility of a testing regime that could better ensure isolation of the infectious and get to grips with the virus swiftly, without the need for ongoing costly restrictions on activities. The result, again, was huge damage to our economic welfare.

At times, public health officials have themselves undermined measures that could have reduced COVID-19 transmission risks at low cost. The public was advised against wearing facemasks because policymakers thought of the market for them as static and their availability as zero-sum—that is, that one person buying a facemask deprived a health care worker of it. They failed to appreciate how quickly businesses and suppliers would ramp up production or innovate as demand surged.

Some public health experts likewise undermined compliance with social distancing guidelines by endorsing participation in political protests or by going out of their way to advise that even infected people may go out and vote on Election Day. In doing so, they muddied the general externality argument about COVID-19 by propagating their own preferences about what activities were important at a time when people were being advised not to participate in other pursuits that may have been more important to them personally.

Of course, politicians of both parties were guilty of encouraging behaviors that worsened the virus's spread at various stages of the pandemic. Trump regularly downplayed the virus and attended high-profile political events where attendees did not comply with social distancing or mask-wearing, while high-profile Democrats, including California Governor Gavin Newsom and Speaker of the House Nancy Pelosi, were seen to flout their own state's rules on indoor dining and salon closures.

Huge congressional relief programs were prioritized over granting more resources to medical innovation or to ensuring rapid, accurate diagnostic testing, even though the economic returns of getting to grips with the public health crisis earlier on would have been huge. Already, political incentives are pushing politicians toward talking about the need for national self-sufficiency in the production of certain medical and pharmaceutical goods, or for updated pandemic plans. We will likely leave this pandemic better prepared for fighting the war that will have just ended than being ready to face the next crisis.

Even now, with vaccines providing a feasible route to end this nightmare soon, there seems a bizarre lack of urgency in ensuring they are rolled out quickly. The Food and Drug Administration is now delaying vaccines approved elsewhere. State-level policymakers are trying to centrally plan the allocation process, resulting, predictably, in images of huge lines in some states and stories of vaccines being thrown away in others. Despite the vaccines actually existing, and Europe showing the risks of a more-transmissible strain likely to bite in the United States soon, policymakers do not appear to be updating their implicit cost-benefit analyses of mitigation measures either, despite both of these realities strengthening the case for greater efforts to reduce transmission of the virus now.

True, mistakes were always going to have been made, given the novel nature of this virus and the fact that such a shock had not before afflicted today's sophisticated modern society. Even the most libertarian among us have recognized that there is more far justification for intervening in market activity during a pandemic than in ordinary times. But it's clear that a host of government failures have made this crisis worse than it needed to be.

The precise measures taken have been contentious, both because they were unprecedented in their intrusiveness (clearly overreaching often) but also because major crises like this can have much longer-lasting impacts on policy.

After wars—which COVID-19 has been analogized to—the size and scope of government never quite seems to fall back to where it was before. People rightly perceived that there was a lot at stake in the response. Some economic historians even believe there is a tradeoff, and that highly coercive governments will tend to deal better with crises such as pandemics, but at the cost of those same coercive tendencies making those countries poorer in normal times and less innovative in finding sustainable solutions to said crises.[1]

It will be important, then, that any future inquest into the pandemic response doesn't just assume that other countries' "better" performance on public health proves the virtues of their forms of government more broadly. Our liberties, and the prosperity they engender, are incredibly precious. If anything, the delicate tradeoffs embedded within this crisis surely show the need for being more discerning about the scope of overall government activity and when it is truly justified for the government to intervene.

We have seen remarkable innovation at the level of households, businesses, and health care professionals in learning to live with the virus. The medical and pharmaceutical sectors have worked at rapid speed to find us treatments and vaccines to help mitigate or end this pandemic. Public health efforts, however—supposedly a core government function—have generally shown little sign of progress from what they were a century ago. Quarantines, shutting things down, hand washing, and facemasks are hardly novel approaches to dealing with a respiratory virus. Maybe, just maybe, governments' ever-broadening scope has taken focus away from innovation in areas where government activity could, in theory, have important benefits.

This book, however, was not primarily about the ins and outs of pandemic-related economics or even the scope of government. It was an introduction to economics through the example of the pandemic. This crisis has highlighted pertinent case studies of timeless economic principles and ideas that are worth remembering. My hope is that if you have made it this far, you will turn this final page having acquired a better understanding of them and be ready to apply the lessons to future economic challenges.

ACKNOWLEDGMENTS

Writing this book proved a more daunting prospect than perhaps I originally envisaged. Just a month or so into the project, three things became clear. First, I wanted to take on more concepts than initially planned, at greater length. Second, writing on a subject that was rapidly evolving would require near-constant revisions on everything from content to verb tenses. Third, the possibility that the pandemic would end or that public interest in the topic might wane, particularly because of a medical innovation that might appear in the near future, meant that there was a relatively short window for publishing the book to ensure its maximum timeliness.

A consequence of these three factors is that I've ended up putting a lot more pressure on my superb Cato Institute colleagues in terms of workload. In particular, I would like to thank Jason Kuznicki and Karen Garvin for their flexible and sterling efforts in content editing and copyediting at speed and our research assistant David Kemp for his ever-willingness to highlight sloppy thinking, produce charts, and make sure my memory did not deceive me in my references and citations.

The concept for this book was conceived in conversation with Jeffrey Miron, Cato's director of economic studies, and David Boaz, Cato's executive vice president. Both have been incredibly supportive of what I was trying to achieve and provided useful comments and feedback on an early draft. Eleanor O'Connor, Cato's managing director for books, oversaw the publication process particularly astutely.

Current and former colleagues and friends who provided extensive, helpful comments on the first draft include Stephen Davies, Oliver Wiseman, Diego Zuluaga, and Len Shackleton. I am deeply indebted to them.

Scott Lincicome, Gene Healy, Steven Hamilton, Chris Edwards, Philip Booth, Steven Horowitz, Alan Reynolds, Rupert Darwall, Alex Tabarrok, John Cochrane, David Henderson, Chris Giles, Todd Zywicki, Sam Bowman, Ben Southwood, Rory Meakin, Sam Dumitriu, and Jonathan Portes either reviewed particular chapters or unwittingly provided important insights for certain sections in conversations or electronic exchanges.

In truth, however, much of this work stands on the shoulders of economists as a broader community. Institutions such as Chicago Booth's Initiative on Global Markets survey group and blogs such as Tyler Cowen and Alex Tabarrok's *Marginal Revolution*, Timothy Taylor's *Conversable Economist*, and John Cochrane's *The Grumpy Economist* proved deep mines of inspiration. I have been astounded at the speed and quality of work produced in relation to the pandemic in the new papers that are published weekly at the National Bureau of Economic Research, many of which are cited here. Kevin Lewis's daily emails, *Politico*'s briefings, and a crossdisciplinary email group of like-minded scholars provided both revelations and challenges to my preconceptions. I wish to thank all who contributed without realizing it.

On a personal level, I would like to thank my parents and broader family for being supportive from across the Atlantic Ocean as I worked hard to finish this.

My former employers—Frontier Economics, the Centre for Policy Studies, and the Institute of Economic Affairs—kept my love of economics alive and got me into a place where I'd feel confident enough to take on this type of book. I would not be in the position to do so at the Cato Institute, however, without the vision of the late R. Evan Scharf, whose named chair I occupy. His widow, Sue Scharf, has always been encouraging of my work, and I would like to thank her family deeply for their ongoing generosity in supporting my role.

Finally, I'd like to express my gratitude for my darling Tessa, whose support and guidance has been unwavering during this process. In our first year of living together, she probably didn't imagine we'd be stuck indoors for months on end, with me cramped during waking hours over a laptop at the kitchen table. This book is dedicated to her. I am grateful for her patience, understanding, and love. The best thing to happen in 2020 was her saying "yes" to becoming my fiancée.

Chapter 1

1. Áine Cain, "9 Retailers that Have Hiked Wages during the Coronavirus Pandemic," *Business Insider*, March 25, 2020.

2. Thomas Franck, "Hardest-hit Industries: Nearly Half the Leisure and Hospitality Jobs Were Lost in April," CNBC, May 8, 2020.

3. Kim Parker, Juliana Menasce Horowitz, and Anna Brown, "About Half of Lower-Income Americans Report Household Job or Wage Loss Due to COVID-19," Pew Research Center, April 21, 2020.

4. Peter Weber, *The Week*, "Most Americans Will Get Coronavirus Stimulus Check in April. Here's How the Program Works," *Yahoo! News*, March 26, 2020.

5. Jeffrey Miron, Peter Van Doren, and Ryan Bourne, "The Value of Living," *Cato at Liberty* (blog), April 20, 2020.

6. Justin Wolfers, "G.D.P. Doesn't Credit Social Distancing, but It Should," *New York Times*, May 14, 2020.

Chapter 2

1. Matt Ridley, "So Where Did the Virus Come From?," *Wall Street Journal*, March 29, 2020.

2. Shing Hei Zhan, Benjamin E. Deverman, and Yujia Alina Chan, "SARS-CoV-2 Is Well Adapted for Humans. What Does This Mean for Re-emergence?," bioRXiv, May 2, 2020, https://doi.org/10.1101/2020.05.01.073262.

3. Roni Caryn Rabin, "First Patient with Wuhan Coronavirus Is Identified in the U.S.," *New York Times*, January 21, 2020.

4. Daniel P. Oran and Eric J. Topol, "Prevalence of Asymptomatic SARS-CoV-2 Infection: A Narrative Review," *Annals of Internal Medicine* 173, no. 5 (June 2020): 362–67, https://doi.org/10.7326/M20-3012; and Steven Sanche, Yen Ting Lin, Chonggang Xu, Ethan Romero-Severson, Nick Hengartner, and Ruian Ke, "High Contagiousness and Rapid Spread of Severe Acute Respiratory Syndrome Coronavirus 2 *Emerging Infectious Diseases* 26, no. July 2020): 1470–77, https://dx.doi.org/10.3201/eid2607.200282.

5. John Osterhoudt and Nick Gillespie, "Should the Coronavirus Lockdowns End Immediately? Hoover Institution's David Henderson vs. University of Michigan's Justin Wolfers," Soho Forum debate video, Reason.com, April 24, 2020.

6. Martin Bodenstein, Giancarlo Corsetti, and Luca Guerrieri, "Social Distancing and Supply Distributions in a Pandemic," Cambridge-INET Working Paper Series no. 2020/17, and Cambridge Working Papers in Economics: 2031, May 2, 2020.

7. Christopher Lee, "Texas Hospital Says Man, 30, Died after Attending a 'Covid Party,'" *New York Times*, July 12, 2020.

8. Dhaval M. Dave, Andrew I. Friedson, Kyutaro Matsuzawa, Joseph J. Sabia, and Samuel Safford, "Black Lives Matter Protests, Social Distancing, and COVID-19," National Bureau of Economic Research (NBER) Working Paper no. 27408, June 2020 (revised August 2020), https://doi.org/10.3386/w27408; and Dhaval M. Dave, Andrew I. Friedson, Kyutaro Matsuzawa, Drew McNichols, Connor Redpath, and Joseph J. Sabia, "Risk Aversion, Offsetting Community Effects, and COVID-19: Evidence from an Indoor Political Rally," NBER Working Paper No. 27522, July 2020 (revised August 2020), https://doi.org/10.3386/w27522.

9. Bizarrely, their decision was endorsed by a prominent public health expert, who apparently did not understand the externality argument either. See, for example: Gregg Gonsalves (@gregggonsalves), "That is, many marching know the risks of #SARSCOV2, as the epidemic is already raging in their communities. They are not acting out of ignorance, which needs to be 'corrected' by the experts," Twitter, June 6, 2020, 6:55 a.m., https://twitter.com/gregggonsalves/status/1269221276071145472?s=20.

10. Edgar K. Browning, "The Myth of Fiscal Externalities," *Public Finance Review* 27, no. 1 (January 1999): 3–18, https://doi.org/10.1177/109114219902700101.

11. J. David Goodman, "How Much Is a View Worth in Manhattan? Try $11 Million," *New York Times*, July 22, 2019.

12. R. H. Coase, "The Problem of Social Cost," *Journal of Economics and Law* 3 (October 1960): 1–44; and Deirdre McCloskey, "The So-Called Coase Theorem," *Eastern Economic Journal* 24, no. 3 (Summer 1998): 367–71.

13. Sam Bowman, "Fighting Covid Is a Binary Choice—and the Majority Favour Lockdown," *Daily Telegraph* (London), October 13, 2020.

14. For a discussion of the economic case for taxes and subsidies, rather than lockdowns, in dealing with this externality, see: Greg Kaplan, Benjamin Moll, and Giovanni Violante, "A Tax-Based Alternative to Lockdowns," University of Chicago, Becker Friedman Institute, Key Economic Findings about COVID-19, September 2, 2020.

15. Jeffrey E. Harris, "The Subways Seeded the Massive Coronavirus Epidemic in New York City," NBER Working Paper no. 27021, April 2020 (revised August 2020), https://doi.org/10.3386/w27021.

16. John McLaren, "Racial Disparity in COVID-19 Deaths: Seeking Economic Roots with Census Data," NBER Working Paper no. 27407, June 2020, https://doi.org/10.3386/w27407; and Christopher R. Knittel and Bora Ozaltun, "What Does and Does Not Correlate with COVID-19 Death Rates," NBER Working Paper no. 27391, June 2020.

17. Daron Acemoglu, Victor Chernozhukov, Iván Werning, and Michael D. Whinston, "Optimal Targeted Lockdowns in A Multi-Group SIR Model," NBER Working Paper no. 27102, May 2020 (revised June 2020), https://doi.org/10.3386/w27391.

18. Thiago de Oliveira Souza, "Externalities, Incentives, Government Failure, and the Coronavirus Outbreak," Social Science Research Network (SSRN), April 23, 2020, https://dx.doi.org/10.2139/ssrn.3583160.

19. M. Keith Chen, Judith A. Chevalier, and Elisa F. Long, "Nursing Home Staff Networks and COVID-19," NBER Working Paper no. 27608, July 2020, https://doi.org/10.3386/w27608.

20. Christopher Weaver, Anna Wilde Mathews, and Jon Kamp, "COVID-19 Cases Jump in Sunbelt Nursing Homes," *Wall Street Journal*, July 11, 2020.

Chapter 3

1. WDW News Today (@WDWNT), "Current crowds at the Magic Kingdom for tonight's showing of Happily Ever After . . . #DisneyWorld," Twitter, March 15, 2020, 8:41 p.m., https://twitter.com/WDWNT/status/1239351087741702145?s=20.

2. "Abigail Disney Slams Tweet Showing Huge Crowds at Magic Kingdom," Fox Business, March 16, 2020.

3. David Boaz, "Who Will Reopen the Economy—the President, the Governors, or the People?," *Cato at Liberty* (blog), April 15, 2020.

4. "Nike Statement on COVID-19," Nike News, March 26, 2020; and Kellie Ell, "Store Closures in North America Begin as Coronavirus Spreads," WWD, March 14, 2020.

5. "Starbucks Will Offer Coffee to Go ONLY across America and Close Some Stores Amid Coronavirus Outbreak," *Daily Mail* (London), March 16, 2020.

6. Scott McCartney, "Why Empty Planes Keep Flying through the Pandemic," *Wall Street Journal*, May 6, 2020.

7. "The State of the Restaurant Industry," OpenTable online database, updated September 9, 2020.

8. Beth McKibben, "Atlanta Mayor Closes Bars and Limits Restaurants to Takeout," Eater Atlanta, March 19, 2020.

9. Sumedha Gupta, Thuy D. Nguyen, Felipe Lozano Rojas, Shyam Raman, Byungkyu Lee, Ana Bento, Kosali I. Simon, and Coady Wing, "Tracking Public and Private Responses to the COVID-19 Epidemic: Evidence from State and Local Government Actions," National Bureau of Economic Research (NBER) Working Paper no. 27027, April 2020, https://doi.org/10.3386/w27027.

10. Raj Chetty, John N. Friedman, Nathaniel Hendren, Michael Stepner, and the Opportunity Insights Team, "Real-Time Economics: A New Platform to Track the Impacts of COVID-19 on People, Businesses, and Communities Using Private Sector Data," https://tracktherecovery.org/.

11. Raj Chetty, John N. Friedman, Nathaniel Hendren, Michael Stepner, and the Opportunity Insights Team, "Real-Time Economics: A New Platform to Track the Impacts of COVID-19 on People, Businesses, and Communities Using Private Sector Data," Opportunity Insights Economic Tracker, May 7, 2020.

12. Chetty et al., "Real-Time Economics."

13. Christopher J. Cronin and William N. Evans, "Private Precaution and Public Restrictions: What Drives Social Distancing and Industry Foot Traffic in the COVID-19 Era?," NBER Working Paper no. 27531, July 2020, https://doi.org/10.3386/w27531.

14. James Sears, J. Miguel Villas-Boas, Vasco Villas-Boas, and Sofia Berto Villas-Boas, "Are We #StayingHome to Flatten the Curve?," California University Department of Agriculture and Resource Economics Working Papers, May 25, 2020 (revised August 6 2020).

15. CityMapper, "% of Stockholm Moving Compared to Usual," City Mapper Mobility Index, https://citymapper.com/cmi/stockholm.

16. Rupali Mehra, "How the Coronavirus Is Affecting Life on Sweden's Tourism Island Gotland," *The Local* (Sweden), April 8, 2020.

17. Asger Lau Andersen, Emil Toft Hansen, Niels Johannesen, and Adam Sheridan, "Pandemic, Shutdown and Consumer Spending: Lessons from Scandinavian Policy Responses to COVID-19," Cornell University, May 10, 2020.

18. John Cochrane, "An SIR Model with Behavior," *The Grumpy Economist* (blog), May 4, 2020.

19. EpiForecasts, "National and Subnational Estimates for the United States of America, Centre for Mathematical Modelling of Infectious Disease. See also "COVID-19 Infections Tracker," https://covid19-projections.com/infections-tracker/.

20. "Effective Reproduction Number," Swiss National COVID-19 Science Task Force, https://ncs-tf.ch/en/situation-report.

21. Simon Wood, "Did COVID-19 Infections Decline before UK Lockdown?," arXiv Cornell University, June 1, 2020.

22. Dhaval M. Dave, Andrew I. Friedson, Kyutaro Matsuzawa, Drew McNichols, and Joseph J. Sabia, "Did the Wisconsin Supreme Court Restart a COVID-19 Epidemic? Evidence from a Natural Experiment," NBER Working Paper no. 27322, June 2020, https://doi.org/10.3386/w27322.

23. Nicholas W. Papageorge, Matthew V. Zahn, Michèle Belot, Eline van den Broek-Altenburg, Syngjoo Choi, Julian C. Jamison, and Egon Tripodi, "Socio-Demographic Factors Associated with Self-Protecting Behavior during the Covid-19 Pandemic," NBER Working Paper no. 27378, June 2020, https://doi.org/10.3386/w27378.

24. Dylan Balla-Elliott, Zoë B. Cullen, Edward L. Glaeser, Michael Luca, and Christopher T. Stanton, "Business Reopening Decisions and Demand Forecasts during the COVID-19 Pandemic," NBER Working Paper no. 27362, June 2020, https://doi.org/10.3386/w27362.

25. Felipe Lozano Rojas, Xuan Jiang, Laura Montenovo, Kosali I. Simon, Bruce A. Weinberg, and Coady Wing, "Is the Cure Worse Than the Problem Itself? Immediate Labor Market Effects of COVID-19 Case Rates and School Closures in the U.S.," NBER Working Paper no. 27127, May 2020, https://doi.org/10.3386/w27127; Sumedha Gupta, Laura Montenovo, Thuy D. Nguyen, Felipe Lozano Rojas, Ian M. Schmutte, Kosali I. Simon, Bruce A. Weinberg, and Coady Wing, "Effects of Social Distancing Policy on Labor Market Outcomes," NBER Working Paper no. 27280, May 2020, https://doi.org/10.3386/w27280; ChaeWon Baek, Peter B. McCrory, Todd Messer, and Preston Mui, "Unemployment Effects of Stay-at-Home Orders: Evidence from High Frequency Claims Data," Institute for Research on Labor and Employment (IRLE) Working Paper 101-20, July 2020; and Raj Chetty, John N. Friedman, Nathaniel Hendren, Michael Stepner, and the Opportunity Insights Team, "How Did COVID-19 and Stabilization Policies Affect Spending and Employment? A New Real-Time Economic Tracker Based on

Private Sector Data," NBER Working Paper no. 27431, June 2020, https://doi.org /10.3386/w27431.

26. Austan Goolsbee and Chad Syverson, "Fear, Lockdown, and Diversion: Comparing Drivers of Pandemic Economic Decline 2020," Becker Friedman Institute Working Paper, June 18, 2020.

27. Marcella Alsan, Luca Braghieri, Sarah Eichmeyer, Minjeong Joyce Kim, Stefanie Stantcheva, and David Y. Yang, "Civil Liberties in Times of Crisis," NBER Working Paper no. 27972, October, 2020, https://doi.org/10.3386/w27972.

28. Edward L. Glaeser, Ginger Zhe Jin, Benjamin T. Leyden, and Michael Luca, "Learning from Deregulation: The Asymmetric Impact of Lockdown and Reopening on Risky Behavior during COVID-19," NBER Working Paper no. 27650, August 2020, https://doi.org/10.3386/w27650.

29. See data from the Opportunity Insights Tracker, "Percent Change in Number of Small Businesses Open: States," www.tracktherecovery.org.

30. Tsutomu Watanabe and Tomoyoshi Yabu, "Japan's Voluntary Lockdown," *COVID Economics: Vetted and Real-Time Papers* 46, Centre for Economic Policy Research (September 1, 2020): 1–31.

Chapter 4

1. "Today's Coronavirus Update: Trump Closes Borders, New York Locks Down," *New York Post*, March 20, 2020.

2. Trudy Ann Cameron, "Euthanizing the Value of a Statistical Life," *Review of Environmental Economics and Policy* 4, no. 2 (Summer 2010): 161–78, https://doi.org/10.1093/reep/req010.

3. Scott D. Grosse, Kurt V. Krueger, and Mercy Mvundura, "Economic Productivity by Age and Sex: 2007 Estimates for the United States," *Medical Care* 47, no. 7, Supplement 1 (July 2009: S94–103, https://doi.org/10.1097/MLR.0b013e31819c9571.

4. H. Spencer Banzhaf, "Retrospectives: The Cold-War Origins of the Value of Statistical Life," *Journal of Economic Perspectives* 28, no. 4 (Fall 2014): 213–26, https://doi.org/10.1257/jep.28.4.213.

5. Thomas J. Kniesner and W. Kip Viscusi, "The Value of a Statistical Life," Vanderbilt Law Research Paper no. 19-15, Social Science Research Network (SSRN), http://dx.doi.org/10.2139/ssrn.3379967.

6. Tim Harford, "How Do We Value a Statistical Life?," *Financial Times*, April 3, 2020.

7. Chris Doucouliagos, T. D. Stanley, and Margaret Giles, "Are Estimates of the Value of a Statistical Life Exaggerated?," *Journal of Health Economics* 31, no. 1 (January 2012): 197–206, https://doi.org/10.1016/j.jhealeco.2011.10.001.

8. Isabel V. Sawhill and Christopher Pulliam, "Six Facts about Wealth in the United States," Brookings Institution, June 25, 2019.

9. Sabah Meddings, "Coronavirus Vaccine: Wanted—Human Guinea Pigs to Be Infected with Covid-19," *The Times* (London), June 7, 2020.

10. "Pandemic Planning Scenarios: Infection Fatality Ratio, Current Best Estimate," Centers for Disease Control and Prevention, September 10, 2020, https://www.cdc.gov/coronavirus/2019-ncov/hcp/planning-scenarios.html.

11. James Sears, J. Miguel Villas-Boas, Vasco Villas-Boas, and Sofia Berto Villas-Boas, "Are We #StayingHome to Flatten the Curve?," California University Department of Agriculture and Resource Economics Working Papers, April 5, 2020 (revised May 2020).

12. For a good summary, see: Joseph E. Aldy and W. Kip Viscusi, "Age Differences in the Value of Statistical Life: Revealed Preference Evidence," *Review of Environmental Economics and Policy* 1, no. 2 (Summer 2007): 241–60, https://doi.org/10.1093/reep/rem014.

13. James Broughel and Michael Kotrous, "The Benefits of Coronavirus Suppression: A Cost-Benefit Analysis of the Response to the First Wave of COVID-19," Mercatus Center, COVID-19 Economic Recovery Working Paper, June 11, 2020.

14. Some nursing homes were aware of these possibilities. See, for example: "No Coronavirus Cases at Nursing Home Where Staff Paid to Live On-site, Owner Says," Becker's Hospital Review, May 19, 2020.

Chapter 5

1. Donald Trump (@RealDonaldTrump), "We cannot let the cure be worse than the problem itself. At the end of the 15 day period, we will make a decision as to which way we want to go!," March 22, 2020, 11:50 p.m., https://twitter.com/realdonaldtrump/status/1241935285916782593?lang=en.

2. Initiative on Global Markets Forum, "Policy for the COVID-19 Crisis," University of Chicago Booth School of Business, March 27, 2020.

3. George Selgin, "The New Deal and Recovery: A New *Alt-M* Series," *Alt-M* (blog), June 12, 2020.

4. Scott Atlas (@SWAtlasHoover), "Famous public health 'experts' testing & isolating asymptomatics, limiting in-person school, restricting businesses . . . That's the DEFINITION of lockdown! Why care? Got another email from a wife of a suicide victim—pleading for me to OPEN America. End the insanity #LockdownsKill," Twitter, October 16, 2020, 4:22 p.m., https://twitter.com/SWAtlasHoover/status/1317199337320054789?s=20.

5. Atlas (@SWAtlasHoover), "Famous public health 'experts.'"

6. Centers for Disease Control and Prevention, "Provisional COVID-19 Death Counts by Sex, Age, and State," updated as of October 14, 2020.

7. James Sears, J. Miguel Villas-Boas, Vasco Villas-Boas, and Sofia Berto Villas-Boas, "Are We #StayingHome to Flatten the Curve?," California University Department of Agriculture and Resource Economics Working Papers, April 5, 2020 (revised May 2020).

8. Patrick G. T. Walker et al. "The Global Impact of COVID-19 and Strategies for Mitigation and Suppression," Imperial College London, March 3, 2020, https://doi.org/10.25561/77735.

9. Michael Greenstone and Vishan Nigam, "Does Social Distancing Matter?," Becker Friedman Institute Working Paper no. 2020-26, March 25, 2020, Social Science Research Network (SSRN), https://dx.doi.org/10.2139/ssrn.3561244.

10. Centers for Disease Control And Prevention, "Excess Deaths Associated with COVID-19: Number of Excess Deaths," updated July 15, 2020.

11. Niall Ferguson, "No More Handshakes," *Times Literary Supplement*, October 30, 2020.

12. Phillip Magness, "SimCity-Style Modeling Flunks the Real-World Test," in *Coronavirus and Disease Modeling*, ed. Peter C. Earle (Great Barrinton, MA: American Institute for Economic Research, 2020).

13. John Cochrane, "Dumb Reopening Might Just Work," *The Grumpy Economist* (blog), May 4, 2020; and Flavio Toxvaerd, "Equilibrium Social Distancing," Cambridge-INET Working Paper Series no. 2020/08, March 2020.

14. Joshua S. Gans, "The Economic Consequences of $\hat{R} = 1$: Towards a Workable Behavioural Epidemiological Model of Pandemics," NBER Working Paper no. 27632, July 2020, https://doi.org/10.3386/w27632.

15. Andrew Atkeson, Karen Kopecky, and Tao Zha, "Four Stylized Facts about COVID-19," NBER Working Paper no. 27719, August 2020, https://doi.org/10.3386/w27719.

16. James H. Fowler, Seth J. Hill, Nick Obradovich, and Remy Levin, "The Effect of Stay-at-Home Orders on COVID-19 Cases and Fatalities in the United States," medRXiv, May 12, 2020, https://doi.org/10.1101/2020.04.13.20063628.

17. Dhaval M. Dave, Andrew I. Friedson, Kyutaro Matsuzawa, Joseph J. Sabia, and Samuel Safford, "Were Urban Cowboys Enough to Control COVID-19? Local Shelter-in-Place Orders and Coronavirus Case Growth," NBER Working Paper no. 27229, May 2020, https://doi.org/10.3386/w27229.

18. Benjamin Born, Alexander Dietrich, and Gernot J. Müller, "The Lockdown Effect: A Counterfactual for Sweden," Centre for Economic Policy Research Discussion Paper no. DP14744, May 11, 2020.

19. Alexander Arnon, John Ricco, and Kent Smetters, "Epidemiological and Economic Effects of Lockdown," Brookings Papers on Economic Activity Conference Drafts, September 24, 2020.

20. Charles Courtemanche, Joseph Garuccio, Anh Le, Joshua Pinkston, and Aaron Yelowitz, "Strong Social Distancing Measures in the United States Reduced the COVID-19 Growth Rate," *Health Affairs* 39, no. 7 (2020): 1237–46, https://doi.org/10.1377/hlthaff.2020.00608.

21. Pedro M Folegatti et al., "Safety and Immunogenicity of the ChAdOx1 nCoV-19 Vaccine against SARS-CoV-2: A Preliminary Report of a Phase 1/2, Single-Blind, Randomised Controlled Trial," *The Lancet*, July 20, 2020, https://doi.org/10.1016/S0140-6736(20)31604-4; and "Coronavirus: Protein Treatment Trial 'a Breakthrough,'" BBC News, July 20, 2020.

22. James Broughel and Michael Kotrous, "The Benefits of Coronavirus Suppression: A Cost-Benefit Analysis of the Response to the First Wave of COVID-19," Mercatus Center, COVID-19 Economic Recovery Working Paper, June 11, 2020.

23. Thomas J. Kniesner and Ryan Sullivan, "The Forgotten Numbers: A Closer Look at COVID-19 Non-Fatal Valuations," Institute of Labor Economics (IZA) Discussion Paper no. 13632, August 2020.

24. Marcella Alsan, Luca Braghieri, Sarah Eichmeyer, Minjeong Joyce Kim, Stefanie Stantcheva, and David Y. Yang, "Civil Liberties in Times of Crisis," NBER Working Paper no. 27972, October 2020, https://doi.org/10.3386/w27972.

25. "Gross Domestic Product, Third Quarter 2020 (Advance Estimate)," Bureau of Economic Analysis, news release, October 29, 2020.

26. Nicola Fuchs-Schündeln, Dirk Krueger, Alexander Ludwig, and Irina Popova, "The Long-Term Distributional and Welfare Effects of Covid-19 School Closures," NBER Working Paper no. 27773, September 2020, https://doi.org/10.3386/w27773.

27. Michael Andrews, "Bar Talk: Informal Social Interactions, Alcohol Prohibition, and Invention," Harvard University Working Paper, March 31, 2020.

28. Julian Kozlowski, Laura Veldkamp, and Venky Venkateswaran, "Scarring Body and Mind: The Long-Term Belief-Scarring Effects of COVID-19," NBER Working Paper no. 27439, June 2020, https://doi.org/10.3386/w27439.

29. Casey Mulligan, "The Economic Cost of Shutting Down "Non-essential" Businesses," *supply and demand (in that order)* (blog), March 26, 2020.

30. Eudora Maria de Castro Ribeiro, "COVID-19: Pandemics, Recessions, and Suicide—Lessons from the Past and Points to the Future," in *COVID Economics, Vetted and Real Time Papers* 36, Centre for Economic Policy Research, (July 10, 2020): 45–79.

31. Sandro Galea, Raina M. Merchant, and Nicole Lurie, "The Mental Health Consequences of COVID-19 and Physical Distancing: The Need for Prevention and Early Intervention," *JAMA Internal Medicine* 180, no. 6 (2020): 817–18, doi:10.1001/jamainternmed.2020.1562.

32. Ann Hsing et al., "A Rapid Assessment of Psychological Distress and Well-Being: Impact of the COVID-19 Pandemic and Shelter-in-Place," April 17, 2020; and William Wan and Heather Long, "'Cries for Help': Drug Overdoses Are Soaring during the Coronavirus Pandemic," *Washington Post*, July, 2020.

33. Jeffrey A. Singer, "Elective Doesn't Mean Non-Essential. Skip Sweeping Coronavirus Bans, Let Doctors Decide," *USA Today*, May 7, 2020.

34. Christopher J. Cronin and William N. Evans, "Nursing Home Quality, COVID-19 Deaths, and Excess Mortality," NBER Working Paper no. 28012, October 2020, https://doi.org/10.3386/w28012.

35. Nicole Fisher, "History—and Psychology—Predict Riots and Protests amid Coronavirus Pandemic Lockdowns," *Forbes*, May 21, 2020.

36. Christopher Ingraham, "Spike in Violent Crime Follows Rise in Gun-Buying amid Social Upheaval," *Washington Post*, July 15, 2020.

37. David M. Cutler and Lawrence H. Summers, "The COVID-19 Pandemic and the $16 Trillion Virus," *Journal of the America Medical Association* 324, no. 15 (October 12, 2020): 1495–96, doi:10.1001/jama.2020.19759.

38. See Opportunity Insights Tracker, "Percent Change in All Consumer Spending, Restaurants & Hotels, States: South Dakota"; and Opportunity Insights Tracker, "Percent Change in All Consumer Spending, Restaurants & Hotels, National," October 16, 2020, www.tracktherecovery.org.

39. Victoria Knight, "No, the WHO Didn't Change Its Lockdown Stance or 'Admit' Trump Was Right," Politifact, October 15, 2020.

Chapter 6

1. Hannah Fry, "Paddle Boarder Chased by Boat, Arrested in Malibu after Flouting Coronavirus Closures," *Los Angeles Times*, April 3, 2020.

2. Executive Order 2020-42 (COVID-19)—Rescinded, Office of Governor Gretchen Whitmer, https://www.michigan.gov/whitmer/0,9309,7-387-90499_90705 -525182—,00.html.

3. John G. Fernald, "Roads to Prosperity? Assessing the Link between Public Capital and Productivity," *American Economic Review* 89, no. 3 (June 1999): 619–38, https://doi.org/10.1257/aer.89.3.619.

4. Gilles Duranton and Matthew A. Turner, "Urban Growth and Transportation," *Review of Economic Studies* 79, no. 4 (October 2012): 1407–40, https://doi .org/10.1093/restud/rds010.

5. Diego Zuluaga, "Sadly, Economic Thinking Is Still Marginal," *Medium*, July 26, 2017.

6. Daron Acemoglu, Victor Chernozhukov, Iván Werning, and Michael D. Whinston, "Optimal Targeted Lockdowns in a Multi-Group SIR Model," National Bureau of Economic Research (NBER) Working Paper no. 27102, May 2020 (revised June 2020), https://doi.org/10.3386/w27102.

7. Varadarajan V. Chari, Rishabh Kirpalani, and Christopher Phelan, "The Hammer and the Scalpel: On the Economics of Indiscriminate versus Targeted Isolation Policies during Pandemics," NBER Working Paper no. 27232, May 2020, https://doi.org/10.3386/w27232.

8. David Baqaee, Emmanuel Farhi, Michael J. Mina, and James H. Stock, "Reopening Scenarios," NBER Working Paper no. 27244, May 2020, https://doi.org /10.3386/w27244.

9. Serina Chang, Emma Pierson, Pang Wei Koh, Jaline Gerardin, Beth Redbird, David Grusky, and Jure Leskovek, "Mobility Network Models of COVID-19 Explain Inequities and Inform Reopening," *Nature*, November 10, 2020, https:// doi.org/10.1038/s41586-020-2923-3.

10. Stephen A. Lauer et al., "The Incubation Period of Coronavirus Disease 2019 (COVID-19) from Publicly Reported Confirmed Cases: Estimation and Application," *Annals of Internal Medicine* 172, no. 9 (May 2020): 577–82, https://doi .org/10.7326/M20-0504.

11. "If You've Been Exposed to Coronavirus," Harvard Health Publishing, March 2020 (as of September 24, 2020).

12. See summary by Salim Hayek, "False-Negative Rate of RT-PCR SARS-CoV-2 Tests," American College of Cardiology, May 18, 2020.

13. Charles Hymas and Gordon Rayner, "Quarantine to Be Cut to 10 Days for People Arriving from Spain," *The Telegraph* (London), July 27, 2020.

14. Joel Achenbach, "CDC Says 2-week Coronavirus Quarantines Can Be Cut to 10 or 7 Days," *Washington Post*, December 2, 2020.

15. Viral V. Acharya, Timothy Johnson, Suresh Sundaresan, and Steven Zheng, "The Value of a Cure: An Asset Pricing Perspective," NBER Working Paper no. 28127, November 2020, https://doi.org/10.3386/w28127.

16. Peter Whoriskey, Douglas MacMillan, and Jonathan O'Connell, "'Doomed to Fail': Why a $4 Trillion Bailout Couldn't Revive the American Economy," *Washington Post*, October 5, 2020.

Chapter 7

1. "Warren Has a Plan for That," Official Elizabeth Warren Shop, Warren Democrats, https://shop.elizabethwarren.com.

2. Elizabeth Warren, "Preventing, Containing, and Treating Infectious Disease Outbreaks at Home and Abroad," *Medium*, January 28, 2020.

3. Elizabeth Warren, "Protecting Our People and Our Economy from Coronavirus," *Medium*, March 2, 2020.

4. Elizabeth Warren, "My Updated Plan to Face the Coronavirus Crisis," *Medium*, March 12, 2020.

5. F. A. Hayek, "The Use of Knowledge in Society," *American Economic Review* 35, no. 4 (September 1945): 519–30.

6. John Kay and Mervyn King, "The Radical Uncertainties of Coronavirus," *Prospect*, March 30, 2020.

7. Frank H. Knight, "Risk, Uncertainty and Profit," University of Illinois at Urbana–Champaign's Academy for Entrepreneurial Leadership Historical Research Reference in Entrepreneurship, 1921.

8. For an example of how this uncertainty may affect optimal policy, see: Michael Barnett, Greg Buchak, and Constantine Yannelis, "Epidemic Responses under Uncertainty," National Bureau of Economic Research (NBER) Working Paper no. 27289, May 2020, https://doi.org/10.3386/w27289.

9. Fabrizio Mazzonna, "Cultural Differences in COVID-19 Spread and Policy Compliance: Evidence from Switzerland," *COVID Economics: Vetted and Real-Time Papers* 33, Centre for Economic Policy Research (June 30, 2020): 163–85.

10. Chris Giles, "Scientists Should Take Lessons from Economists on Virus Response," March 19, 2020.

11. Jagadeesh Gokhale, Bernd Raffelhüschen, and Jan Walliser, "The Burden of German Unification: A Generational Accounting Approach," Federal Reserve Bank of Cleveland, Working Papers (Old Series) 9412, revised 1994.

12. RTT News, "South Korea Jobless Rate Rises in September," *Business Insider*, October 16, 2020.

13. David Argente, Chang-Tai Hsieh, and Munseob Lee, "The Cost of Privacy: Welfare Effects of the Disclosure of COVID-19 Cases," Becker Friedman Institute for Economics Working Paper no. 2000-64, May 15, 2020 (revised July 22, 2020), Social Science Research Network (SSRN), https://dx.doi.org/10.2139/ssrn.3601143.

14. Laurence Kotlikoff and Michael Mina, "Beat Covid without a Vaccine," *Wall Street Journal,* October 1, 2020.

15. Klaus Desmet and Romain Wacziarg, "Understanding Spatial Variation in COVID-19 across the United States," NBER Working Paper no. 27329, June 2020 (revised July 2020), https://doi.org/10.3386/w27329.

16. "Las Vegas Mayor Slammed for Suggesting Workers Could Be COVID-19 'Control Group,'" ABC News, April 23, 2020.

17. Chris Edwards, "Top-Down Regulations for COVID-19?," *Cato at Liberty* (blog), April 23, 2020.

18. "Fauci: Why the Public Wasn't Told to Wear Masks When the Coronavirus Pandemic Began," *The Hill*, June 16, 2020.

Chapter 8

1. Joseph A. Benitez, Charles J. Courtemanche, and Aaron Yelowitz, "Racial and Ethnic Disparities in COVID-19: Evidence from Six Large Cities," National Bureau of Economic Research (NBER) Working Paper no. 27592, July 2020, https://doi.org/10.3386/w27592.

2. Coady Wing, Daniel H. Simon, and Patrick Carlin, "Effects of Large Gatherings on the COVID-19 Epidemic: Evidence from Professional and College Sports," July 30, 2020, Social Science Research Network, http://dx.doi.org/10.2139/ssrn.3657625.

3. Dhaval M. Dave, Andrew I. Friedson, Kyutaro Matsuzawa, Joseph J. Sabia, and Samuel Safford, "Black Lives Matter Protests, Social Distancing, and COVID-19," NBER Working Paper no. 27408, August 2020, https://doi.org/10.3386/w27408.

4. Avik Roy, "The Most Important Coronavirus Statistic: 42% of U.S. Deaths Are from 0.6% of the Population," *Forbes*, May 26, 2020.

5. John P. A. Ioannidis, Cathrine Axfors, and Despina G. Contopoulos-Ioannidis, "Second versus First Wave of COVID-19 Deaths: Shifts in Age Distribution and in Nursing Home Fatalities," medRXiv, November 30, 2020, https://doi.org/10.1101/2020.11.28.20240366.

6. Klaus Desmet and Romain Wacziarg, "Understanding Spatial Variation in COVID-19 across the United States," NBER Working Paper no. 27329, June 2020 (revised July 2020), https://doi.org/10.3386/w27329.

7. John M. Barrios and Yael Hochberg, "Risk Perception through the Lens of Politics in the Time of the COVID-19 Pandemic," NBER Working Paper no. 27008, April 2020, https://doi.org/10.3386/w27008.

8. Hunt Allcott, Levi Boxell, Jacob C. Conway, Billy A. Ferguson, Matthew Gentzkow, and Benny Goldman, "What Explains Temporal and Geographic Variation in the Early US Coronavirus Pandemic?," NBER Working Paper no. 27965, October, 2020, https://doi.org/10.3386/w27965.

9. Francine D. Blau, Josefine Koebe, and Pamela A. Meyerhofer, "Who Are the Essential and Frontline Workers?," NBER Working Paper no. 27791, September 2020, https://doi.org/10.3386/w27791.

10. Jeffrey E. Harris, "Reopening under COVID-19: What to Watch For," NBER Working Paper no. 27166, May 2020 (revised August 2020), https://doi.org/10.3386/w27166.

11. Harris, "Reopening under COVID-19."

12. Holman W. Jenkins Jr., "The Other Media Blackout," *Wall Street Journal*, October 30, 2020.

Chapter 9

1. Megan Twohey, Steve Eder, and Marc Stein, "Need a Coronavirus Test? Being Rich and Famous May Help," *New York Times*, March 18, 2020.

2. Denise Roland and Joshua Robinson, "How Are the Rich and Famous Jumping the Test Queues? In England, by Paying $425," *Wall Street Journal*, March 21, 2020.

3. Daniel Desrochers, "Rand Paul Defends His Decision Not to Self-Quarantine after He Was Tested for COVID-19," *Lexington Herald Leader*, March 23, 2020.

4. Desrochers, "Rand Paul Defends His Decision not to Self-Quarantine."

5. Food and Drug Administration, "FDA Takes Significant Step in Coronavirus Response Efforts, Issues Emergency Use Authorization for the First 2019 Novel Coronavirus Diagnostic," news release, February 4, 2020.

6. Shawn Boburg, Robert O'Harrow Jr., Neena Satija, and Amy Goldstein, "Inside the Coronavirus Testing Failure: Alarm and Dismay among the Scientists Who Sought to Help," *Washington Post*, April 3, 2020.

7. Casey B. Mulligan, "Economic Activity and the Value of Medical Innovation during a Pandemic, National Bureau of Economic Research (NBER) Working Paper no. 27060, April 2020, https://doi.org/10.3386/w27060.

8. Ed Yong, "How the Pandemic Will End," *The Atlantic*, March 25, 2020.

9. Ed Yong, "How the Pandemic Defeated America," *The Atlantic*, August 4, 2020.

10. Richard Harris, "Rapid, Cheap, Less Accurate Coronavirus Testing Has a Place, Scientists Say," NPR, July 22, 2020.

11. Joshua Gans, "Validation of the Value of Rapid Tests," *Plugging the Gap* (blog), October 9, 2020; Andrew Pekosz et al., "Antigen-Based Testing but Not Real-Time PCR Correlates with SARS-CoV-2 Virus Culture," medRXiv, October 5, 2020, https://doi.org/10.1101/2020.10.02.20205708.

12. Daniel B Larremore et al., "Test Sensitivity Is Secondary to Frequency and Turnaround Time for COVID-19 Surveillance," medRXiv, September 8, 2020, https://doi.org/10.1101/2020.06.22.20136309.

13. Alex Tabarrok, "Frequent, Fast, and Cheap Is Better Than Sensitive," *Marginal Revolution* (blog), July 24, 2020; and John Cochrane, "Beat Covid without a Vaccine," *The Grumpy Economist* (blog), October 2, 2020.

14. Ted Bergstrom, Carl T. Bergstrom, and Haoran Li, "Frequency and Accuracy of Proactive Testing for COVID-19," medRxiv, September 8, 2020, https://doi.org/10.1101/2020.09.05.20188839.

15. Joshua Gans, "The Slovakian Model," *Plugging the Gap* (blog), November 20, 2020.

16. Andrew Atkeson, Michael Droste, and Michael J. Mina, and James H. Stock, "Economic Benefits of COVID-19 Screening Tests," medRXiv, October 22, 2020, https://doi.org/10.1101/2020.10.22.20217984.

17. Matt Ridley, *How Innovation Works: And Why It Flourishes in Freedom* (New York: HarperCollins, 2020).

18. Germán Gutiérrez and Thomas Philippon, "The Failure of Free Entry," NBER Working Paper no. 26001, June 2019, https://doi.org/10.3386/w26001.

19. "Coronavirus (COVID-19) Update: White House Press Briefing by FDA Commissioner Stephen M. Hahn, M.D.," U.S. Food and Drug Administration, March 7, 2020.

20. "Coronavirus (COVID-19) Update: FDA Issues New Policy to Help Expedite Availability of Diagnostics," U.S. Food and Drug Administration, February 29, 2020.

21. Philippe Aghion, Antonin Bergeaud, and John Van Reenen, "The Impact of Regulation on Innovation," Harvard University Working Paper, March 2019.

22. On telehealth, see: "4 Things to Know about Trump's Emergency Plan on Coronavirus," *Politico*, March 13, 2020. On testing, see: Ed Silverman, "FDA Moves to Boost Coronavirus Testing Capacity by Giving States More Power," *Stat*, March 16, 2020. On flying, see: Transportation Security Administration, "Hand Sanitizer," https://www.tsa.gov/travel/special-procedures?field_disability _type_value=15. On doctor consultations, see: "The Doctor Will Zoom You Now," *Wall Street Journal*, April 26, 2020.

23. Mike Palicz, "DOT Waives Hours of Service Regulations for Truck Drivers Providing Relief to Coronavirus Outbreak," Americans for Tax Reform, March 16, 2020.

24. U.S. Environmental Protection Agency, "COVID-19 Implications for EPA's Enforcement and Compliance Assurance Program," March 26, 2020.

25. Alcohol and Tobacco Tax and Trade Bureau, "Production of Hand Sanitizer to Address the COVID-19 Pandemic," March 26, 2020.

26. Catherine Carlock, "Gov. Baker Bans Reusable Bags at Grocery Stores, Lifts Local Plastic Bag Bans," *Boston Business Journal*, March 25, 2020.

27. Ryan Bourne and Chris Edwards, "Economic Recovery and Minimum Wages," *The Hill*, April 28, 2020.

28. Vincent Geloso and Jamie Bologna Pavlik, "Economic Freedom and the Economic Consequences of the 1918 Pandemic," August 4, 2020, https://doi.org /10.1111/coep.12504.

Chapter 10

1. "Purell for $400? U.S. Lawmaker Urges Amazon to Tamp Down Price Gouging," Reuters, March 4, 2020.

2. "Amazon Battles Sharp Price Rises of Coronavirus Products," *Financial Times*, March 3, 2020.

3. Elisa Braun, "France Slaps Price Controls on Hand Sanitizer," *Politico EU*, March 4, 2020.

4. "CMA to Crack Down on Coronavirus Price Increases," Competition Policy International, March 8, 2020.

5. "Amazon Battles Sharp Price Rises of Coronavirus Products."

6. "Harris, Warren Announce Bill to Stop Price Gouging during the COVID-19 Pandemic," office of Kamala D. Harris, press release, April 10, 2020.

7. "Harris, Warren Announce Bill to Stop Price Gouging."

8. "Harris, Warren Announce Bill to Stop Price Gouging."

9. Jonathan Hartley, "Inattention and Prices over Time: Experimental Evidence from 'The Price Is Right' (1972–2019)," October 11, 2019, https://dx.doi.org /10.2139/ssrn.3469008.

10. Raj Chetty, John N. Friedman, Nathaniel Hendren, Michael Stepner, and the Opportunity Insights Team, "How Did COVID-19 and Stabilization Policies Affect Spending and Employment? A New Real-Time Economic Tracker Based on Private Sector Data," National Bureau of Economic Research (NBER) Working Paper no. 27431, June 2020, https://doi.org/10.3386 /w27431.

11. Katie Conner, "Is There Still a Meat Shortage? The Current Situation with Chicken, Beef, Pork Prices and Supply," CNET, June 12, 2020.

12. "Changes in Demand and Disrupted Supply Chains Feed into Shortages at the Store," Marketplace, April 13, 2020.

13. Ben Fox Rubin, "Three Months into the Pandemic, Price Gouging Is Still a Real Problem," CNET, June 18, 2020.

14. Rubin, "Three Months into the Pandemic."

15. "How COVID-19 Affected U.S. Consumer Prices in March," Reuters, April 10, 2020.

16. Russ Roberts, "Price Gouging Could Actually Fix Our Face Mask Shortage," *Medium*, May 4, 2020.

17. Roberts, "Price Gouging Could Actually Fix Our Face Mask Shortage."

18. Luis Cabral and Lei Xu, "Seller Reputation and Price Gouging: Evidence from the COVID-19 Pandemic," *VOX EU*, May 7, 2020.

19. Adrienne Vogt, "These Unknown Brands Took Over Store Shelves while Purell and Clorox Disappeared," CNN Business, August 5, 2020.

20. "Coronavirus: Sharp to Use TV Factory to Make Surgical Masks," BBC News, March 2, 2020.

21. Olivia Rockeman, Yueqi Yang, and Jeff Green, "COVID Survival Guide: Pivot to PPE and Make It Last," Bloomberg, October 3, 2020.

22. Heather Morton, "Price Gouging State Statutes," National Conference of State Legislatures, March 30, 2020.

23. "Consumer Protection: Price Gouging," office of Attorney General Mark R. Herring, https://www.oag.state.va.us/consumer-protection/index.php?option=com _content&view=article&id=181.

24. "Consumer Protection: Price Gouging."

25. Initiative on Global Markets Forum, "Price Gouging," University of Chicago Booth School of Business, May 2, 2012.

26. Juan Camilo Castillo, "Who Benefits from Surge Pricing?," Stanford University, December 28, 2019; and Peter Cohen, Robert Hahn, Jonathan Hall, Steven Levitt, and Robert Metcalfe, "Using Big Data to Estimate Consumer Surplus: The Case of Uber," NBER Working Paper no. 22627, September 2016, https://doi .org/ 10.3386/w22627.

27. Chungsang Tom Lam and Meng Liu, "Demand and Consumer Surplus in the On-demand Economy: the Case of Ride Sharing," October 11, 2017.

28. Roberts, "Price Gouging Could Actually Fix Our Face Mask Shortage."

29. Paula Froelich, "Danish Store Instills Pricing Trick to Stop Hand Sanitizer Hoarders," *New York Post*, March 21, 2020.

30. Eva Batey, "San Francisco Emergency Order Says Delivery Apps Must Cap Restaurant Fees at 15 Percent," Eater San Francisco, April 10, 2020.

31. Steven Suranovic, "Surge Pricing and Price Gouging: Public Misunderstanding as a Market Imperfection," International Institute for Educational Planning Working Paper no. 2015-20, December 2015.

Chapter 11

1. Andy George, "How to Make a $1500 Sandwich in Only 6 Months," September 15, 2015, YouTube video, 3:43, https://www.youtube.com/watch?v=URvWSsAgtJE.

2. Daniel J. Ikenson, "Why We Trade," *Cato at Liberty* (blog), August 10, 2016.

3. David H. Autor, David Dorn, and Gordon H. Hanson, "The China Shock: Learning from Labor Market Adjustment to Large Changes in Trade," National Bureau of Economic Research (NBER) Working Paper no. 21906, January 2016, https://doi.org/10.3386/w21906.

4. Xavier Jaravel and Erick Sager, "What Are the Price Effects of Trade? Evidence from the U.S. and Implications for Quantitative Trade Models," Centre for Economic Policy Research (CEPR) Discussion Paper no. 13902, August 2019.

5. Lorenzo Caliendo, Maximiliano Dvorkin, and Fernando Parro, "Trade and Labor Market Dynamics: General Equilibrium Analysis of the China Trade Shock," *Econometrica* 87, no. 3 (May 2019): 741–835, https://doi.org/10.3982/ECTA13758.

6. Robert C. Feenstra, Hong Ma, and Yuan Xu, "US Exports and Employment," NBER Working Paper no. 24056, November 2017, https://doi.org/10.3386/w24056.

7. Initiative on Global Markets Forum, "Free Trade," University of Chicago Booth School of Business, March 13, 2012.

8. Marco Rubio, "We Need a More Resilient American Economy," *New York Times*, April 20, 2020.

9. Robert E. Lighthizer, "The Era of Offshoring U.S. Jobs Is Over," May 11, 2020.

10. Robert E. Lighthizer, "How to Make Trade Work For Workers," *Foreign Affairs*, July/August 2020.

11. Michael Lind, "On Domestic Sourcing," Moving the Chains symposium, American Compass, June 9, 2020.

12. Steve Davies, "Going Viral," Institute of Economic Affairs, April 29, 2020.

13. Sabrina Rodriguez, "Burning through Hundreds of Millions of N-95 Masks," *Politico Weekly Trade* (newsletter), April 14, 2020.

14. Rodriguez, "Burning through Hundreds of Millions of N-95 Masks."

15. Scott Lincicome, "On 'Supply-Chain Repatriation,' It's Buyer (and Nation) Beware," *National Review Online*, April 28, 2020.

16. Martin Sandbu, "Globalisation and National Resilience Can Coexist Despite Covid-19," *Financial Times*, April 1, 2020.

17. Barthélémy Bonadio, Zhen Huo, Andrei A. Levchenko, and Nitya Pandalai-Nayar, "Global Supply Chains in the Pandemic," NBER Working Paper no. 27224, May 2020 (revised August 2020), https://doi.org/10.3386/w27224.

18. Francesco Caselli, Miklós Koren, Milan Lisicky, and Silvana Tenreyro, "Diversification through Trade," NBER Working Paper no. 21498, August 2015, https://doi.org/10.3386/w21498.

19. Justin T. Westbrook, "America Is Running Out of Pickup Trucks," *Jalopnik*, May 4, 2020.

20. Lind, "On Domestic Sourcing."

21. Scott Lincicome, "Doomed to Repeat It: The Long History of America's Protectionist Failures," Cato Institute Policy Analysis no. 819, August 22, 2017.

22. Scott Lincicome, "What If Politicians Are the Biggest Medical Supply Chain Risk?," *Cato at Liberty* (blog), September 9, 2020.

23. Lincicome, "On 'Supply-Chain Repatriation'"; and Inu Manak and Logan Kolas, "Supply Chains and Interdependence: Is This Really a Problem That Needs Solving?," *Cato at Liberty* (blog), June 17, 2020.

24. Sam Jones, "Swiss Keep Calm and Rest on Their Months of Stockpiles," *Financial Times*, March 26, 2020.

25. "About the Strategic National Stockpile," Public Health Emergency, U.S. Department of Health and Human Services.

26. Lincicome, "On 'Supply-Chain Repatriation.'"

27. Caleb Watney and Alec Stapp, "Masks for All: Using Purchase Guarantees and Targeted Deregulation to Boost Production of Essential Medical Equipment," COVID-19 Crisis Response Policy Briefs, Mercatus Center, April 8, 2020.

28. Alex Tabarrok, "Sicken Thy Neighbor Trade Policy," *Marginal Revolution* (blog), March 29, 2020.

Chapter 12

1. Sam Peltzman, "The Effects of Automobile Safety Regulation," *Journal of Political Economy* 83, no. 4 (August 1975): 677–726, https://www.jstor.org/stable /1830396?seq=1.

2. Steven D. Levitt and Jack Porter, "Sample Selection in the Estimation of Air Bag and Seat Belt Effectiveness," *Review of Economics and Statistics* 83, no. 4 (November 2001): 603–15, https://doi.org/10.1162/003465301753237696.

3. Michael Munger, "The Dangers of Safety Equipment," *New York Times*, January 6, 2017.

4. Mark Wilson, "Wearing Masks May Have a Surprising Unintended Consequence," *Fast Company*, May 8, 2020; and Michael Crowe, "CDC, WHO Clash on Effectiveness of Masks in Preventing Spread of COVID-19," King 5 News, May 10, 2020.

5. Youpei Yan, Jude Bayham, Eli P. Fenichel, and Aaron Richter, "Do Face Masks Create a False Sense of Security? A COVID-19 Dilemma," medRXiv, May 27, 2020, https://doi.org/10.1101/2020.05.23.20111302.

6. Yan et al., "Do Face Masks Create a False Sense of Security?"

7. Renee C. Wurth, "By All Means, Wear a Face Mask. Just Don't Think It Will Make You Invincible," *The Guardian* (London), April 11, 2020.

8. Olga Perski, David Simons, Robert West, and Susan Michie, "Face Masks to Prevent Community Transmission of Viral Respiratory Infections: A Rapid Evidence Review Using Bayesian Analysis," Qeios, May 1, 2020, https://doi.org/ 10.32388/1SC5L4.

9. Tom Jefferson et al., "Physical Interventions to Interrupt or Reduce the Spread of Respiratory Viruses: Systematic Review: Part 1—Face Masks, Eye Protection and Person Distancing: Systematic Review and Meta-Analysis," medRXiv, April 7, 2020, https://doi.org/10.1101/2020.03.30.20047217; and C. Raina MacIntyre

and Abrar Ahmad Chughtai, "Facemasks for the Prevention of Infection in Healthcare and Community Settings," *British Medical Journal* 350 (April 9, 2015): h694, https://doi.org/10.1136/bmj.h694.

10. Shuo Feng, Chen Shen, Nan Xia, Wei Song, Mengzhen Fan, and Benjamin J Cowling, "Rational Use of Face Masks in the COVID-19 Pandemic," *The Lancet Respiratory Medicine* 8, no. 5 (May 2020): 434–36, 1 May, 2020, https://doi.org /10.1016/S2213-2600(20)30134-X.

11. Timo Mitze, Reinhold Kosfeld, Johannes Rode, and Klaus Wälde, "Face Masks Considerably Reduce COVID-19 Cases in Germany: A Synthetic Control Method Approach," Institute of Labor Economics (IZA) Discussion Paper no. 13319, June 2020.

12. Daniel C. Payne et al., "SARS-CoV-2 Infections and Serologic Responses from a Sample of U.S. Navy Service Members—USS *Theodore Roosevelt*, April 2020," *Morbidity and Mortality Weekly Report* 69, no. 23 (June 2020): 714–21, http://dx .doi.org/10.15585/mmwr.mm6923e4.

13. Alexander Karaivanov, Shih En Lu, Hitoshi Shigeoka, Cong Chen, and Stephanie Pamplona, "Face Masks, Public Policies and Slowing the Spread of COVID-19: Evidence from Canada," NBER Working Paper no. 27891, October 2020, https://doi.org/10.3386/w27891.

14. Faith Karimi, "Two Hairstylists Who Had Coronavirus Saw 140 Clients. No New Infections Have Been Linked to the Salon, Officials Say," CNN, June 11, 2020.

15. Renyi Zhang, Yixin Li, Annie L. Zhang, Yuan Wang, and Mario J. Molina, "Identifying Airborne Transmission as the Dominant Route for the Spread of COVID-19," Proceedings of the National Academy of Sciences of the United States of America (PNAS), June 11, 2020, https://doi.org/10.1073/pnas.2009637117.

16. Nancy H. L. Leung et al., "Respiratory Virus Shedding in Exhaled Breath and Efficacy of Face Masks," *Nature Medicine* 26, no. 5 (May 2020): 676–80, https://doi.org/10.1038/s41591-020-0843-2; and Anna Davies et al., "Testing the Efficacy of Homemade Masks: Would They Protect in an Influenza Pandemic?," *Disaster Medicine and Public Health Preparedness* 7, no. 4 (August 2013): 413–18, doi:10.1017/dmp.2013.43.

17. Wei Lyu and George L. Wehby, "Community Use of Face Masks and COVID-19: Evidence from a Natural Experiment of State Mandates in the US," *Health Affairs* 39, no. 8 (June 2020): 1419–25, https://www.healthaffairs.org/doi/10 .1377/hlthaff.2020.00818.

18. Derek K. Chu et al., "Physical Distancing, Face Masks, and Eye Protection to Prevent Person-to-Person Transmission of SARS-CoV-2 and COVID-19: A Systematic Review and Meta-analysis," *The Lancet* 395, no. 10242 (June 2020): 1973–87, https://doi.org/10.1016/S0140-6736(20)31142-9.

19. Monica Gandhi and George Rutherford, "Facial Masking for Covid-19— Potential for 'Variolation' as We Await a Vaccine," *New England Journal of Medicine*, September 8, 2020, https://doi.org/10.1056/NEJMp2026913.

20. Matt Novak, "Dr. Fauci Made the Coronavirus Pandemic Worse by Lying about Masks," *Gizmodo*, June 16, 2020.

21. David Wallace-Wells, "People Don't Trust Public-Health Experts Because Public-Health Experts Don't Trust People," *New York Magazine*, June 20, 2020.

22. Craig Timberg, "How Do Masks Change Human Behavior? An Italian Scientist Who Has Studied Cow Sociability Decided to Find Out," *Washington Post*, June 5, 2020.

23. Steven Horwitz and Donald J. Boudreaux, "Economics Show Why Politicians' Mask Mandates Don't Work," *Detroit News*, August 26, 2020.

24. Daniel Jacob Hemel and Anup Malani, "Immunity Passports and Moral Hazard," University of Chicago, Public Law Working Paper no. 743, May 2020, http://dx.doi.org/10.2139/ssrn.3596569.

25. Robert Gearty, "Texas Hospital Says Man, 30, Died after Attending a 'Covid Party,'" *Fox News*, July 11, 2020.

26. Alex Tabarrok, "Immunity Passes Must Be Combined with Variolation," *Marginal Revolution* (blog), April 5, 2020.

27. Apoorva Mandavilli, "You May Have Antibodies after Coronavirus Infection. But Not for Long," *New York Times*, June 18, 2020.

28. James Gallagher, "Covid Reinfection: Man Gets Covid Twice and Second Hit 'More Severe',"' BBC News, October 12, 2020.

29. Tom Chivers, "How Far Away Are 'Immunity Passports'?," *UnHerd*, April 7, 2020.

30. Christopher T. Robertson et al., "Indemnifying Precaution: Economic Insights for Regulation of a Highly Infectious Disease," *Journal of Law and the Biosciences* 7, no. 1 (May 2020), doi:10.1093/jlb/lsaa032.

31. Joshua S. Gans, "The Economic Consequences of $\hat{R} = 1$: Towards a Workable Behavioural Epidemiological Model of Pandemics," NBER Working Paper no. 27632, July 2020, https://doi.org/10.3386/w27632.

32. Rajmohan Rajaraman, Zhifeng Sun, Ravi Sundaram, and Anil Kumar S. Vullikanti, "Network Effects of Risk Behavior Change Following Prophylactic Interventions," *PLoS ONE* 8, no. 8 (2013): e64653, https://doi.org/10.1371/journal.pone.0064653.

33. Manuel Hoffmann, Roberto Mosquera, and Adrian Chadi, "Vaccines at Work," IZA Discussion Paper no. 12939, January 2020.

34. Ali Moghtaderi and Avi Dor, "Immunization and Moral Hazard: The HPV Vaccine and Uptake of Cancer Screening," NBER Working Paper no. 22523, https://doi.org/10.3386/w22523.

35. "Pfizer and BioNTech Announce Publication of Results from Landmark Phase 3 Trial of BNT162B2 COVID-19 Vaccine Candidate in the New England Journal of Medicine," Pfizer, press release, December 10, 2020; "Moderna Announces Primary Efficacy Analysis in Phase 3 COVE Study for Its COVID-19 Vaccine Candidate and Filing Today with U.S. FDA for Emergency Use Authorization," Moderna, press release, November 30, 2020; and Centers for Disease Control and Prevention, "Influenza (Flu): How Well Flu Vaccines Work," https://www.cdc.gov/flu/vaccines-work/vaccineeffect.htm.

Chapter 13

1. John Cochrane, "Bailout Redux," *The Grumpy Economist* (blog), April 20, 2020.

2. John H. Cochrane, "Lessons from the Financial Crisis," *Regulation* 32, no. 4 (Winter 2009–2010): 34–37.

3. Arnold Kling, "Anti-fragile Arnold Hates This Bailout," *askblog* (blog), April 25, 2020.

4. "The NBER's Recession Dating Procedure," National Bureau of Economic Research (NBER), January 7, 2008.

5. Richard Alm and W. Michael Cox, "Creative Destruction," Library of Economics and Liberty.

6. Jeffrey A. Miron, "Bailout or Bankruptcy?" *Cato Journal* 29, no. 1 (Winter 2009): 1–17.

7. Jonathan Portes, "Economists Usually Worry about Bailing Out Private Firms and Increasing National Debt. But Right Now, We Should Be Doing Both," *Prospect*, March 17, 2020.

8. Megan McArdle, "A Libertarian's Unlikely Pandemic Plea: Subsidize Everything," *Washington Post*, March 17, 2020.

9. Initiative on Global Markets Forum, "Stimulus and Stabilizers," University of Chicago Booth School of Business, May 19, 2020.

10. Cochrane, "Bailout Redux."

11. Eamonn Butler, "Public Choice: A Primer," Institute of Economic Affairs, March 25, 2012.

12. "Airline Bailout Shouldn't Be Cleared for Takeoff," *Boston Globe*, March 18, 2020.

13. Veronique de Rugy and Gary D. Leff, "The Case against Bailing Out the Airline Industry," Mercatus Center, COVID-19 Crisis Response Policy Brief, March 25, 2020.

14. Will Horton, "How the U.S. Is Distributing Airline Bailout Funds in COVID-19 Relief Deal," *Forbes*, April 15, 2020.

15. "Leading Lobbying Industries in the United States in 2019, by Total Lobbying Spending," Statista, March 4, 2020.

16. "Industry Profile: Air Transport," OpenSecrets.Org, Center for Responsive Politics, https://www.opensecrets.org/federal-lobbying/industries/summary?cycle=2019&id=M01.

17. "Industry Profile: Air Transport, Summary," OpenSecrets.Org, Center for Responsive Politics, https://www.opensecrets.org/federal-lobbying/industries/summary?cycle=2019&id=T1100.

18. "Airlines: Money to Congress," OpenSecrets.Org, Center for Responsive Politics, https://www.opensecrets.org/industries/summary.php?ind=T1100&cycle=2018&recipdetail=A&sortorder=U.

19. Salvatore Nunnari, "The Political Economy of the U.S. Auto Industry Crisis," Working Paper, California Institute of Technology Division of the Humanities and Social Sciences, May 17, 2011.

20. Michael Dorsch, "Bailout for Sale? The Vote to Save Wall Street," Public Choice 155, no. 3/4 (June 2013): 211–28.

21. David R. Henderson, "Rent Seeking," Library of Economics and Liberty.

22. Jessica Wehrman, "Airlines Boosted Lobbying as Pandemic Spread," *Roll Call*, April 23, 2020.

23. "Airline CEOs Issue Letter to Congress Urging Swift Action on Bipartisan Aid Package," Airlines for America, March 21, 2020.

24. Michael Smith, "Three Essays on the Political Economy of Corporate Bailouts," (doctoral thesis, Columbia University 2014), https://doi.org/10.7916/D8QZ283M.

25. Lisa Martine Jenkins, "Amid Coronavirus, Voters Reluctant to Fly, but Split on Potential Airline Bailout," *Morning Consult*, March 20, 2020.

26. Sara Fischer, "Axios Harris Poll 100: Corporate Trust Soars during the Pandemic," Harris Poll, July 30, 2020.

27. Leslie Josephs, "How Airline Workers Won a $32 Billion Lifeline in the Contentious Coronavirus Relief Bill," CNBC, March 27, 2020.

28. Christopher Neilson, John Eric Humphries, and Gabriel Ulyssea, "Information Frictions and Access to the Paycheck Protection Program," NBER Working Paper no. 27624, July 2020, https://doi.org/10.3386/w27624.

29. Alexander W. Bartik, Zoe B. Cullen, Edward L. Glaeser, Michael Luca, Christopher T. Stanton, and Adi Sunderam, "The Targeting and Impact of Paycheck Protection Program Loans to Small Businesses," NBER Working Paper no. 27623, July 2020, https://doi.org/10.3386/w27623.

30. David Boaz, "Trillion-Dollar Spending Bills Bring Out the Lobbyists," *Cato at Liberty* (blog), May 1, 2020.

Chapter 14

1. Greg Iacurci, "She Got a Forgivable Loan. Her Employees Hate Her for It," CNBC, April 22, 2020.

2. Peter Ganong, Pascal Noel, and Joseph Vavra, "US Unemployment Insurance Replacement Rates during the Pandemic," Becker Friedman Institute Working Paper no. 2020-62, August 2020.

3. "Economic Effects of Additional Unemployment Benefits of $600 per Week," Congressional Budget Office, June 4, 2020.

4. Scott Horsley, "Bitter Taste for Coffee Shop Owner, as New $600 Jobless Benefit Drove Her to Close," NPR, April 21, 2020; and Kurt Huffman, "Our Restaurants Can't Reopen until August," *Wall Street Journal*, April 21, 2020.

5. Arindrajit Dube, "The Impact of the Federal Pandemic Unemployment Compensation on Employment: Evidence from the Household Pulse Survey (Preliminary)," Arin Dube Working Papers, July 31, 2020; and Joseph Altonji et al., "Employment Effects of Unemployment Insurance Generosity during the Pandemic," Tobin Center for Economic Policy, Yale University, July 14, 2020.

6. "Summary of Commentary on Current Economic Conditions by Federal Reserve District," *Beige Book*, Board of Governors of the Federal Reserve System, September 2, 2020.

7. "Summary of Commentary on Current Economic Conditions."

8. "Summary of Commentary on Current Economic Conditions."

9. "Summary of Commentary on Current Economic Conditions."

10. For a formal model of this thinking on behalf of employees, see: Corina Boar and Simon Mongey, "Dynamic Trade-Offs and Labor Supply under the CARES Act," University of Chicago, Becker Friedman Institute, Key Economics Findings about COVID-19, August 19, 2020.

11. Ioana Elena Marinescu, Daphné Skandalis, and Daniel Zhao, "Job Search, Job Posting and Unemployment Insurance during the COVID-19 Crisis," July 30, 2020.

12. Initiative on Global Markets Forum, "Jobs and Unemployment Insurance," University of Chicago Booth School of Business, July 18, 2020.

13. Kate Davidson (@KateDavidson), "An employer in manufacturing, located in the northeast, said jobs in the $11-$13/hr range have gone infilled [sic] for the past eight weeks. He said he hears the same from contacts across the country 'Thus stimulus money is encouraging people to stay home,'" Twitter, July 30, 2020, 4:52 p.m., https://twitter.com/KateDavidson/status/1288940503493484545.

14. "Economists vs. Common Sense," *Wall Street Journal*, August 2, 2020.

15. Ramesh Ponnuru, "The Unemployment-Benefit Question," The Corner, *National Review Online*, July 23, 2020.

16. Kurt Mitman and Stanislav Rabinovich, "Optimal Unemployment Benefits in the Pandemic," Centre for Economic Policy Research (CEPR) Discussion Paper no. DP14915, June 2020.

17. Steven Hamilton (@SHamiltonian), "Linking the phaseout of the UI bonus to economic indicators creates an endogeneity loop that could slow the recovery," Twitter, August 2, 2020, 11:45 p.m., https://twitter.com/SHamiltonian/status/1290131533957705728?s=2.

18. Kate Davidson, "Is $600 a Week in Extra Unemployment Aid Deterring People from Seeking Work?," *Wall Street Journal*, July 29, 2020.

19. Abhijit V. Banerjee and Esther Duflo, *Good Economics for Hard Times* (New York: Public Affairs, 2019).

20. Henrik Jacobsen Kleven, Camille Landais, and Emmanuel Saez, "Taxation and International Migration of Superstars: Evidence from the European Football Market," *American Economic Review* 103, no. 5 (2013): 1892–1924, https://dx.doi.org/10.1257/aer.103.5.1892.

21. Henrik Jacobsen Kleven, Camille Landais, Emmanuel Saez, and Esben Schultz, "Migration and Wage Effects of Taxing Top Earners: Evidence from the Foreigners' Tax Scheme in Denmark," CEPR Discussion Paper no. 9410, March 2013.

22. Ufuk Akcigit, Salomé Baslandze, and Stefanie Stantcheva, "Taxation and the International Mobility of Inventors," Cato Institute Research Briefs in Economic Policy no. 63, November 9, 2016.

23. Charles I. Jones, "Taxing Top Incomes in a World of Ideas," NBER Working Paper no. 25725, April 2019, https://doi.org/10.3386/w25725.

24. Two such proposals have been advanced, one for the U.S. and one for the UK: Robert E. Litan, "Want Herd Immunity? Pay People to Take the Vaccine," Brookings Institution op-ed, August 18, 2020; and Sam Bowman and Ryan Bourne, "Arms Out to Help Out: The Case for a Covid Vaccine Payment," CapX, October 19, 2020.

25. McKenzie Stauffer, "BYU-Idaho Threatens Suspension for Students Intentionally Getting COVID-19 to Sell Plasma," 2KUTV, October 13, 2020.

26. Billy Binion, "Andrew Cuomo to Chicken Wings: You're Not Real Food," *Reason*, July 24, 2020.

27. Tyler Cowen (@TylerCowen), "Ask who is the least cost avoider? And govt. can still ban some sectors and activities for a while. You are presenting a recipe for never reopening again," Twitter, April 15, 2020, 9:52 p.m., https://twitter.com /tylercowen/status/1250602840332161024?s=20.

28. Justin Wolfers (@JustinWolfers), "The whole point of making employers liable for risking the lives of their staff is to prevent them from exposing their staff to undue risk. Businesses are asking for the right to expose their workers to fatal risks with no consequences. It's bad economics and bad policy," Twitter, April 15, 2020, 9:19 p.m., https://twitter.com/JustinWolfers/status/12505946439070 51520?s=20.

29. Tyler Cowen and Trace Mitchell, "Legal Liability and COVID-19 Recovery," Mercatus Center, COVID-19 Economic Recovery Policy Briefs, May 8, 2020.

30. Daniel Jacob Hemel and Daniel B. Rodriguez, "A Public Health Framework for COVID-19 Business Liability," *Journal of Law and Biosciences* 7, no. 1 (September 22, 2020), https://doi.org/10.1093/jlb/lsaa074.

Chapter 15

1. Luis Garicano, "I Did Not Stammer When the Queen Asked Me about the Meltdown," *The Guardian* (London), November 17, 2008.

2. Nassim Nicholas Taleb, *The Black Swan: The Impact of the Highly Improbable* (New York: Random House, 2007).

3. Benjamin Halliburton, "COVID-19 Is a Black Swan," *Forbes*, March 19, 2020.

4. Bill Gates, "The Next Outbreak? We're Not Ready," Ted Talk, 2015.

5. Bernard Avishai, "The Pandemic Isn't a Black Swan but a Portent of a More Fragile Global System," *New Yorker*, April 21, 2020.

6. Lyle Adriano, "How This Broker Helped a University Get Pandemic Cover," Insurance Business America, May 4, 2020.

7. Dan Diamond, "Inside America's 2-Decade Failure to Prepare for Coronavirus," Politico, April 11, 2020.

8. "Pandemic Influenza Plan," Public Health Emergency, U.S. Department of Health and Human Services, November 2005.

9. Barack Obama and Richard Lugar, "Grounding a Pandemic," *New York Times*, June 6, 2005.

10. Alex Azar, "Preventing the Next Global Health Disaster," Real Clear World, April 11, 2018.

11. "An HHS Retrospective on the 2009 H1N1 Influenza Pandemic to Advance All Hazards Preparedness," June 15, 2012.

12. "DHS Has Not Effectively Managed Pandemic Personal Protective Equipment and Antiviral Medical Countermeasures," Department of Homeland Security, August 26, 2014.

13. "Partly False Claim: Trump Fired Entire Pandemic Response Team in 2018," Reuters, March 25, 2020.

14. Diamond, "Inside America's 2-Decade Failure."

15. "GHS Index: Global Health Security Index: Building Collective Action and Accountability," *The Economist* Intelligence Unit and Johns Hopkins Bloomberg School of Public Health, October 2019.

16. Noah Smith (@Noahpinion), "Libertarians: Government sucks, let's hollow out the civil service *Pandemic comes, hollowed-out civil service is unable to respond effectively* Libertarians: See, told you government sucks," Twitter, March 8, 2020, 2:59 p.m., https://twitter.com/Noahpinion/status/12367282372852 28544.

17. *Facing 21st Century Public Health Threats: Our Nation's Preparedness and Response Capabilities, Part I*, Before the U.S. Senate Committee on Health, Education, Labor and Pensions, 115th Congress, (January 17, 2018) (statement of Scott Gottlieb, Commissioner of Food and Drugs, Department of Health and Human Services). January 17, 2018.

18. Chris Edwards, "Coronavirus and NIH/CDC Funding," *Cato at Liberty* (blog), March 16, 2020.

19. Bryan Caplan, "State *Priorities*, Not State 'Capacity,'" Library of Economics and Liberty, Aprils 29, 2020.

20. Data available at World Bank, "Government Effectiveness," Worldwide Governance Indicators, https://info.worldbank.org/governance/wgi/Home/Reports.

21. Ryan Bourne (@MrRBourne), "Except there's no correlation between state capacity in OECD & deaths/population. Some say 'that shows you're measuring state capacity wrong.' But it's tautology to say good performance = good state capacity, & judge state capacity from covid performance," Twitter, October 1, 2020, 1:09 p.m., https://twitter.com/MrRBourne/status/1311714797491281931; and Ryan Bourne (@MrRBourne), "Take this other index across more countries—government effectiveness. Same thing. No correlation at all between this measure and COVID-19 performance in terms of deaths. Our prior judgment of state capacity values appear unlinked to pandemic performance," Twitter, October 1, 2020, 1:09 p.m., https://twitter.com/MrRBourne/status/1311714800750260228.

22. Andrew Healy and Neil Malhotra, "Myopic Voters and Natural Disaster Policy," *American Political Science Review* 103, no. 3 (August 2009): 387–406.

23. Derek Thompson, "What's Behind South Korea's COVID-19 Exceptionalism?," *The Atlantic*, May 6, 2020.

24. Ed Yong, "How the Pandemic Defeated America," *The Atlantic*, August 4, 2020.

25. Robert E. Wright, "Why the Political Class Freaked Out," American Institute for Economic Research, April 9, 2020.

26. Massimo Pulejo and Pablo Querubín, "Electoral Concerns Reduce Restrictive Measures during the COVID-19 Pandemic," National Bureau of Economic Research (NBER) Working Paper no. 27498, July 2020, https://doi.org/10 .3386/w27498.

27. Marcella Alsan, Luca Braghieri, Sarah Eichmeyer, Minjeong Joyce Kim, Stefanie Stantcheva, and David Y. Yang, "Civil Liberties in Times of Crisis," NBER Working Paper no. 27972, October 2020, https://doi.org/10.3386/w27972.

28. Avishai, "The Pandemic Isn't a Black Swan."

Chapter 16

1. William D. Cohan, "Grim as It Is Now, Larry Summers Guesses Recovery Could Be Faster Than Anticipated," *Vanity Fair*, April 2, 2020.

2. Julian Kozlowski, Laura Veldkamp, and Venky Venkateswaran, "Scarring Body and Mind: The Long-Term Belief-Scarring Effects of COVID-19," National Bureau of Economic Research (NBER) Working Paper no. 27439, June 2020, https://doi.org/10.3386/w27439.

3. Rosie Perper, "Trump's Senior Economic Adviser Referred to Americans Returning to Work as 'Human Capital Stock,'" *Business Insider*, May 26, 2020.

4. John Springford (@JohnSpringford), "On the V-shaped recovery debate: it's in government's gift, surely? If they do enough to keep workers attached to firms, keep firms solvent, and then stimulate a recovery when the virus is contained (ie, run big deficits), then why not?," Twitter, April 14, 2020, 10:27 a.m., https://twitter.com/JohnSpringford/status/1250068170007883779.

5. Alex Miller, "Premier League Faces Prospect of Losing £1.2BILLION If Season Is Abandoned with Doubts Raised over Whether Top Flight Is Insured for Money They Would Owe Sky and BT," *Mail on Sunday* (London), March 28, 2020.

6. Jason Burt, "Exclusive: Play Now or Risk No Football until Next Year, Premier League to Tell Players," *Telegraph*, May 12, 2020.

7. Tom Gott, "The 68 Premier League Players Out of Contract on June 30," *90 Min*, March 16, 2020.

8. Raj Chetty, John N. Friedman, Nathaniel Hendren, Michael Stepner, and the Opportunity Insights Team, "How Did COVID-19 and Stabilization Policies Affect Spending and Employment? A New Real-Time Economic Tracker Based on Private Sector Data," NBER Working Paper no. 27431, June 17, 2020, https://doi.org/10.3386/w27431.

9. Chetty et al., "How Did COVID-19 and Stabilization Policies Affect Spending and Employment?"

10. Personal Savings Rate data are from "Personal Income and Outlays, August 2020," U.S. Bureau of Economic Analysis, October 1, 2020, https://www.bea.gov/news/2020/personal-income-and-outlays-august-2020.

11. David Gelles, "Are Companies More Productive in a Pandemic?," *New York Times*, June 23, 2020; Marita Zimmermann, Amy E. Benefield, and Benjamin M. Althouse, "They Stumble That Run Fast: The Economic and COVID-19 Transmission Impacts of Reopening Industries in the US," medRXiv, June 15, 2020, https://doi.org/10.1101/2020.06.11.20128918; and Dimitris Papanikolaou and Lawrence D. W. Schmidt, "Working Remotely and the Supply-side Impact of Covid-19," NBER Working Paper no. 27330, June 2020, https://doi.org/10.3386/w27330.

12. Scott R. Baker, Nicholas Bloom, and Stephen J. Terry, "Using Disasters to Estimate the Impact of Uncertainty," NBER Working Paper no. 27167, May 2020, https://doi.org/10.3386/w27167.

13. Robert W. Fairlie, "The Impact of Covid-19 on Small Business Owners: The First Three Months after Social-Distancing Restrictions," NBER Working Paper no. 27462, July 2020 (revised August 2020), https://doi.org/10.3386/w27462.

14. Chetty et al., "How Did COVID-19 and Stabilization Policies Affect Spending and Employment?"

15. David Altig et al., "Firms Expect Working from Home to Triple," *macroblog* (blog), Federal Reserve Bank of Atlanta, May 28, 2020.

16. David Autor and Elisabeth Reynolds, "The Nature of Work after the COVID Crisis: Too Few Low-Wage Jobs," Hamilton Project, July 16, 2020.

17. Data are from "Business Employment Dynamics," U.S. Bureau of Labor Statistics, April 29, 2020, https://www.bls.gov/news.release/cewbd.toc.htm.

18. Austan Goolsbee and Chad Syverson, "Fear, Lockdown, and Diversion: Comparing Drivers of Pandemic Economic Decline 2020," Becker Friedman Institute Working Paper, June 18, 2020.

19. Jose Maria Barrero, Nick Bloom, and Steven J. Davis, "COVID-19 Is Also a Reallocation Shock," Becker Friedman Institute Working Paper, June 25, 2020.

20. Barrero et al., "COVID-19 Is Also a Reallocation Shock."

21. Ryan Bourne and Chris Edwards, "Economic Recovery and Minimum Wages," *The Hill*, April 28, 2020.

Conclusion

1. Vincent Geloso and Ilia Murtazashvili, "Can Governments Deal with Pandemics?," Working Paper, Social Science Research Network, August 11, 2020.

Note: Page numbers with "n" indicate endnotes; page numbers with "f" indicate figures.

RYAN BOURNE occupies the R. Evan Scharf Chair for the Public Understanding of Economics at the Cato Institute and is a columnist for the *Daily Telegraph* and *ConservativeHome*. He has written on a number of economic issues, including fiscal policy, inequality, price and wage controls, and infrastructure spending, and has contributed to numerous books, including: *Flaws and Ceilings: Price Controls and the Damage they Cause*; *Taxation, Spending, and Economic Growth*; and *A Fiscal Cliff: New Perspectives on the U.S. Federal Debt Crisis*. He is coauthor, along with Kwasi Kwarteng and Jonathan Dupont, of *A Time for Choosing: Free Enterprise in Twenty-First Century Britain*.

Before joining Cato, Bourne was Head of Public Policy at the Institute of Economic Affairs and Head of Economic Research at the Centre for Policy Studies (both in the UK). He has extensive broadcast and print media experience and has appeared on BBC News, CNN, Sky News, CNBC, and Fox Business Network. Bourne holds a BA and an MPhil in economics from the University of Cambridge.

Founded in 1977, the Cato Institute is a public policy research foundation dedicated to broadening the parameters of policy debate to allow consideration of more options that are consistent with the principles of limited government, individual liberty, and peace. To that end, the Institute strives to achieve greater involvement of the intelligent, concerned lay public in questions of policy and the proper role of government.

The Institute is named for *Cato's Letters*, libertarian pamphlets that were widely read in the American Colonies in the early 18th century and played a major role in laying the philosophical foundation for the American Revolution.

Despite the achievement of the nation's Founders, today virtually no aspect of life is free from government encroachment. A pervasive intolerance for individual rights is shown by government's arbitrary intrusions into private economic transactions and its disregard for civil liberties. And while freedom around the globe has notably increased in the past several decades, many countries have moved in the opposite direction, and most governments still do not respect or safeguard the wide range of civil and economic liberties.

To address those issues, the Cato Institute undertakes an extensive publications program on the complete spectrum of policy issues. Books, monographs, and shorter studies are commissioned to examine the federal budget, Social Security, regulation, military spending, international trade, and myriad other issues. Major policy conferences are held throughout the year, from which papers are published thrice yearly in the *Cato Journal*. The Institute also publishes the quarterly magazine *Regulation*.

In order to maintain its independence, the Cato Institute accepts no government funding. Contributions are received from foundations, corporations, and individuals, and other revenue is generated from the sale of publications. The Institute is a nonprofit, tax-exempt, educational foundation under Section 501(c)3 of the Internal Revenue Code.

Cato Institute
1000 Massachusetts Avenue NW
Washington, DC 20001
www.cato.org